Data Just Right

Data Just Right

Introduction to Large-Scale Data & Analytics

Michael Manoochehri

✦✦Addison-Wesley

Upper Saddle River, NJ • Boston • Indianapolis • San Francisco
New York • Toronto • Montreal • London • Munich • Paris • Madrid
Capetown • Sydney • Tokyo • Singapore • Mexico City

Many of the designations used by manufacturers and sellers to distinguish their products are claimed as trademarks. Where those designations appear in this book, and the publisher was aware of a trademark claim, the designations have been printed with initial capital letters or in all capitals.

The author and publisher have taken care in the preparation of this book, but make no expressed or implied warranty of any kind and assume no responsibility for errors or omissions. No liability is assumed for incidental or consequential damages in connection with or arising out of the use of the information or programs contained herein.

For information about buying this title in bulk quantities, or for special sales opportunities (which may include electronic versions; custom cover designs; and content particular to your business, training goals, marketing focus, or branding interests), please contact our corporate sales department at corpsales@pearsoned.com or (800) 382-3419.

For government sales inquiries, please contact governmentsales@pearsoned.com.

For questions about sales outside the United States, please contact international@pearsoned.com.

Visit us on the Web: informit.com/aw

Library of Congress Cataloging-in-Publication Data

Manoochehri, Michael.
  Data just right : introduction to large-scale data & analytics / Michael Manoochehri.
        pages   cm
  Includes bibliographical references and index.
  ISBN 978-0-321-89865-4 (pbk. : alk. paper)—ISBN 0-321-89865-6 (pbk. : alk. paper)
  1. Database design. 2. Big data. I. Title.
  QA76.9.D26M376 2014
  005.74'3—dc23

                                                      2013041476

ISBN-13: 978-0-321-89865-4
ISBN-10: 0-321-89865-6
Text printed in the United States on recycled paper at RR Donnelley in Crawfordsville, Indiana.
First printing, December 2013

❖

This book is dedicated to my parents,
Andrew and Cecelia Manoochehri,
who put everything they had into making sure
that I received an amazing education.

❖

Contents

Foreword

The array of tools for collecting, storing, and gaining insight from data is huge and getting bigger every day. For people entering the field, that means digging through hundreds of Web sites and dozens of books to get the basics of working with data at scale. That's why this book is a great addition to the Addison-Wesley Data & Analytics series; it provides a broad overview of tools, techniques, and helpful tips for building large data analysis systems.

Michael is the perfect author to provide this introduction to Big Data analytics. He worked on the Cloud Platform Developer Relations team at Google, helping developers with BigQuery, Google's hosted platform for analyzing terabytes of data quickly. He brings his breadth of experience to this book, providing practical guidance for anyone looking to start working with Big Data or anyone looking for additional tips, tricks, and tools.

The introductory chapters start with guidelines for success with Big Data systems and introductions to NoSQL, distributed computing, and the CAP theorem. An introduction to analytics at scale using Hadoop and Hive is followed by coverage of real-time analytics with BigQuery. More advanced topics include MapReduce pipelines, Pig and Cascading, and machine learning with Mahout. Finally, you'll see examples of how to blend Python and R into a working Big Data tool chain. Throughout all of this material are examples that help you work with and learn the tools. All of this combines to create a perfect book to read for picking up a broad understanding of Big Data analytics.

—*Paul Dix, Series Editor*

Preface

Did you notice? We've recently crossed a threshold beyond which mobile technology and social media are generating datasets larger than humans can comprehend. Large-scale data analysis has suddenly become magic.

The growing fields of distributed and cloud computing are rapidly evolving to analyze and process this data. An incredible rate of technological change has turned commonly accepted ideas about how to approach data challenges upside down, forcing companies interested in keeping pace to evaluate a daunting collection of sometimes contradictory technologies.

Relational databases, long the drivers of business-intelligence applications, are now being joined by radical NoSQL open-source upstarts, and features from both are appearing in new, hybrid database solutions. The advantages of Web-based computing are driving the progress of massive-scale data storage from bespoke data centers toward scalable infrastructure as a service. Of course, projects based on the open-source Hadoop ecosystem are providing regular developers access to data technology that has previously been only available to cloud-computing giants such as Amazon and Google.

The aggregate result of this technological innovation is often referred to as *Big Data*. Much has been made about the meaning of this term. Is Big Data a new trend, or is it an application of ideas that have been around a long time? Does Big Data literally mean lots of data, or does it refer to the process of approaching the value of data in a new way? George Dyson, the historian of science, summed up the phenomena well when he said that Big Data exists "when the cost of throwing away data is more than the machine cost." In other words, we have Big Data when the value of the data itself exceeds that of the computing power needed to collect and process it.

Although the amazing success of some companies and open-source projects associated with the Big Data movement is very real, many have found it challenging to navigate the bewildering amount of new data solutions and service providers. More often than not, I've observed that the processes of building solutions to address data challenges can be generalized into the same set of common use cases that appear over and over.

Finding efficient solutions to data challenges means dealing with trade-offs. Some technologies that are optimized for a specific data use case are not the best choice for others. Some database software is built to optimize speed of analysis over flexibility, whereas the philosophy of others favors consistency over performance. This book will help you understand when to use one technology over another through practical use cases and real success stories.

Who This Book Is For

There are few problems that cannot be solved with unlimited money and resources. Organizations with massive resources, for better or for worse, can build their own bespoke systems to collect or analyze any amount of data. This book is not written for those who have unlimited time, an army of dedicated engineers, and an infinite budget.

This book is for everyone else—those who are looking for solutions to data challenges and who are limited by resource constraints. One of the themes of the Big Data trend is that anyone can access tools that only a few years ago were available exclusively to a handful of large corporations. The reality, however, is that many of these tools are innovative, rapidly evolving, and don't always fit together seamlessly. The goal of this book is to demonstrate how to build systems that put all the parts together in effective ways. We will look at strategies to solve data problems in ways that are affordable, accessible, and by all means practical.

Open-source software has driven the accessibility of technology in countless ways, and this has also been true in the field of Big Data. However, the technologies and solutions presented in this book are not always the open-source choice. Sometimes, accessibility comes from the ability of computation to be accessed as a service.

Nonetheless, many cloud-based services are built upon open-source tools, and in fact, many could not exist without them. Due to the great economies of scale made possible by the increasing availability of utility-computing platforms, users can pay for supercomputing power on demand, much in the same way that people pay for centralized water and power.

We'll explore the available strategies for making the best choices to keep costs low while retaining scalability.

Why Now?

It is still amazing to me that building a piece of software that can reach everyone on the planet is not technically impossible but is instead limited mostly by economic inequity and language barriers. Web applications such as Facebook, Google Search, Yahoo! Mail, and China's Qzone can potentially reach hundreds of millions, if not billions, of active users. The scale of the Web (and the tools that come with it) is just one aspect of why the Big Data field is growing so dramatically. Let's look at some of the other trends that are contributing to interest in this field.

The Maturity of Open-Source Big Data

In 2004, Google released a famous paper detailing a distributed computing framework called MapReduce. The MapReduce framework was a key piece of technology that Google used to break humongous data processing problems into smaller chunks. Not too long after, another Google research paper was released that described BigTable, Google's internal, distributed database technology.

Since then, a number of open-source technologies have appeared that implement or were inspired by the technologies described in these original Google papers. At the same time, in response to the inherent limits and challenges of using relational-database models with distributed computing systems, new database paradigms had become more and more acceptable. Some of these eschewed the core features of relational databases completely, jettisoning components like standardized schemas, guaranteed consistency, and even SQL itself.

The Rise of Web Applications

Data is being generated faster and faster as more and more people take to the Web. With the growth in Web users comes a growth in Web applications.

Web-based software is often built using application programming interfaces, or APIs, that connect disparate services across a network. For example, many applications incorporate the ability to allow users to identify themselves using information from their Twitter accounts or to display geographic information visually via Google Maps. Each API might provide a specific type of log information that is useful for data-driven decision making.

Another aspect contributing to the current data flood is the ever-increasing amount of user-created content and social-networking usage. The Internet provides a friction-less capability for many users to publish content at almost no cost. Although there is a considerable amount of noise to work through, understanding how to collect and analyze the avalanche of social-networking data available can be useful from a marketing and advertising perspective.

It's possible to help drive business decisions using the aggregate information collected from these various Web services. For example, imagine merging sales insights with geographic data; does it look like 30% of your unique users who buy a particular product are coming from France and sharing their purchase information on Facebook? Perhaps data like this will help make the business case to dedicate resources to targeting French customers on social-networking sites.

Mobile Devices

Another reason that scalable data technology is hotter than ever is the amazing explosion of mobile-communication devices around the world. Although this trend primarily relates to the individual use of feature phones and smartphones, it's probably more accurate to as think of this trend as centered on a user's identity and device independence. If you both use a regular computer and have a smartphone, it's likely that you have the ability to access the same personal data from either device. This data is likely to be stored somewhere in a data center managed by a provider of infrastructure as a service. Similarly, the smart TV that I own allows me to view tweets from the Twitter users I follow as a screen saver when the device is idle. These are examples of ubiquitous computing: the ability to access resources based on your identity from arbitrary devices connected to the network.

Along with the accelerating use of mobile devices, there are many trends in which consumer mobile devices are being used for business purposes. We are currently at an early stage of ubiquitous computing, in which the device a person is using is just a tool for accessing their personal data over the network. Businesses and governments are starting to recognize key advantages for using 100% cloud-based business-productivity software, which can improve employee mobility and increase work efficiencies.

In summary, millions of users every day find new ways to access networked applications via an ever-growing number of devices. There is great value in this data for driving business decisions, as long as it is possible to collect it, process it, and analyze it.

The Internet of . . . Everything

In the future, anything powered by electricity might be connected to the Internet, and there will be lots of data passed from users to devices, to servers, and back. This concept is often referred to as the *Internet of Things*. If you thought that the billions of people using the Internet today generate a lot of data, just wait until all of our cars, watches, light bulbs, and toasters are online, as well.

It's still not clear if the market is ready for Wi-Fi-enabled toasters, but there's a growing amount of work by both companies and hobbyists in exploring the Internet of Things using low-cost commodity hardware. One can imagine network-connected appliances that users interact with entirely via interfaces on their smartphones or tablets. This type of technology is already appearing in televisions, and perhaps this trend will finally be the end of the unforgivable control panels found on all microwave ovens.

Like the mobile and Web application trends detailed previously, the privacy and policy implications of an Internet of Things will need to be heavily scrutinized; who gets to see how and where you used that new Wi-Fi-enabled electric toothbrush? On the other hand, the aggregate information collected from such devices could also be used to make markets more efficient, detect potential failures in equipment, and alert users to information that could save them time and money.

A Journey toward Ubiquitous Computing

Bringing together all of the sources of information mentioned previously may provide as many opportunities as red herrings, but there's an important story to recognize here. Just as the distributed-computing technology that runs the Internet has made personal communications more accessible, trends in Big Data technology have made the process of looking for answers to formerly impossible questions more accessible.

More importantly, advances in user experience mean that we are approaching a world in which technology for asking questions about the data we generate—on a once unimaginable scale—is becoming more invisible, economical, and accessible.

How This Book Is Organized

Dealing with massive amounts of data requires using a collection of specialized technologies, each with their own trade-offs and challenges. This book is organized in parts that describe data challenges and successful solutions in the context of common use cases. Part I, "Directives in the Big Data Era," contains Chapter 1, "Four Rules for Data Success." This chapter describes why Big Data is such a big deal and why the promise of new technologies can produce as many problems as opportunities. The chapter introduces common themes found throughout the book, such as focusing on building applications that scale, building tools for collaboration instead of silos, worrying about the use case before the technology, and avoiding building infrastructure unless absolutely necessary.

Part II, "Collecting and Sharing a Lot of Data," describes use cases relevant to collecting and sharing large amounts of data. Chapter 2, "Hosting and Sharing Terabytes of Raw Data," describes how to deal with the seemingly simple challenge of hosting and sharing large amounts of files. Choosing the correct data format is very important, and this chapter covers some of the considerations necessary to make good decisions about how data is shared. It also covers the types of infrastructure necessary to host a large amount of data economically. The chapter concludes by discussing data serialization formats used for moving data from one place to another.

Chapter 3, "Building a NoSQL-Based Web App to Collect Crowd-Sourced Data," is an introduction to the field of scalable database technology. This chapter discusses the history of both relational and nonrelational databases and when to choose one type over the other. We will also introduce the popular Redis database and look at strategies for sharding a Redis installation over multiple machines.

Scalable data analytics requires use and knowledge of multiple technologies, and this often results in data being siloed into multiple, incompatible locations. Chapter 4, "Strategies for Dealing with Data Silos," details the reasons for the existence of data silos and strategies for overcoming the problems associated with them. The chapter also takes a look at why data silos can be beneficial.

Once information is collected, stored, and shared, we want to gain insight about our data. Part III, "Asking Questions about Your Data," covers use cases and technology involved with asking questions about large datasets. Running queries over massive data can often require a distributed solution. Chapter 5, "Using Hadoop, Hive, and Shark to Ask Questions about Large Datasets," introduces popular scalable tools for running queries over ever-increasing datasets. The chapter focuses on Apache Hive, a tool that converts SQL-like queries into MapReduce jobs that can be run using Hadoop.

Sometimes querying data requires iteration. Analytical databases are a class of software optimized for asking questions about datasets and retrieving the results very quickly. Chapter 6, "Building a Data Dashboard with Google BigQuery," describes the use cases for analytical databases and how to use them as a complement for batch-processing tools such as Hadoop. It introduces Google BigQuery, a fully managed analytical database that uses an SQL-like syntax. The chapter will demonstrate how to use the BigQuery API as the engine behind a Web-based data dashboard.

Data visualization is a rich field with a very deep history. Chapter 7, "Visualization Strategies for Exploring Large Datasets," introduces the benefits and potential pitfalls of using visualization tools with large datasets. The chapter covers strategies for visualization challenges when data sizes grow especially large and practical tools for creating visualizations using popular data analysis technology.

A common theme when working with scalable data technologies is that different types of software tools are optimized for different use cases. In light of this, a common use case is to transform large amounts of data from one format, or shape, to another. Part IV, "Building Data Pipelines," covers ways to implement pipelines and workflows for facilitating data transformation. Chapter 8, "Putting It Together: MapReduce Data Pipelines," introduces the concept of using the Hadoop MapReduce framework for processing large amounts of data. The chapter describes creating practical and accessible MapReduce applications using the Hadoop Streaming API and scripting languages such as Python.

When data processing tasks become very complicated, we need to use workflow tools to further automate transformation tasks. Chapter 9, "Building Data Transformation Workflows with Pig and Cascading," introduces two technologies for expressing very complex MapReduce tasks. Apache Pig is a workflow-description language that makes it easy to define complex, multistep MapReduce jobs. The chapter also introduces Cascading, an elegant Java library useful for building complex data-workflow applications with Hadoop.

When data sizes grow very large, we depend on computers to provide information that is useful to humans. It's very useful to be able to use machines to classify, recommend, and predict incoming information based on existing data models. Part V, "Machine Learning for Large Datasets," contains Chapter 10, "Building a Data Classification System with Mahout," which introduces the field of machine learning. The chapter will also demonstrate the common machine-learning task of text classification using software from the popular Apache Mahout machine-learning library.

Interpreting the quality and meaning of data is one of the goals of statistics. Part VI, "Statistical Analysis for Massive Datasets," introduces common tools and use cases for statistical analysis of large-scale data. The programming language R is the most popular open-source language for expressing statistical analysis tasks. Chapter 11, "Using R with Large Datasets," covers an increasingly common use case: effectively working with large data sets with R. The chapter covers R libraries that are useful when data sizes grow larger than available system memory. The chapter also covers the use of R as an interface to existing Hadoop installations.

Although R is very popular, there are advantages to using general-purpose languages for solving data analysis challenges. Chapter 12, "Building Analytics Workflows Using Python and Pandas," introduces the increasingly popular Python analytics stack. The chapter covers the use of the Pandas library for working with time-series data and the iPython notebook, an enhanced scripting environment with sharing and collaborative features.

Not all data challenges are purely technical. Part VII, "Looking Ahead," covers practical strategies for dealing with organizational uncertainty in the face of data-analytics innovations. Chapter 13, "When to Build, When to Buy, When to Out-source," covers strategies for making purchasing decisions in the face of the highly innovative field of data analytics. The chapter also takes a look at the pros and cons of building data solutions with open-source technologies.

Finally, Chapter 14, "The Future: Trends in Data Technology," takes a look at current trends in scalable data technologies, including some of the motivating factors driving innovation. The chapter will also take a deep look at the evolving role of the so-called Data Scientist and the convergence of various data technologies.

Acknowledgments

This book would not have been possible without the amazing technical and editorial support of Robert P. J. Day, Kevin Lo, Melinda Rankin, and Chris Zahn. I'd especially like to thank Debra Williams Cauley for her mentorship and guidance.

I'd also like to thank my colleagues Wesley Chun, Craig Citro, Felipe Hoffa, Ju-kay Kwek, and Iein Valdez as well as the faculty, staff, and students at the UC Berkeley School of Information for help in developing the concepts featured in this book.

About the Author

Michael Manoochehri is an entrepreneur, writer, and optimist. With the help of his many years of experience working with enterprise, research, and nonprofit organizations, his goal is to help make scalable data analytics more affordable and accessible. Michael has been a member of Google's Cloud Platform Developer Relations team, focusing on cloud computing and data developer products such as Google BigQuery. In addition, Michael has written for the tech blog *ProgrammableWeb.com*, has spent time in rural Uganda researching mobile phone use, and holds an M.A. in information management and systems from UC Berkeley's School of Information.

Directives in the
Big Data Era

Four Rules for Data Success

The first rule of any technology used in a business is that automation applied to an efficient operation will magnify the efficiency. The second is that automation applied to an inefficient operation will magnify the inefficiency.
—Bill Gates

The software that you use creates and processes data, and this data can provide value in a variety of ways. Insights gleaned from this data can be used to streamline decision making. Statistical analysis may help to drive research or inform policy. Real-time analysis can be used to identify inefficiencies in product development. In some cases, analytics created from the data, or even the data itself, can be offered as a product.

Studies have shown that organizations that use rigorous data analysis (when they do so effectively) to drive decision making can be more productive than those that do not.[1] What separates the successful organizations from the ones that don't have a data-driven plan?

Database technology is a fast-moving field filled with innovations. This chapter will describe the current state of the field, and provide the basic guidelines that inform the use cases featured throughout the rest of this book.

When Data Became a BIG Deal

Computers fundamentally provide the ability to define logical operations that act upon stored data, and digital data management has always been a cornerstone of digital computing. However, the volume of digital data available has never been greater than at the very moment you finish this sentence. And in the time it takes you to read this sentence, terabytes of data (and possibly quite a lot more) have just been generated by computer systems around the world. If data has always been a central part of computing, what makes Big Data such a big deal now? The answer: accessibility.

---

1. Brynjolfsson, Erik, Lorin Hitt, and Heekyung Kim. "Strength in Numbers: How Does Data-Driven Decisionmaking Affect Firm Performance?" (2011).

The story of data accessibility could start with the IT version of the Cambrian explosion: in other words, the incredible rise of the personal computer. With the launch of products like the Apple II and, later, the Windows platform, millions of users gained the ability to process and analyze data (not a lot of data, by today's standards) quickly and affordably. In the world of business, spreadsheet tools such as VisiCalc for the Apple II and Lotus 1-2-3 for Windows PCs were the so-called killer apps that helped drive sales of personal computers as tools to address business and research data needs. Hard drive costs dropped, processor speeds increased, and there was no end to the amount of applications available for data processing, including software such as Mathematica, SPSS, Microsoft Access and Excel, and thousands more.

However, there's an inherent limitation to the amount of data that can be processed using a personal computer; these systems are limited by their amount of storage and memory and by the ability of their processors to process the data. Nevertheless, the personal computer made it possible to collect, analyze, and process as much data as could fit in whatever storage the humble hardware could support. Large data systems, such as those used in airline reservation systems or those used to process government census data, were left to the worlds of the mainframe and the supercomputer.

Enterprise vendors who dealt with enormous amounts of data developed **relational database management systems** (RDBMSs), such as those provided by Microsoft SQL Server or Oracle. With the rise of the Internet came a need for affordable and accessible database backends for Web applications. This need resulted in another wave of data accessibility and the popularity of powerful open-source relational databases, such as PostgreSQL and MySQL. WordPress, the most popular software for Web site content management, is written in PHP and uses a MySQL database by default. In 2011, WordPress claimed that 22% of all new Web sites are built using WordPress.[2]

RDBMSs are based on a tried-and-true design in which each record of data is ideally stored only once in a single place. This system works amazingly well as long as data always looks the same and stays within a dictated size limit.

Data and the Single Server

Thanks to the constantly dropping price of commodity hardware, it's possible to build larger and beefier computers to analyze data and provide the database backend for Web applications. However, as we've just seen, there is a limit to the amount of processing power that can be built into a single machine before reaching thresholds of considerable cost. More importantly, a single-machine paradigm provides other limitations that start to appear when data volume increases, such as cases in which there is a need for high availability and performance under heavy load or in which timely analysis is required.

By the late 1990s, Internet startups were starting to build some of the amazing, unprecedented Web applications that are easily taken for granted today: software that

---

2. http://wordpress.org/news/2011/08/state-of-the-word/

provides the ability to search the entire Internet, purchase any product from any seller anywhere in the world, or provide social networking services for anyone on the planet with access to the Internet. The massive scale of the World Wide Web, as well as the constantly accelerating growth of the number of total Internet users, presented an almost impossible task for software engineers: finding solutions that potentially could be scaled to the needs of every human being to collect, store, and process the world's data.

Traditional data analysis software, such as spreadsheets and relational databases, as reliable and widespread as it had been, was generally designed to be used on a single machine. In order to build these systems to be able to scale to unprecedented size, computer scientists needed to build systems that could run on clusters of machines.

The Big Data Trade-Off

Because of the incredible task of dealing with the data needs of the World Wide Web and its users, Internet companies and research organizations realized that a new approach to collecting and analyzing data was necessary. Since off-the-shelf, commodity computer hardware was getting cheaper every day, it made sense to think about distributing database software across many readily available servers built from commodity parts. Data processing and information retrieval could be farmed out to a collection of smaller computers linked together over a network. This type of computing model is generally referred to as **distributed computing**. In many cases, deploying a large number of small, cheap servers in a distributed computing system can be more economically feasible than buying a custom built, single machine with the same computation capabilities.

While the hardware model for tackling massive scale data problems was being developed, database software started to evolve as well. The relational database model, for all of its benefits, runs into limitations that make it challenging to deploy in a distributed computing network. First of all, sharding a relational database across multiple machines can often be a nontrivial exercise. Because of the need to coordinate between various machines in a cluster, maintaining a state of data consistency at any given moment can become tricky. Furthermore, most relational databases are designed to guarantee data consistency; in a distributed network, this type of design can create a problem.

Software designers began to make trade-offs to accommodate the advantages of using distributed networks to address the scale of the data coming from the Internet. Perhaps the overall rock-solid consistency of the relational database model was less important than making sure there was always a machine in the cluster available to process a small bit of data. The system could always provide coordination eventually. Does the data actually have to be indexed? Why use a fixed schema at all? Maybe databases could simply store individual records, each with a different schema, and possibly with redundant data.

This rethinking of the database for an era of cheap commodity hardware and the rise of Internet-connected applications has resulted in an explosion of design philosophies for data processing software.

If you are working on providing solutions to your organization's data challenges, the current era is the Era of the Big Data Trade-Off. Developers building new data-driven applications are faced with all manner of design choices. Which database back-end should be used: relational, key–value, or something else? Should my organization build it, or should we buy it? How much is this software solution worth to me? Once I collect all of this data, how will I analyze, share, and visualize it?

In practice, a successful data pipeline makes use of a number of different technologies optimized for particular use cases. For example, the relational database model is excellent for data that monitors transactions and focuses on data consistency. This is not to say that it is impossible for a relational database to be used in a distributed environment, but once that threshold has been reached, it may be more efficient to use a database that is designed from the beginning to be used in distributed environments.

The use cases in this book will help illustrate common examples in order to help the reader identify and choose the technologies that best fit a particular use case. The revolution in data accessibility is just beginning. Although this book doesn't aim to cover every available piece of data technology, it does aim to capture the broad use cases and help guide users toward good data strategies.

More importantly, this book attempts to create a framework for making good decisions when faced with data challenges. At the heart of this are several key principles to keep in mind. Let's explore these Four Rules for Data Success.

Build Solutions That Scale (Toward Infinity)

I've lost count of the number of people I've met that have told me about how they've started looking at new technology for data processing because their relational database has reached the limits of scale. A common pattern for Web application developers is to start developing a project using a single machine installation of a relational database for collecting, serving, and querying data. This is often the quickest way to develop an application, but it can cause trouble when the application becomes very popular or becomes overwhelmed with data and traffic to the point at which it is no longer acceptably performant.

There is nothing inherently wrong with attempting to scale up a relational database using a well-thought-out sharding strategy. Sometimes, choosing a particular technology is a matter of cost or personnel; if your engineers are experts at sharding a MySQL database across a huge number of machines, then it may be cheaper overall to stick with MySQL than to rebuild using a database designed for distributed networks. The point is to be aware of the limitations of your current solution, understand when a scaling limit has been reached, and have a plan to grow in case of bottlenecks.

This lesson also applies to organizations that are faced with the challenge of having data managed by different types of software that can't easily communicate or share with one another. These **data silos** can also hamper the ability of data solutions to scale. For example, it is practical for accountants to work with spreadsheets, the Web site development team to build their applications using relational databases, and financial to use a variety of statistics packages and visualization tools. In these situations, it can become difficult to ask questions about the data across the variety of software used throughout the company. For example, answering a question such as "how many of our online customers have found our product through our social media networks, and how much do we expect this number to increase if we improved our online advertising?" would require information from each of these silos.

Indeed, whenever you move from one database paradigm to another, there is an inherent, and often unknown, cost. A simple example might be the process of moving from a relational database to a key–value database. Already managed data must be migrated, software must be installed, and new engineering skills must be developed. Making smart choices at the beginning of the design process may mitigate these problems. In Chapter 3, "Building a NoSQL-Based Web App to Collect Crowd-Sourced Data," we will discuss the process of using a NoSQL database to build an application that expects a high level of volume from users.

A common theme that you will find throughout this book is use cases that involve using a collection of technologies that deal with issues of scale. One technology may be useful for collecting, another for archiving, and yet another for high-speed analysis.

Build Systems That Can Share Data (On the Internet)

For public data to be useful, it must be accessible. The technological choices made during the design of systems to deliver this data depends completely on the intended audience. Consider the task of a government making public data more accessible to citizens. In order to make data as accessible as possible, data files should be hosted on a scalable system that can handle many users at once. Data formats should be chosen that are easily accessible by researchers and from which it is easy to generate reports. Perhaps an API should be created to enable developers to query data programmatically. And, of course, it is most advantageous to build a Web-based dashboard to enable asking questions about data without having to do any processing. In other words, making data truly accessible to a public audience takes more effort than simply uploading a collection of XML files to a privately run server. Unfortunately, this type of "solution" still happens more often than it should. Systems should be designed to share data with the intended audience.

This concept extends to the private sphere as well. In order for organizations to take advantage of the data they have, employees must be able to ask questions themselves. In the past, many organizations chose a data warehouse solution in an attempt to merge everything into a single, manageable space. Now, the concept of becoming a data-driven organization might include simply keeping data in whatever silo is the best fit for the use case and building tools that can glue different systems together. In this case, the focus is more on keeping data where it works best and finding ways to share and process it when the need arises.

Build Solutions, Not Infrastructure

With apologies to true ethnographers everywhere, my observations of the natural world of the wild software developer have uncovered an amazing finding: Software developers usually hope to build cool software and don't want to spend as much time installing hard drives or operating systems or worrying about that malfunctioning power supply in the server rack. Affordable technology for **infrastructure as a service** (inevitably named using every available spin on the concept of "clouds") has enabled developers to worry less about hardware and instead focus on building Web-based applications on platforms that can scale to a large number of users on demand.

As soon as your business requirements involve purchasing, installing, and administering physical hardware, I would recommend using this as a sign that you have hit a roadblock. Whatever business or project you are working on, my guess is that if you are interested in solving data challenges, your core competency is not necessarily in building hardware. There are a growing number of companies that specialize in providing infrastructure as a service—some by providing fully featured virtual servers run on hardware managed in huge data centers and accessed over the Internet.

Despite new paradigms in the industry of infrastructure as a service, the mainframe business, such as that embodied by IBM, is still alive and well. Some companies provide sales or leases of in-house equipment and provide both administration via the Internet and physical maintenance when necessary.

This is not to say that there are no caveats to using cloud-based services. Just like everything featured in this book, there are trade-offs to building on virtualized infrastructure, as well as critical privacy and compliance implications for users. However, it's becoming clear that buying and building applications hosted "in the cloud" should be considered the rule, not the exception.

Focus on Unlocking Value from Your Data

When working with developers implementing a massive-scale data solution, I have noticed a common mistake: The solution architects will start with the technology first, then work their way backwards to the problem they are trying to solve. There is nothing wrong with exploring various types of technology, but in terms of making investments in a particular strategy, always keep in mind the business question that your data solution is meant to answer.

This compulsion to focus on technology first is the driving motivation for people to completely disregard RDBMSs because of NoSQL database hype or to start worrying about collecting massive amounts of data even though the answer to a question can be found by statistical analysis of 10,000 data points.

Time and time again, I've observed that the key to unlocking value from data is to clearly articulate the business questions that you are trying to answer. Sometimes, the answer to a perplexing data question can be found with a sample of a small amount of data, using common desktop business productivity tools. Other times, the problem is more political than technical; overcoming the inability of admins across different departments to break down data silos can be the true challenge.

Collecting massive amounts of data in itself doesn't provide any magic value to your organization. The real value in data comes from understanding pain points in your business, asking practical questions, and using the answers and insights gleaned to support decision making.

Anatomy of a Big Data Pipeline

In practice, a data pipeline requires the coordination of a collection of different technologies for different parts of a data lifecycle.

Let's explore a real-world example, a common use case tackling the challenge of collecting and analyzing data from a Web-based application that aggregates data from many users. In order for this type of application to handle data input from thousands or even millions of users at a time, it must be highly *available*. Whatever database is used, the primary design goal of the data collection layer is that it can handle input without becoming too slow or unresponsive. In this case, a key–value data store, examples of which include MongoDB, Redis, Amazon's DynamoDB, and Google's Google Cloud Datastore, might be the best solution.

Although this data is constantly streaming in and always being updated, it's useful to have a cache, or a source of truth. This cache may be less performant, and perhaps only needs to be updated at intervals, but it should provide *consistent* data when required. This layer could also be used to provide data snapshots in formats that provide interoperability with other data software or visualization systems. This caching layer might be flat files in a scalable, cloud-based storage solution, or it could be a relational database backend. In some cases, developers have built the collection layer and the cache from the same software. In other cases, this layer can be made with a hybrid of relational and nonrelational database management systems.

Finally, in an application like this, it's important to provide a mechanism to ask aggregate questions about the data. Software that provides quick, near-real-time analysis of huge amounts of data is often designed very differently from databases that are designed to collect data from thousands of users over a network.

In between these different stages in the data pipeline is the possibility that data needs to be transformed. For example, data collected from a Web frontend may need to be converted into XML files in order to be interoperable with another piece of software. Or this data may need to be transformed into JSON or a data serialization format, such as Thrift, to make moving the data as efficient as possible. In large-scale data systems, transformations are often too slow to take place on a single machine. As in the case of scalable database software, transformations are often best implemented using distributed computing frameworks, such as Hadoop.

In the Era of Big Data Trade-Offs, building a system data lifecycle that can scale to massive amounts of data requires specialized software for different parts of the pipeline.

The Ultimate Database

In an ideal world, we would never have to spend so much time unpacking and solving data challenges. An ideal data store would have all the features we need to build our applications. It would have the availability of a key–value or document-oriented database, but would provide a relational model of storing data for the best possible consistency. The database would be hosted as a service in the cloud so that no infrastructure would have to be purchased or managed. This system would be infinitely scalable and would work the same way if the amount of data under management consisted of one megabyte or 100 terabytes. In essence, this database solution would be the magical, infinitely scalable, always available database in the sky.

As of this publication, there is currently no such magic database in the sky— although there are many efforts to commercialize cutting-edge database technology that combine many of the different data software paradigms we mentioned earlier in the chapter.

Some companies have attempted to create a similar product by providing each of the various steps in the data pipeline—from highly available data collection to transformation to storage caching and analysis—behind a unified interface that hides some of these complexities.

Summary

Solving large-scale data challenges ultimately boils down to building a scalable strategy for tackling well-defined, practical use cases. The best solutions combine technologies designed to tackle specific needs for each step in a data processing pipeline. Providing high availability along with the caching of large amounts of data as well as high-performance analysis tools may require coordination of several sets of technologies. Along with this, more complex pipelines may require data-transformation techniques and the use of specific formats designed for efficient sharing and interoperability.

The key to making the best data-strategy decisions is to keep our core data principles in mind. Always understand your business needs and use cases before evaluating technology. When necessary, make sure that you have a plan to scale your data solution—either by deciding on a database that can handle massive growth of data or by having a plan for interoperability when the need for new software comes along. Make sure that you can retrieve and export data. Think about strategies for sharing data, whether internally or externally. Avoid the need to buy and manage new hardware. And above all else, always keep the questions you are trying to answer in mind before embarking on a software development project.

Now that we've established some of the ground rules for playing the game in the Era of the Big Data Trade-Off, let's take a look at some winning game plans.

II

Collecting and Sharing a Lot of Data

2

Hosting and Sharing Terabytes
of Raw Data

Poor fellow, he suffers from files.
—Aneurin Bevan

The two truths of the Internet are "no one knows you're a dog," and it's easy to share lots of data with the world—right?

Sharing large amounts of open data should be common practice for governments and research organizations. Data can help inform intelligent policy making as well as provide innovative kindling for investigative journalism, but it's not really easy to find public and municipal datasets. In fact, municipalities that provide loads of publicly available data are often celebrated in the media as innovative pioneers rather than competent governments just doing their jobs. Even when data is freely available, it can be shared using data formats that are nearly impossible for people and computer programs alike to consume in a meaningful way. The sharing of public data online—a task that should seemingly be simple and even taken for granted—is currently the exception rather than the norm. In 2011, the famous Web comic XKCD even published a telling panel that described the process of sending [large] files across the Internet as "something early adopters are still figuring out how to do."[1]

Despite all of these problems, storing and sharing large amounts of data as thousands or even millions of separate documents is no longer a technological or economic impossibility.

This chapter will explore the technical challenges faced as part of the seemingly simple task of sharing a large collection of documents for public consumption—and what technologies are available to overcome these challenges. Our goal is to understand how to make great choices when faced with similar situations and which tools can help.

---

1. http://xkcd.com/949/

Suffering from Files

Imagine you are the CIO of a large corporation. Within your organization, your employees are data consumers, each of whom plays a variety of different roles. Many of your employees are interested in processing accounting reports—but due to their roles, they should not be privy to sensitive human resources information. Some of your employees are software developers and will need to access data programmatically to build applications. In some cases, your users will be less technical and will thus need to access data such as company metrics using a dashboard. Your fellow executives might have access to almost all of the data produced by a company, but what they are really after is a high-level understanding of the major trends.

When faced with the challenge of sharing many gigabytes and even terabytes of data, a variety of potential implementation choices appear. These choices are influenced by factors such as cost, audience, and expertise. Different types of users have different types of data consumer needs. Remember one of our data mantras: Focus on unlocking the value of your data. If you are planning on sharing a great deal of data, your efforts will be useless if users can't access the data in a meaningful way.

The Challenges of Sharing Lots of Files

In order to successfully deal with the problem of sharing lots of files, you first have to understand each of the challenges involved.

Choosing How to Store the Data

The first challenge is determining how to physically store as well as enable the ability to share your files in a scalable and economical way. Although it is simple to just post a bunch of files on any Web server, the cost of storage and bandwidth must scale with the amount of data and the number of users.

The examples in this chapter focus primarily on dealing with a large number of static files. We'll talk more about database technologies in subsequent chapters.

Choosing the Right Data Format

The second data-sharing challenge is to decide the format that you should provide for your users. This decision depends on your intended audience. Should your files be easy for computer programmers to use or easy for the average person to upload into a spreadsheet? What about space: Should you use the most compact format possible or optimize for human readability? In some cases, you should strive to provide a variety of formats for the various use cases you hope to support.

How to Present the Data

The third consideration to address involves how you allow users to access your data. A municipality that aims to share information with its local citizens should provide online data dashboards with well-designed visualizations so that the technically challenged can participate. However, data journalists and researchers need more than just dashboards; they need lots of big, raw, machine-readable data for detailed analysis. The municipality should also invest in ways to provide programmatic access via Web-based APIs to encourage the development of software applications that consume the data on demand.

Solving the Problem

The rest of this chapter focuses on the first two challenges: dealing with strategies for storage and sharing and understanding which format is the best solution for a particular use case. We will cover various use cases and strategies for processing, analyzing, and visualizing data in the chapters to come.

Imagine we have lots of open data in many files. If you are part of a government, one major goal of sharing data is to maximize accessibility, a factor that will be key to your design. Unfortunately, I can think of very few local governments that have done a great job sharing public data.

In order to solve our problem, let's revisit our game plan for data success. Let's take a look at how we can share our data with the world by building as little infrastructure as possible. Let's work hard to consider our data consumers' needs; we will also keep in mind our data challenge and our audience. Instead of choosing a file format simply because it is popular or familiar, let's deploy our data in a format appropriate to our audience.

Storage: Infrastructure as a Service

You're not still serving files from a server in your office, are you? Unfortunately, many organizations are still sharing files with the outside world using in-house infrastructure. Over the past few years, technological advances that were developed to serve the needs of massive Internet companies have become widely available and economical for the average application developer. Providers like Rackspace, Amazon, Google, and many others have begun to offer services that can be thought of as utility computing, or computing as a service. In fact, the pricing and business model of this type of computing is starting to mimic the models used for public utilities such as power and water companies. For the price of, say, buying a few hard drives and some server hardware, it's now possible to buy access to the equivalent of many more machines, using the same storage and serving infrastructure that manages the world's largest Web sites.

In this infrastructure-as-a-service (IAAS) model of computing, many physical machines are connected together in a network cluster, in some respects acting like a single, large computer. Data belonging to a single user might be physically stored in small chunks on many different physical machines. The hardware used is typically cheap and easily replaceable. Most importantly, redundancy is built into these systems. The difficult challenge of dealing with hardware failure is handled by the IAAS providers as data is replicated to introduce further recovery from failure.

There are many benefits to this type of storage model, as well as many potential trade-offs. In terms of cost, these systems are able to use economies of scale to drive down the costs of individual customer storage. For an economically restricted organization, in order to host and share a huge number of files, this model is the only economically feasible way to share data at high availability without incurring exorbitant storage or bandwidth costs.

Using an IAAS storage solution fulfills several of the guiding principles we discussed in the first chapter. First, this solution allows us to plan for scale: If massive increases in storage or bandwidth occur, our solution will be able to handle it. Also, this model helps us avoid building infrastructure by allowing us to worry about our data rather than purchasing and maintaining our own hardware, hiring systems administrators, or thinking about backups or electricity.

The Network Is Slow

The network is really slow. The average global Internet data transfer speed in 2012 was 2.3 megabits per second (Mbps), with the United States clocking in at around 5.3 Mbps.[2] Imagine having to transfer your 25 gigabytes of data from one place to another at a consistent speed of 5.3 Mbps. At this rate, the transfer will take close to 11 hours. Projects like Google Fiber that aim to increase the average Internet connection toward the 1,000 Mbps range using optical fiber seem promising, but they may not be widespread in the United States for many years. The solutions to many of the issues we've raised inherently favor use of distributed, ubiquitous computing systems. However, network latency will often rear its head when it comes to *big* data challenges.

Choosing the Right Data Format

Let's consider a practical use case. A local government has just installed devices that track the position and speed of each bus in the transit system every minute. This data is used to determine how well these busses stick to their planned schedules. However, because this is a civic project, the city wants to make the raw data available to people who would like to run their own analyses. How should the city structure the data so that others are easily able to make use of it?

A common format for sharing data is comma-separated value (CSV) files. CSV files feature a record of data with each field in the record separated by a comma. Separate records are defined by a line break. While the "C" in CSV often stands for "comma," it's not uncommon to find formats that are delimited by other characters, such as tabs, spaces, or other, more esoteric symbols. Listing 1.1 shows CSV creation in Python.

Listing 1.1 Creating a CSV file using Python

```
import csv

my_csv_file = open('/tmp/sample.csv', 'w')
csv_writer = csv.writer(my_csv_file)
```

---

2. www.theverge.com/2012/5/1/2990469/average-global-internet-speed-drop-us

```
sample_row = ('Michael', 1234, 23.46, 'San Francisco, California')

# Write a CSV row
csv_writer.writerow(sample_row)

# Result: Michael,1234,23.46,"San Francisco, California"
```

CSV is definitely a great format for "flat" data—that is, data that can be represented in a single line. Log data, such as that coming from Web servers and sensors, is well represented in this format. CSV can be fairly compact as text-based data goes: It's the data, pure and simple, with little markup or structure to get in the way. Also, it is definitely easy for most people to use CSV, as it can be imported into spreadsheets, ingested into databases, and easily parsed programmatically. For logs or records that don't require data modeling beyond flat rows, CSV can be extremely useful.

Most importantly, CSV is an excellent format for *sequential access* of data. In other words, it's simple for a computer program to grab one, two, or 1,000 rows at a time from the middle of a file and just start processing. In a distributed processing system, this is helpful for breaking up large programming tasks into many smaller ones. Do you have a huge CSV file that is overwhelming the memory of your single machine? Just split it up and process the fragments.

Although CSV has many positives going for it, there are cases in which it can be a pretty bad format for sharing a large amount data. First of all, it lacks much in the way of standardization. Certainly there have been attempts at official CSV standards,[3] but in practice, there is little regularity in how developers create CSV output. Unfortunately, this sometimes means that people will add a few header lines, use peculiar delimiters between fields, or escape strings in eccentric ways. CSV also doesn't provide a standard way of referring to information about the file itself; when working with collections of CSVs, any information about the type or date that the data represents is sometimes found in the filename itself. In fact, CSV files basically lack any metadata at all, requiring those using them for sharing data to provide additional information about the file somewhere else.

CSV is very bad at describing data that does not fit well into discreet rows. In practice, real world data often has many dimensions, and not all of these dimensions necessarily fit into the rigid structure of CSV's rectangular regularity. Take, for example, data about the number of people registered for political parties in the United States, organized state by state. All states have representatives from the two major parties and many of the much smaller ones. However, some states may have specific parties not found in other states. Therefore, the list of parties will be different sizes for different states. Expressing this data in CSV format provides a data-modeling challenge. Does one create columns of data for every possible political party? Is the list of parties concatenated into a single string and stored in a field all by itself? These representations are not a natural fit for a fixed-size-row structure.

---

3. http://tools.ietf.org/html/rfc4180

Another problem (which we will explore in the next section) is that CSV files are not necessarily human readable; a file that describes a collection of numerical values will be difficult to understand at a glance as it will appear to just be a mishmash of numbers.

Choose CSV when your data is easily expressed in a flat row or if you want to ensure compatibility with nearly everything. CSV format is easy to parse and load, and it will always be easily supported by spreadsheets, databases, and all kinds of other software applications due to its ubiquity. However, don't expect CSV to do anything special; it's not a format that is going to go out of its way to help you. If your audience is more likely to be less technical, CSV may be a good fit. If you expect your data to be used by software developers, they may prefer structured data formats such as JSON (see ahead).

XML: Data, Describe Thyself

If you've worked with data of any kind, you've certainly encountered the Extensible Markup Language, or **XML**. Because of its widespread use and software support, XML is another obvious contender for being the primary file format for sharing huge numbers of files with your consumers.

XML is the way to go to store structured source files from which you can convert to another format. For example, if you have a collection of structured documents that may need to be transformed into a variety of other formats, XML is a great choice to use as the "source of truth" file format.

JSON: The Programmer's Choice

XML is the best at what it was designed for—document interoperability—but it's not always the best choice as a format for hosting a large collection of files. In some cases, the overhead of XML's structure and mission does not match well with the object-oriented focus of many programming languages.

JSON (which stands for JavaScript Object Notation) is a data interchange specification that has gained much popularity with developers. As the name implies, a JSON object is valid JavaScript, so it is obviously an easy data format to use for JavaScript applications. However, JSON is not just for JavaScript, as parsers exist for many major programming languages.

JSON syntax is very simple, and often models data much closer to the original state than the corresponding XML representation. In other words, because XML is structured in a tree-like model, in some cases using it in an object-oriented programming environment can be difficult. XML's model and extensibility features mean that it can model *any* type of data, but there are cases in which the overhead of pulling out nodes from an XML object is less convenient that simply referring to the data in object notation as with JSON. A file in JSON can potentially be faster to parse than a similar document encoded in XML due to a lighter-weight syntax. Placing a collection of newline-delimited JSON objects together in a file makes the format easy to parse programmatically, in the same way that CSV provides sequential access to data.

JSON also shares some of the less desirable characteristics of XML: It is certainly a verbose format, and it will take up additional storage space and bandwidth. Like XML, each field in a JSON record has some description involved, resulting in quite a lot of markup for the amount of data described. Although it is a good format for passing messages from one place to another, JSON is not designed for extensibility, and it lacks some of the fancy schema and validation features found in XML.

Finally, there's another excellent reason to consider hosting data in JSON: It is often trivial to import JSON objects into many types of popular, open-source, nonrelational databases. We will take a look at some of this technology in Chapter 3, "Building a NoSQL-Based Web App to Collect Crowd-Sourced Data."

Hosting a collection of data in newline-delimited JSON format is a good start for data exchange when coders are involved, and this format will make application developers and nonrelational database administrators happy. JSON is not a great format for a general population that expects to be able to load files directly into a spreadsheet (for that application, use CSV).

Listing 1.2 provides a brief comparison of the structure of CSV, XML, and JSON formats.

Listing 1.2   **Comparison of CSV, XML, and JSON**

```
# CSV example
first_name,last_name,book,date
"Michael", "Manoochehri", "Data Just Right",2013


<!-- XML Example -->
<xml>
  <author>Michael Manoochehri</author>
  <list>
    <book position="1">Data Just Right</book>
  </list>
</xml>


// JSON example
{
"name": "Michael",
"book":{"title":"Data Just Right","date":"2013"}
}
```

Character Encoding

Character encoding is the process by which a computer represents all the characters and symbols necessary for exchanging information, such as the ones you are reading right now. A very simple example of character encoding is Morse code, which represents letters in the alphabet as pulses that can be transmitted over a wire or visually.

Years ago, due to limitations in hardware (and probably a linguistic bias by American geeks working on early computing systems), many computers often represented textual characters in a format known as the American Standard Code for Information Interchange, or **ASCII**. ASCII worked great for representing characters from the English language. It worked so well that the Johnson administration even made ASCII a federal standard in 1968.[4]

What worked well in the United States didn't exactly translate to users who communicate in languages with characters that differ from those in the English alphabet. In fact, many countries ended up creating their own encoding standards that, although similar to ASCII, were incompatible with ASCII in various ways. This obviously caused all kinds of frustrating problems in the software world.

Fortunately, by the late 1980s, a group of very smart computer scientists began to come up with solutions to this alphabet soup (pardon the pun). Their solution was the **Unicode Standard**, which aims to define a set of standard encodings for all the characters in the world. Unicode is typically implemented using one of several standards, the most common ones being UTF-8 and UTF-16. The UTF-8 standard was famously first developed on the back of a placemat and implemented in a matter of a few days.[5] Because most of the technologies that encompass the Big Data movement grew up after its creation, Unicode is almost universally supported by the software featured in this chapter and others. Many of the technologies and tools in this book will natively use one of these encodings.

Unfortunately, it's not uncommon to encounter situations in which enormous amounts of data are tied up in files encoded with some version of ASCII or some other non–Unicode scheme. Sometimes, non–Unicode data is created accidentally or unwittingly. Another source of non–Unicode data may come from legacy software, such as the decades-old reservations systems that are still being used by some airlines. Some older desktop software might only be able to export data in obsolete encoding formats.

The message here is simple: If you've got lots of data lying around that is not already encoded in UTF-8 or UTF-16, then convert it!

Working with text files? Try these classics.

When working with large amounts of text data, sometimes the quickest way to solve a problem is to use some of the original Unix command-line utilities, such as split, grep, and sed. After many decades, this software is still in widespread use today; thanks to open-source implementations of Unix such as GNU/Linux, the utilities might even be used more than ever before!

Do you have annoying header information in your CSV file? Remove the first two lines of a file and place the result in a new file:

```
sed '1,2d' file > newfile
```

---

4. www.presidency.ucsb.edu/ws/index.php?pid=28724
5. www.cl.cam.ac.uk/~mgk25/ucs/utf-8-history.txt

Is the data in your source file delimited by an odd character, such the caret (^)? Replace those pesky characters with commas!

```
sed 's/\^/,/g' original_file > new_file
```

When working with extremely large text files with millions of lines, it's possible to have a bad record on a particular line; but how can you display it? With sed, it's easy to print out a particular line number, such as line number 3,451,234:

```
sed '3451234q;d' your_large_file.csv
```

Another great utility for dealing with very large files is split, which, as the name implies, splits large files into smaller ones. For example, if you have a very large file that you need to split into chunks of 500 Mb at most while preserving the integrity of line endings (avoiding broken lines), use this command:

```
split -C 500m your_large_file.csv
```

There's a lot more that can be done with Unix command-line text-processing utilities. Sometimes the best (and quickest) solution is the simplest.

File Transformations

We've only briefly touched upon the challenges of working with many files in a variety of data formats. In practice, converting many files from one format to another can be a very involved process. What if you've got a lot of data in a particular format, and you need to convert it to another format? This data transformation process can sometimes be daunting.

Transforming a large collection one document at time can take enormous amounts of time. Fortunately, it is also a task well suited to distributed systems. When confronted with hundreds and even thousands of separate documents, it's helpful to run these tasks in parallel using a large number of distributed resources.

The most popular open-source distributed computing framework is **Hadoop**. Hadoop is an open-source implementation of the MapReduce framework, which allows data processing tasks to be split across a large number of separate machines. Hadoop was originally inspired by Google's MapReduce research paper (but it is by no means the only implementation of MapReduce). In Chapter 9, "Building Data Transformation Workflows with Pig and Cascading," we'll take a look at how to build an end-to-end data-transformation pipeline using the open-source Cascading workflow framework.

Data in Motion: Data Serialization Formats

XML, JSON, and even plain old CSV files can all be considered members of a class of objects used in the process of converting data into bits that a computer can understand and move from one place to another. This process is known as **data serialization**.

Data systems often make use of many machines across a network. Some machines specialize in collecting data from a large number of inputs quickly. Others are tasked with running batch processes that analyze the data. When building systems that move data from one system to another, sending the output of one process to the input of another is a common task. Unfortunately, the network is always going to be the slowest step in this process. To help provide the most efficient data transfer, it's beneficial to represent data in the most compact way possible.

Earlier in this chapter, we saw that XML is great for converting from one document format to another but is not always the best choice for data interoperability, especially when data sizes are very large. Recall that JSON also shares this characteristic with XML. The markup in XML and JSON produces files larger than the data that either format represents, resulting in more time being taken to physically move data from one place to another. Although it's possible to compress files in these data formats before sending them off, the developer still needs to handle the compression and decompression steps himself.

As Internet companies began to deal with the challenges of Web scale data, they quickly realized that the overhead of moving data between systems could result in considerable cost and latency. Similarly, it was found that systems built with a variety of technologies (for example, using C++ for some applications and Python for others) benefitted from the use of a common language for passing data back and forth.

A naïve approach to this problem would be to convert data into some type of byte array: basically, a binary representation of the data. This approach might reduce the size of the data, but, unfortunately, each system would have to know beforehand exactly how the data was serialized so that it could later be deserialized. Hard coding the encoding and decoding functions into the application would work, but it would be problematic if anything about the data model changed. If an application pipeline depended on multiple systems built with different programming languages, the work involved in changing these functions would be considerable.

Several solutions to this problem were created independently, but they all work in similar ways. In general, the first step is to provide a description of the data, or schema, and define it somewhere that is common to both sender and receiver. The second step is to build a standard interface with programming language support to serialize the data into both the message sender and receiver.

Apache Thrift and Protocol Buffers

When data sizes grow very large, the overhead of data transfer between systems can add up. This might not be an issue at the megabyte scale, but as data grows to gigabytes and beyond, the cost and latency of moving data back and forth can become a huge issue. Two different technologies that take similar approaches to solving this problem are Apache Thrift and Protocol Buffers.

Apache Thrift is an open-source project originally developed at Facebook to provide a generic data solution for data serialization. Thrift allows developers to define a configuration file that describes the data that will be serialized. A code generator is run to produce a server that handles the data serialization in the language specified.

Google's Protocol Buffers are very similar to Thrift, and the software to compile Protocol Buffers is also available to use as open-source software.

Like Thrift, Protocol Buffers are used in a variety of projects. While Protocol Buffers are generally used for moving data around, some organizations are using Protocol Buffers for persistent files. For example, OpenStreetMap is currently converting its available map data from XML to a static format known as PBF (protocol buffer binary format).

Apache Avro

Apache Avro is a relatively new data serialization format that combines some of the best features of all the technologies we have described previously. Unlike Apache Thrift or Protocol Buffers, Avro data is self-describing and uses a JSON-schema description to describe each individual field. However, *unlike* XML or JSON, this schema is not incorporated into every field but instead is provided as a JSON object included with the data itself. Avro also natively supports compression so that developers don't have to spend much time worrying about building this logic themselves.

Avro is currently used in the Hadoop community, but it deserves to be more widely used in other applications. Some developers are exploring the possibility of reading and writing data in the Avro format as static files. Programming language support for Avro has been growing, and over time it's possible that it may become more of a de facto standard for data serialization.

Summary

Sharing a large set of documents seems like a simple task, but the reality is that many organizations that should be sharing data in the most accessible ways possible simply aren't.

Are you hosting a massive collection of files? In order to maintain scalability and affordability in the face of massive amounts of storage and bandwidth, distributed storage services provided by infrastructure-as-a-service providers are generally the only economical solution.

Choosing a file format for your hosted files can be a challenge, but not if you know how your audience may use your data. CSV files are trivial to parse and are universally supported by everything from spreadsheets to database software to programming languages. However, CSV is not able to model complex data structures easily. XML is a great format for providing an unambiguous source of data that can be used for converting documents from one format to another. It is well supported and is best used for providing unambiguous structure for document data. However, it is not necessarily the best format for software developers who wish to quickly serialize, transfer, and parse data. Although JSON is not as extensible as XML or as simple as CSV, its ease of use for data transfer certainly makes it a popular format for programmers and nonrelational database administrators.

Both XML and JSON formats carry a lot of baggage from the markup used to describe data. As data needs scale, more large data source providers are moving from text-based file formats (such XML or JSON) to language-agnostic binary formats designed for data transfer efficiency.

If you are in a situation in which you are building software systems to process or transfer large amounts of data, you may gain an efficiency boost by using a data-serialization format. Both Thrift and Protocol Buffers are open-source and well supported by community efforts. Avro is an exciting new approach to data serialization that combines many of the features found in the formats described in this chapter.

3

Building a NoSQL-Based Web App to Collect Crowd-Sourced Data

Memory is the new disk and disk is the new tape.
—Jim Gray

There was a time, not too long ago, when developers building Web applications with open-source databases always chose either MySQL or PostgreSQL. Although these relational databases are still extremely popular for many types of applications, in the past few years a bewildering amount of new nonrelational and distributed database projects have appeared. Some of these tools are designed to handle the performance needs of dealing with Internet-scale data and do so by distributing the workload over multiple machines.

The rapid innovation we are seeing in the world of distributed database technology is the result of open-source velocity, lower costs for commodity hardware, and the increasing accessibility of cloud computing. Although distributed database technologies allow small, frugal teams to handle and build amazingly scalable Web applications, the sheer amount of available choices can be a challenge.

In this chapter, we take a look at the landscape of scalable database systems—technologies that are built to handle high volumes of data transfer and be distributed over many machines. We also explore a very common application design pattern in which constant streams of data are either inserted or read from a database that millions of clients may be accessing at once. This application model can be found in many use cases, from social multiplayer games to social messaging applications and even in the backends that aggregate data from Internet of Things devices.

Relational Databases: Command and Control

The majority of digital data transactions we make every day—whether visiting a Web site, using an ATM machine, or making an airline reservation—are handled by a

relational database. The relational database concept owes everything to the work of Edgar F. Codd, a former Royal Air Force pilot and World War II veteran.

Codd has a unique place in computer science history. As digital computing was being developed in the 1960s, early databases were structured in a hierarchical manner, meaning that data was structured as a collection of parent–child relationships. This type of database was sometimes convenient for the application storing the data, especially when the data itself was inherently hierarchical (for example, a classification of plant species). However, when the underlying data expressed complex relationships or had no inherent hierarchy, modeling data using a hierarchical database model was very clumsy. The biggest problem was the lack of a feature that we take for granted today: free-form search capabilities. In order to traverse the data stored in this manner, a user had to have a knowledge of the hierarchical structure. It became clear that a more flexible and generalizable model was necessary to make sense of ever-growing datasets.

Codd's relational model is currently so ubiquitous that the concept is well known even to the casual database user, but let's revisit the basic characteristics. Codd proposed that each record of data be described using **tuples**, which are discrete sets of values that can be individually referenced by a unique identifier. In many applications, tuples are simply ordered lists of values, and each value can be retrieved by referencing a position in the list. In most programming languages, tuples are **zero-based**, meaning that the first element is referenced by "0," the second by "1," and so on. In Codd's relational database model, each element in the database record is accessed not by number, but by a name known as an **attribute**. For example, if I were to store a data record of Edgar Codd's name, I could define an attribute as `first_name` to reference "Edgar" and another attribute as `last_name` to store "Codd." Tuples of the same type can be organized into tables, which can then be cross-referenced to each other based on an existing relationship.

A key component to the success of the relational database model is the idea of **normalization**: In Codd's view, each unit of data should exist only once in a single table. This cuts down on redundancy and storage costs. More importantly, normalization makes it possible to keep data consistent by having to change values only in a single location. In Codd's system, a column in each table can be designated as a **primary key**, which is an attribute value that is used to retrieve a single record unambiguously. The primary key could be used to connect these relationships using some type of syntactical query. The **Structured Query Language** (SQL) was later created by other IBM researchers to express relational queries. Codd's concept provides the ability to ask a variety of questions about the data in various tables so long as the data can be related in some way.

Let's take a look at the simple example of using a relational table in Listing 3.1. Our example database holds two types of values: identities of computer scientists and information about countries. Unless some very sweeping changes happen at the United Nations, we can assume that each record in the "countries" table is unique, so we can treat the country name as a primary key. On the other hand, it's possible for two humans to have exactly the same name. Therefore, in our "people" table, we need to add an additional, unique numerical attribute called id as our primary key, as we can't guarantee that there are not two distinct Edgar Codds. Finally, we can use an SQL query that returns a relationship between the names of the computer scientists and which country they are from.

Listing 3.1 **A simple relational database model and SQL query**

```
Table #1: countries
Name                    abbreviation
-----------------------------------------------------------
United Kingdom          UK
United States           USA


Table #2: people
Id    first           last            nationality
-----------------------------------------------------------
1     Edgar           Codd            United Kingdom
2     Alan            Turing          United Kingdom
3     Eric            Brewer          United States

/* Example SQL Query */
SELECT
  people.id, people.first, people.last, countries.abbreviation
FROM
  people, nationality
WHERE
  countries.name = "United Kingdom";

# Result
1, Edgar, Codd, UK
2, Alan, Turing, UK
```

Relational databases allow for a very flexible model for storing and querying data. Putting work into the design of the schema of data provides great benefits, such as the ability to express a variety of queries. The relational database model provides an accessible interface to complex data problems and a method for unlocking the value of data.

Codd published his ideas about the relational database model in 1970. At first, Codd's employer, IBM, took its time commercializing this technology. It took nearly a decade for IBM to develop a product based on Codd's theories for database design. While Big Blue was taking its time bringing the relational database to market, many others were recognizing the value of Codd's relational concept. Among these was none other than Larry Ellison, who helped found a company with the inauspicious name Software Development Laboratories. This company later evolved into Oracle, and Ellison's commercial success made him one of the richest people in the world. The relational database market sparked intense competition throughout the 1990s, with behemoths including Sybase and Microsoft joining Oracle and IBM in the scrum for major enterprise dollars. The relational database market wasn't just a boon for proprietary software vendors. Many popular open-source relational databases were developed, including the popular projects MySQL and PostgreSQL. Although Codd never attained the massive financial success of Ellison, his work was so influential it earned him a Turing Award (sometimes called the computer science Nobel Prize) in 1981.

The Relational Database ACID Test

As relational databases were brought to market, Codd was not completely satisfied with the design of various implementations. He went on to publish a set of rules that he believed must be met in order for a database to qualify as "relational." Some of these rules described standards for data consistency, including the need for all information in a relational database (including table and column names) to be represented in only one way. Other rules, which are still debated today, include the manner in which a relational database should represent NULL values.

The former Royal Air Force pilot's rules for relational databases were never completely realized by most mainstream software packages. Whether a piece of software fulfilled all of Codd's rules or simply most of them, relational databases all shared similar utility and flexibility that have helped them become the dominant manner of interacting with digital data. Databases that generally conform to a relational model are described as exhibiting four traits known as **ACID**—an acronym representing the terms atomicity, consistency, isolation, and durability. In summary, these four rules attempt to prevent unexpected or erratic results. **Atomicity** and **consistency** refer to relational databases' goals of preventing partial insertions and to maintaining a valid state from one transaction to another. **Isolation** refers to the ability of a database to handle multiple transactions at the same time without conflicts. **Durability** means that a database retains the last known correct state in the event of errors or crashes.

When launching a piece of software, technological limitations and decisions about acceptable compromises outweigh the goal of conforming to a particular idealized architecture. Codd publicly voiced a distaste for products that billed themselves as relational but did not conform to his strict idealization of the relational concept. Codd's tension would foreshadow an even larger deviation of database architecture from the ideal relational model in the decades to follow.

Relational Databases versus the Internet

One of the many reasons that the relational database concept became the dominant form of data management is that it strives to provide a great deal of data consistency. Surely a database administrator should be wary of transactions that leave the database in an uncertain state. Despite these consistency features, the relational model has been disrupted by the same humble invention that disrupted so many other aspects of daily life: the Internet. All of a sudden, application development was shifting to the Web. Applications of all types, from business software to email to video, were being built not for a single user on a desktop, but for anyone who had access to an Internet connection. Much of the growth of open-source database MySQL was due to the availability of easy-to-use integrations with Web-friendly scripting languages such as Perl and PHP.

Codd's concept of database structure imposes an upfront understanding of the data. Schemas and relationships must be defined before making a single insert. The relational model also requires a bit of work on the part of the software itself. Consider the process of an application writing a record to a relational database; data might be represented using more than one table. The database itself must take care to ensure that data is consistent after the write has occurred, which takes a bit of computational overhead.

However, as the user base of a Web site grows, so does the need to handle the scale of data. Some of the early Web pioneers such as Amazon and Google found that relational databases were not always the right tool for the job. The priorities of existing relational database systems were geared more toward consistency than availability.

Consider an online messaging system in which users post and share comments publicly with other users. A relational database design architecture might define a table to keep track of individual users, with each user being assigned a unique identifier. In order to facilitate message sharing, we would also require a table relating each posted message to information about the target recipient. Although heavily simplified, this type of system is not unlike the many comment and blog systems currently used on the Web.

Now imagine the Web site has gone viral and that millions of users access this online system at all times. How can we handle the scale? With computing prices dropping every day, servers and hard disks are available to handle quite a lot of transactional processing. At some point, a single machine might not be able to handle the load of many thousands of queries every second. Furthermore, Web traffic, log data, and other factors may mean that, over time, it might not be possible to continually upgrade a single server. The need for higher capacity and plenty of data throughput requires other strategies.

Although commodity computer hardware tends to become cheaper over time, continually upgrading to more massive server hardware has been historically economically infeasible. Spending twice as much money on a huge, single machine may not provide double the performance. In contrast, smaller, more modest servers remain inexpensive. In general, it makes more economic sense to scale horizontally: in other words, to simply add more cheap machines to the system rather than try to put a single relational database on one expensive, massive server.

In order to guarantee performance of this Web application, one might consider splitting the relational tables across a collection of machines. Perhaps each table could reside on a different machine; it might be possible to split, or **shard**, individual tables of a relational database system off to a dedicated server. At some point, the table with the most data might again become too large to host on a single machine. Situations like this create bottlenecks in our system. When faced with the onslaught of Web-scale data, the popular relational database model begins to create very challenging problems. With the hardware available, Codd's idealized concepts of database design simply don't support the realities of Web traffic.

Codd's rules were already being bent as relational database software was being made available in the market place. In order to cope with the new needs of the Web-scale data world, database developers started to question the rigid requirements defined by Codd's relational model. Since users favor responsive Web sites, many Web applications require quick database reads over the need for consistent database insertions. Instead of worrying about consistency, what if a database was optimized for availability? Similarly, hard drives are cheap, and storage is getting cheaper all the time. Could Codd's distaste for redundant data be reconsidered, allowing for the same data stored in many places? The implications of Internet-sized data were beginning to expose limitations in Codd's relational database concepts. In fact, the creators of Web-scale distributed databases had started to shrug their shoulders about the need to maintain ACID compliance. Application developers started to differentiate between software requirements that favored a large number of database reads versus a small number of database writes. Some developers began to ponder the consequences of reduced consistency. What would really happen if, say, some users were provided database results that were slightly staler than others?

CAP Theorem and BASE

When data sizes scale to very large volumes, data application developers often have to deal with a variety of trade-offs. Often, the only economically viable option is to distribute a single database across a large number of either physical or virtual machines hosted on a cluster of commodity servers. In 2000, UC Berkeley professor and Inktomi co-founder Dr. Eric Brewer proposed a model for understanding how distributed computing systems such as a distributed database system might operate. Brewer's conjecture begins by defining three important characteristics of distributed systems: consistency, availability, and partition tolerance, or **CAP**. **Consistency** refers to the ability for each machine to have access to exactly the same data at any given time. **Availability** describes the ability of a system to respond to requests. Finally, if a system can function successfully in the event of a partial failure (perhaps if one of the servers in the system crashes or loses power), then the system exhibits **partition tolerance**. Brewer's famous conjecture stated that it is impossible for a distributed system to exhibit all three of these characteristics at the same time. Many research papers and even books have been devoted to studying different aspects of CAP.

Let's illustrate the consequences of the CAP theorem with an example. Imagine a data system in which a relational database on one machine is mirrored, for redundancy, using a second machine. Every time a database update is made on the primary machine, the data is also sent to the other machine to make the same update. At first glance, this design solves both the availability and the partition tolerance problem: If one machine goes down, the other is available, and the system itself may continue to run.

Unfortunately, the consistency of the system is compromised. How will the two servers maintain sync once the broken machine comes back online? Will the primary machine block existing connections for a short time, affecting system availability, in order to make sure data is consistent with the other machine? Dealing with data at scale using multiple machines presents challenges like this all the time.

The consequences of the CAP theorem freed database designers to come up with alternative ways of thinking about scalability. In a clever play on words, an alternative to the rules of ACID compliance came to be known as **BASE**, short for "basically available, soft state, eventually consistent." In 2008, Dan Pritchett, then a technical fellow at eBay, published an ACM article entitled "BASE: An Acid Alternative,"[1] in which he stated that while "ACID is pessimistic and forces consistency at the end of every operation, BASE is optimistic and accepts that the database consistency will be in a state of flux."

Put simply, BASE systems strive to maximize some aspect of CAP, such as availability or partition tolerance, by allowing parts of the database system to exist in different states of consistency. For example, when using many machines, a database write event to one machine might not be available to the entire system. The state of this type of system will become consistent—eventually. In an ACID-compliant relational database, we would expect data from an insertion to be available to the system and all users immediately. However, in our distributed system, while a database insertion is happening on one machine a client could be requesting data stored on another. If two clients request the same piece of data from separate machines, the two values retrieved may be out of sync. Developers that follow the guidelines of BASE architecture accept that these inconsistencies tend to be less important when compared to the need of the system to be able to scale well.

Why can't a relational database model be distributed across many machines? The answer is simple: It can. However, as we've seen, the process of distributing a relational database over a large pool of machines exposes a great deal of complexity for the database administrator.

Relational databases are the best design for applications in which data is absolutely required to be inserted in a consistent state. The canonical example of this is a financial transaction database—users will not tolerate a database that provides inconsistent responses about money. For some types of Web content, applications are mostly geared toward a specific task, such as serving many users with content that doesn't change very much. Sometimes, an application is focused on being able to collect data very quickly and using many machines, and immediate consistency of the data is not a requirement. For these applications, a different architecture may be more useful.

Nonrelational Database Models

Let's take a look at the use cases, advantages, and disadvantages of nonrelational databases. There are many types of nonrelational database models, but we will focus on the two most popular types: key–value stores and document stores. These classes of

---

1. http://queue.acm.org/detail.cfm?id=1394128

databases refer to general design concepts rather than strict categories, as features of one type are often found in the other.

Key–Value Database

It goes without saying that Amazon.com attracts a large number of users, and, out of necessity, the company has been on the cutting edge of application scalability. A seminal paper about the nonrelational database technology behind Amazon's Dynamo database, entitled "Amazon's Highly Available Key–Value Store," describes a set of use cases for which relational databases are not ideal. "For many services," the paper states, "such as those that provide best seller lists, shopping carts, customer preferences, session management, sales rank, and product catalog, the common pattern of using a relational database would lead to inefficiencies and limit scale and availability." [2] When data volumes grow, reading from and writing to a relational database while maintaining ACID compliance can be computationally expensive.

A key–value store looks a lot like a big hash table. Each record in the database is an object identified by a unique key. The value that is addressed by this key can basically be anything: a string, a JSON or XML document, a binary blob, or a number of other things. A key characteristic of these databases is that the system doesn't really know anything about the data being stored; all access to data comes from the key. Key–value stores are the right choice for applications that generally retrieve database information based on a single key.

This design makes for very good performance for database writes. Another advantage is that the design lends itself toward being easy to scale and replicate across a network of machines. Because each record in the database is simply a value addressed by a unique key, the data itself can reside on any machine on the network as long as the system knows how it can be located. One way to scale this type of database is to keep a secondary table of key-range to machine mappings. When a piece of data is defined, this table may be referred to by the secondary table and the request sent to the proper machine.

On the other hand, a general disadvantage of the design of a key–value store is that data cannot be accessed by value. In other words, it is impossible to query a key–value data store for all records that contain a particular set of values. The only way to query a key–value database is by specifying a request by key or, in some cases, a range of keys.

Listing 3.2 demonstrates some examples of using a key–value store to query for data.

Listing 3.2 **Organizing data by key using a key-value data store**

```
> SET book:1 "Data Just Right"
> SET author:1 "Michael Manoochehri"

> GET book:1
"Data Just Right"
```

---

2. http://s3.amazonaws.com/AllThingsDistributed/sosp/amazon-dynamo-sosp2007.pdf, p. 1

```
> GET author:1
"Michael Manoochehri"
```

Some examples of open-source key–value stores are Apache Cassandra and LinkedIn's Project Voldemort. We will take a closer look at building a scalable data solution using the open-source Redis database, which is the most popular in-memory key–value store, later in this chapter.

Document Store

Every day, we interact with numerous documents of various types, both physical and virtual, such as business cards, receipts, tax returns, and playlists. Some of these documents have similar characteristics, such as the time they were created or the information they might contain about a particular person. Other documents contain data completely unique to the document type; an online application may have any number of different fields, for example. The data from this variety of documents might be difficult to express using the rigid schemas found in relational databases. Not only that: What if the schema of a variety of documents needed to be changed? In these cases, it might be the right time to look into using a document store.

A document store is a type of database that stores data as a collection of—you guessed it—documents. These documents themselves may be XML representations, JSON objects, and even specific binary formats (see Chapter 2 for a closer look at these formats). In contrast to a relational database—in which every record in a table must adhere to the same schema—a document store can contain a variety of records with completely different schemas. In other words, each record might have a completely different structure. Although this is also true of most key–value stores, the difference is that document stores usually allow the user to ask questions about the actual data in the database, rather than interrogating simply using the key.

A canonical example that illustrates the differences between a document store and a relational database can be found in serving the information necessary to construct a page for a typical blog. Blog pages not only feature page content and a title but also additional content such as an author name, links to related posts, and even user comments. If this information was stored in a relational database, the queries necessary to build a single page would require accessing a large number of tables.

The user of a document store takes a different approach; all of the content for a single page is stored in a single, large record. These records remain independent of one another, and changing one does not affect the rest of the blog post records. If one of the blog pages contains a completely different chunk of information (say, links to photo URLs for a slideshow), this information can be added to any document without worrying about the schema of the others. The relational database, on the other hand, would represent all of the information as relationships between existing, normalized tables. If a slideshow feature was needed, a new "slideshow" table, with a strictly defined schema, would need to be created. In addition, relationships to the rest of the content of the page would need to be defined, likely by a key relating it to a unique blog post ID.

In our example, the main advantage of the document store is that it can produce the entire set of data necessary to produce a blog page with a single query. If the blog's visitor traffic becomes huge, the database records could be split across many machines without worrying as much about exactly what records ended up on which machine. The query could simply be routed to a single machine, the entire page content retrieved at once, and the blog page rendered in a single pass. For very high-volume Web sites with many more readers than content writers, a document store is likely to be the best choice for a database backend.

Now imagine that some of the blog's database records featured an author whose last name was misspelled (this is a use case that I have personally experienced quite a few times). When using a relational database, author information would be stored in only one place: a single record in the authors table. Since the data found in a relational database should be completely normalized, the misspelled value can be easily changed by issuing a single SQL statement. In contrast, the document database stores the information about authors in each and every record. If an author produces many blog posts, that author's name is repeated over and over in every record the author is associated with. Many of these documents could contain a misspelled author name, so we would need to iterate over all of the broken records and update them one at a time. Usually this is done by writing a function that iterates over each individual document containing the misspelled name field and changing it if found. The normalization and consistency of the relational database has made this error correction process more computationally simple and predictable.

Listing 3.3 illustrates inserting and retrieving data from a document store—in this case, MongoDB. In contrast to a key–value store, it is possible to query for records based on the data itself rather than having to rely on the key.

Listing 3.3 Inserting and retrieving data using a document store

```
# Insertion of two documents with different schemas
> db.example.insert({"name":"michael",
                     "book":"Data Just Right"})
> db.example.insert({"name":"edgar",
                     "book":"The Relational Model for Database Management",
                     "employers":["Royal Air Force","IBM"]})

> db.example.find()

{
   "_id" : ObjectId("51ab96791a4b9b1009e2c459"),
   "name" : "michael",
   "book" : "Data Just Right"
}

{
   "_id" : ObjectId("51ab9a041a4b9b1009e2c45c"),
   "name" : "edgar",
```

```
    "book" : "The Relational Model for Database Management",
    "employers" : [ "Royal Air Force", "IBM" ]
}

# Retrieve documents that contain a particular name
> db.example.find({"name":"michael"})

{
    "_id" : ObjectId("51ab96791a4b9b1009e2c459"),
    "name" : "michael",
    "book" : "Data Just Right"
}

# Retrieve documents that contain a particular employer
> db.example.find({"employers":"Royal Air Force"})

{
    "_id" : ObjectId("51ab9a041a4b9b1009e2c45c"),
    "name" : "edgar",
    "book" : "The Relational Model for Database Management",
    "employers" : [ "Royal Air Force", "IBM" ]
}
```

Document stores are the right choice when you need a scalable database solution and querying over the content of the data (and not just the key) is important. Examples of this type of database include open-source software such as MongoDB and CouchDB.

Leaning toward Write Performance: Redis

On the surface, the multitude of distributed databases seems to cover a lot of the same use cases. As a result, newcomers often face a great deal of confusion when trying to choose a nonrelational database solution. In reality, each of the popular nonrelational databases are very opinionated. Some are geared toward being easily distributed across many machines at the expense of consistency. Others focus on raw speed of data writes and reads. When trying to choose between one or the other, you must be opinionated as well. The most important goal as a database decider is understanding your particular use case.

For this example, let's choose a primary goal for our application and select an appropriate database solution for reaching this goal. Along the way, we will learn about the challenges faced when scaling our choice of database. An increasingly common use case is applications that handle a great deal of database insertions very quickly. Small developer teams might want to build a Web application that can handle many messages from thousands or even millions of users. Perhaps the use case is an application that scrolls a set of tweets that mention a particular television show during a broadcast. Similarly, an application might require aggregating data from thousands of weather sensors around the world. This design pattern is also common in the online gaming world. Many social multiplayer games offer the ability for a game to be replayed, with statistics about the gaming environment broadcast publicly. In this case, a continuous stream of data might be streamed into the application backend from thousands or even millions of players at all times.

In the previous example, flexibility in querying is less important than the ability to collect data very fast. For applications like this, a key–value store is a good choice, as the simplicity of this model makes database writes as fast as possible. The key–value design also lends itself well to distributed applications, in which the choice of which part of the database to shard is not particularly crucial. One database that meets many of these criteria is the open-source key–value store Redis. The Web site DB-Engines.com,[3] which provides a ranking of the most popular database software using metrics such as search engine result sizes and the amount of technical questions posted on forums such as StackOverflow.com, claims that Redis is also the most popular key–value data store.

Redis has many interesting features that make it a good choice for applications that require very fast read and write performance. It is primarily an "in-memory" database, meaning that it stores the entire database using your server's available memory. This might seem like a big limitation, as you will need to provide adequate hardware (whether physical or virtual) for your application, and once the power goes out, your data will presumably be lost. Not so fast! Redis can also provide the "D" of ACID compliance—durability—as it provides configurable options for persisting the in-memory data to disk. In other words, Redis provides both a volatile, but performant, layer for reading and writing data and a persistent on-disk cache for durability.

Like everything in the data world, great advantage must come at the expense of something else, and in this case, that something else is consistency. For example, if the in-memory database is set to persist data to disk every ten seconds, and the memory fails in that time (due to power failure), data will be lost. A high-volume Web application recording the scores of thousands of online game players may produce a considerable amount of data. It is also possible to tell Redis to persist every single in-memory database write to disk individually, thus providing very good durability. Unfortunately, this reduces Redis' performance quite a bit, negating the advantage of using a memory-based system in the first place. On top of all this, Redis also has an easy-to-configure replication feature, which allows a primary instance to stream updates to a secondary server asynchronously.

Redis is excellent at setting and getting data quickly based on the data's keys—but as it is a key–value store, it does not allow queries to access the values referred to by the keys. If your application requires a different type of functionality, such as the need to quickly retrieve data based on a particular aspect of the data itself, then a different type of nonrelational database, such as a document store, may be more appropriate.

---

3. http://db-engines.com/en/ranking

Listing 3.4 demonstrates basic commands for how to insert and retrieve single values, lists, and hash structures using the Redis command-line interface.

Listing 3.4   Examples of using Redis for single values, lists and hashes

```
# Setting values by key
> SET user:1:name 'Michael'
> SET user:2:name 'Ben'

# Retrieve a list of keys matching a pattern
> KEYS user*

1) "user:2:name"
2) "user:1:name"

# Retrieving a value using the respective key
> GET user:2:name

"Ben"

# Using lists - LPUSH adds values to the head of a list
> LPUSH names 'Jared'
> LPUSH names 'Melinda'

# Retrieve a range of values from a list
> LRANGE names 0 1

1) "Melinda"
2) "Jared"

# RPUSH adds values to the tail of the list
> RPUSH names 'Debra'
> LRANGE names 0 2

1) "Melinda"
2) "Jared"
3) "Debra"

# Using hashes - HMSET sets fields to their respective values for a
# hash stored at a key
> HMSET employees:1 name 'Michael' city 'San Francisco' role 'Author'

# Retrieve the "name" attribute of the hash "employees:1"
> HGET employees:1  name

"Michael"
```

```
# Retrieve all keys and values of the hash "employees:1"
> HGETALL employees:1

1) "name"
2) "Michael"
3) "city"
4) "San Francisco"
5) "role"
6) "Author"
```

The contents of computer memory do not persist when the power shuts off. Storing persistent data is the role of the disk. Redis is an "in-memory" data store, so what happens when someone trips over a power cord and your server turns off? Does the entire database get erased? Well, not really: Redis augments the performance of the in-memory system by providing the ability to persist data to disk. When data volumes are enormous, we must consider various trade-offs. For example, do we need to have complete consistency at all times? Is it reasonable for our application to potentially lose the last minute of data if the power suddenly goes out? There are many applications that don't really require persistence at all, and for these, it's also possible to turn off Redis persistence completely.

Sharding across Many Redis Instances

Building applications that serve many users requires database administrators to think about what to do in situations in which the amount of data hurling toward your system is constantly growing. This characteristic, known as **scalability**, is a key goal of high-throughput databases used in Web scale applications.

The simple application that we've built using Redis is able to collect lots of data very quickly. In fact, it's become so useful that your boss has asked you to build a system that can handle 50 times as much data. In the spirit of picking the right tool for the job, you might not need to do anything! Redis write performance is very good, and additional computer resources may not be necessary.

At some point, however, you may need to use multiple machines, whether physical or virtual, to handle the traffic and data of your application. Redis is limited by the amount of available memory in a machine, and there is only so much one can add to a single server before it gets to be prohibitively expensive. Also important is replication of the database for crucial applications. If the single machine that is your primary interface with the world goes down for any reason, you will need another machine ready to pick up the slack. It's not important that these two machines are completely in sync—as we've learned, making sure that the data between each is exactly consistent at any given time is not always necessary—but for real life applications, durability is a concern.

What we really want is for our distributed key–value store to automatically be able to handle the addition of new machines to our cluster. Ideally, our database will be able to detect the additional machines and evenly distribute some of our existing data to these machines accordingly. Because the data needs to be distributed, incoming database requests can be automatically routed to the correct node on the network. This ability to simply add individual machines to a pool without worrying too much about configuration of new application logic is known as **linear scalability**, and in practice, it can be difficult to achieve. Anytime a single piece of data needs to be accessed by more than one machine, there is potential for bottlenecks to appear. For example, if one machine is writing a piece of data, and another wants to do the same thing at the same time, the result will be a resource conflict. These problems are challenging, but luckily there are a variety of strategies available for distributing, or **sharding,** data across many machines.

One way to shard data across multiple Redis instances is to decide on a key range beforehand. This is the easiest way to accomplish this, but there's a drawback: It is not robust as data scale gets large. For example, imagine that your application collects the latest scores from thousands of players from an online game. If you have two instances of Redis, your application might be instructed to send scores from usernames starting with A through C to one instance, and scores from players with names starting from D to F to another instance, and so on.

Automatic Partitioning with Twemproxy

Underneath it all, Redis is really designed to be a performant single-server database. Although the fact that Redis is a key–value data store makes it a bit easier to distribute an entire dataset across various instances in a cluster pool, we still need to choose and implement some kind of sharding strategy, as described earlier, to make it work. As of the release of this book, the developers of Redis have indeed been working on a native, fault-tolerant version of the standalone server that allows for automatic cluster management.

In this example, we will demonstrate an open-source technology developed at Twitter, called Twemproxy (originally called nutcracker), to help partition our data needs among a pool of Redis instances, either running on a single machine or running across multiple machines. Twemproxy accepts requests from clients and uses a configured hashing function to decide which instance in the pool of machines is responsible for handling the request. Twemproxy is able to not only speak to Redis instances but also talk to Memcached, another popular in-memory key–value store that is often used as a data cache for high-traffic applications. According to the Redis development team, Twemproxy is the recommended way to shard your data needs among multiple Redis instances.

Twemproxy can also handle errors or other situations. If a particular instance in a pool of Redis machines is down, Twemproxy can be instructed to hold off for a short time before retrying the request. It can also be instructed to eject nodes from the pool if they are down due to failure.

When Twemproxy receives a request to get or set the value for a particular key, how does it know which machine to alert? Twemproxy supports a variety of hashing algorithms, including random hashing, but we need something more consistent. The Ketama algorithm, an open-source hashing algorithm and library written at Last.fm,[4] provides a strategy known as *consistent hashing*.[5] We'll choose this option as our default Twemproxy hashing strategy for our pool of Redis servers.

Twemproxy runs as a daemon and can be configured using a file in YAML format. In Listing 3.5, we demonstrate a configuration file for a pool called `redispool1`, which consists of Redis instances.

Listing 3.5   Configuring Twemproxy for using two Redis instances on a single machine

```
redispool1:
  listen: 127.0.0.1:22121
  hash: fnv1a_64
  distribution: ketama
  auto_eject_hosts: true
  redis: true
  server_retry_timeout: 1000
  server_failure_limit: 1
  servers:
   - 127.0.0.1:6379:1
   - 127.0.0.1:6379:2
```

Alternatives to Using Redis

Redis, although a very good choice for high-throughput applications that require good performance, is not the best choice for all large data applications. As we've seen, the simplicity and memory-based design of Redis means that performance is optimized towards read/write performance, not for consistency.

Furthermore, as we've seen in the previous example, sharding is not an automatic process. The key–value design of Redis makes sharding across many machines a much easier task than with a relational database, but deploying an application reliably across a pool of instances, even with Twemproxy, takes some configuration work.

Project Voldemort is another open-source key–value data store, inspired by Amazon's Dynamo database. It has a simple interface, much like Redis, but a great deal of built-in features to help scale pools of machines as linearly as possible. Although Redis generally exhibits less latency, Voldemort is also a great choice for key–value store applications that require scaling.

Apache Cassandra blends the properties of a key–value store with that of a tabular architecture reminiscent of relational databases. Unlike most key–value stores, Cassandra allows users to query data based on value. Like Voldemort, Cassandra also emphasizes scalability. Cassandra doesn't generally perform database reads and writes

---

4. www.last.fm/user/RJ/journal/2007/04/10/rz_libketama_-_a_consistent_hashing_algo_for_memcache_clients
5. www8.org/w8-papers/2a-webserver/caching/paper2.html

as quickly as Redis, but the ease of scalability and ability to run more complex query capabilities might make it more useful for some applications. Cassandra is also well integrated with Apache Hadoop, and can be used as both an input and output for Hadoop MapReduce jobs.

Finally, it's not impossible to distribute traditional relational databases as data sizes get larger and larger; it's just that it can be more difficult. Some of the techniques for sharding as described earlier can be applied to relational databases. Furthermore, a variety of open-source and commercial relational database sharding software is available. However, as we will see in the next section, the future might belong to new types of database designs that accept a small set of trade-offs to attempt to provide the best of both worlds: a blend of nonrelational scalability and relational consistency.

NewSQL: The Return of Codd

Database administrators often prefer using SQL because it abstracts away much of the complexity of building queries and a huge number of users are already familiar with it. A collection of new database designs attempt to bring together features found in distributed nonrelational databases with the consistency guarantees afforded by relational designs. Some of these projects are (perhaps lamentably) known as "NewSQL" database designs. As with Redis, improving performance by placing the database in memory is another common pattern being used by next-generation systems.

VoltDB was created in part by Michael Stonebraker, who was instrumental in the creation of popular open-source relational database PostgreSQL and the commercial analytical database Vertica. VoltDB is a relational, ACID-compliant database that shares some of the same performance boosts as Redis. Volt uses an in-memory data model along with snapshots of the data to create persistence. Although the need for the entire dataset to fit in memory creates the same sort of size limitations that Redis faces, VoltDB is also designed to scale easily by simply adding more servers to the system.

MemSQL is another in-memory database that is growing in popularity; it uses a variety of best practices to be performant and can be queried using standard SQL. One interesting approach that MemSQL takes to boost query performance is to dynamically compile SQL statements into C++ code. MemSQL then runs this generated C++ as shared libraries. MemSQL also automatically scales linearly as more machines are added to a cluster pool.

Google's Spanner is a database that has evolved from the company's requirements for global computing. According to the public research paper about Spanner, the software "provides externally consistent reads and writes, and globally-consistent reads across the database at a timestamp" and "looks like a relational database instead of a key–value store."[6] Spanner is designed to scale across multiple data centers and exhibit a high level of consistency at the expense of some latency.

---

6. http://research.google.com/archive/spanner-osdi2012.pdf

Summary

The most common architecture for storing data, the relational database model, was a result of the work of database pioneers such as Edgar Codd. The relational database model is designed to provide consistency, a flexible query model, and predictability. Many Web and mobile applications must handle both a constant barrage of incoming data and the need to scale up predictably as the amount of users and clients grows. As data sizes get larger and the need for databases to be tolerant of faults increases, the effort needed to scale and replicate relational database systems tends to make them impractical for high-throughput applications with huge data volumes. A common solution to deal with the problem of massive amounts of data is to use alternative architectures that eschew the traditional architectural choices of relational databases. These are often referred to broadly as **NoSQL** technologies. Two of the most popular non-relational databases are key–value stores and document stores. Key–value data stores allow each record in a database to be accessed by a single key. The data does not need to match a pre-existing schema. This architecture allows for very fast performance, but key–value stores lack the ability to query data by value. In contrast, document stores provide the ability to query against the document itself. Document stores are excellent choices when the data retrieved is best used in single-document form (such as Web site content) or when your database schema is very fluid.

Even in the crowded world of open-source nonrelational data stores, various solutions are designed to excel for one particular use case or another. Some database technologies are designed to be performant under heavy load, at the expense of consistency across nodes. Others types of databases specialize in being as easy to scale across a cluster of machines or as flexible with schema changes as possible. For small- or medium-sized applications that require a strong guarantee of consistency and a flexible querying model, relational databases are still the best choice.

For applications that require high throughput for database writes, a great choice is to use a key–value data store. Much like a hash table, key–value architecture stores data as a collection of unique key–value pairs, resulting in very quick data storage and retrieval. This speed comes at the expense of being able to query data by value. Unlike a document store, only the value of the key can be used to access data. The most popular open-source technology that uses this approach is Redis, which combines an in-memory key–value system with automatic snapshots to disk. Fault tolerance can be provided to some degree by configuring snapshots of data to a persistent disk. Although the ability to completely hold a dataset in memory is both a source of speed and a potential liability, Redis can be used in a distributed manner using client-side sharding. Twemproxy, which provides a hashing proxy layer that automatically distributes keys to a pool of Redis instances, is currently the best way to shard a database across a pool of separate Redis instances.

The distributed database space is still evolving rapidly. A number of new software solutions are combining the structured compliance of Edgar Codd's relational model with the potential for scalability found in key–value and document databases.

4

Strategies for Dealing with Data Silos

Some form of automation will ultimately provide an effective answer to business intelligence problems.
—H. P. Luhn (1958)

Asking a simple question about the data flowing through your organization can be like opening up Pandora's box, exposing communication inefficiencies that belie the promises of an all-digital world. Within an organization, useful data can live everywhere and in every form. Some of this data is transactional, structured, well-regulated data with dedicated personnel tasked to watch over it all the time. What happens when data is unstructured? How much of your organization's data lives in disparate spreadsheets, in Web applications, or in blobs of text such as email records and social media posts?

There are many reasons, both social and technical, for data to become stranded in silos. Traditionally, the usual solution to this problem has been to extract data from disparate sources into a central repository. Recent advances in data analytics technology have prompted organizations to think about new ways to approach these challenges. This chapter takes a look at how the growth of data created by new technology is forcing organizations to reevaluate strategies for dealing with data silos.

A Warehouse Full of Jargon

Business intelligence, or simply BI, is a term as old as digital computing, and seemingly an entire industry of consultants exist simply to define BI models and processes. But what exactly does BI mean? The term refers to a number of concepts involved in using data to drive and justify business decisions. In practice, this often means providing some ability for an organization to find answers to questions about various kinds of data stored in disparate places.

Using metrics to inform decision making isn't just a concept native to the realm of large enterprises. In 2011, Marc Andreessen published a famous editorial in the

Wall Street Journal entitled "Why Software is Eating the World."[1] Andreessen makes the argument that industries that have been traditionally involved with physical media—from photography to music to advertising—have all become dominated, or "eaten," by software firms. Apple opened its iTunes Music Store in 2003, and in just five years it had become the largest music retailer in the United States. It took less than two more years for iTunes to become the largest music retailer in the world. In the advertising industry, marketers can now view real-time metrics for their online ad campaigns, enabling them to quickly iterate their messaging in ways that were never possible using newspapers or television.

This software revolution is affecting more than the world of media. Andreessen contends that the leading companies in almost any industry, from manufacturing to retail to finance, will ultimately be software companies. In this model, organizations that can become even more efficient, faster moving, and better at making strategic decisions will ultimately have an advantage. And in the world of software, one way to become more efficient and make the best possible decisions is to become skillful at analyzing data.

An early, if not the earliest, mention of "business intelligence" can be found in IBM researcher H.P. Luhn's fascinating 1958 research paper "A Business Intelligence System,"[2] which begins with a statement that does not seem at all out of place in the Internet age: "Information is now being generated and utilized at an ever-increasing rate because of the accelerated pace and scope of human activities" (p. 314). Luhn goes on to describe the design of a hypothetical computer system that could use "automated processes" to inform business decisions. The system as described could be built using the existing technology of the day, such as microfilm and magnetic tape.

In the present day, the business intelligence software and consulting market is massive and covers a wide variety of tools that include aspects of data processing, analysis, and reporting. Huge database companies dominate the BI landscape, with highly specialized companies filling out needs of niche markets. Visualization and reporting products act as a window into the backend systems that are used to integrate organizational data. There are even large, well-supported, open-source BI projects (such as Pentaho and the Eclipse BIRT project).

H.P. Luhn's career spanned an era that saw a transition between computing systems that stored instructions on punch cards to that of commercially available all-digital computers of the 1960s. Although his proposed design incorporated the cutting edge technology of the day, Luhn's business intelligence system design had an unfortunate efficiency bottleneck. Just like today, a lot of existing business data was stored on paper. Luhn thought that the transcription of older records would pose a problem because in most cases it wouldn't be economically feasible to perform that job by hand. This disparity between paper and digital media resulted in a hypothetical data silo

---

1. http://online.wsj.com/article/SB10001424053111903480904576512250915629460.html
2. Luhn, H.P. 1958. "A Business Intelligence System." IBM Journal of Research and Development 2: 314–319; available at http://ieeexplore.ieee.org/xpl/articleDetails.jsp?arnumber=5392644.

problem—one in which a disparity between two physical information stores blocked easy interoperability between the data source and the data processing system. Luhn had imagined that a growth in the adoption of analog to digital bridge technology, such as typewriters with simultaneous ticker tape printout, could eliminate this disparity.

Although the dream of a truly paperless office has been a common meme throughout the past few decades (paper use actually doubled between 1980 and 2000[3]), casual business information is rapidly being generated digitally. Unstructured but useful sources of information are becoming the norm as consumer and business platforms converge. Emails, customer reviews, tweets, and user groups can be both valuable sources of "business information" and a nightmare to search, store, and query. Some business applications are mirroring features found in social media, enabling employees to stream posts of data to company-wide social media platforms. As a result, data becomes more fractured, more unstructured, and simply *more*, period.

The Problem in Practice

Let's look at an example of a typical data silo challenge. Customers generate data of all kinds, and this generated data is difficult to control. A customer might report her location as "California" in one transaction and use the abbreviation "CA" in another. Customers also generate support questions, post messages on your company's Facebook page, send emails, and typically do everything in their power to ensure that whatever ideal data model you want to conform to will be disregarded. Dealing with customer data can be difficult enough, but what about all the other data required to understand your business? This might include data from your product inventory, human resources, advertising, finance, and any number of applications crucial to business decisions.

In order to make any sense of this data, it must often be cleaned, or transformed into a more **normalized** form. Erroneous data must be corrected or discarded, and dates must all be converted into the same format. More importantly, if data sets are to be joined in any meaningful way, common keys must be available. In other words, a user's ID must be the exact same value in the purchase database as it is in your customer support logs.

Once this data is processed, it must be stored in a way that enables users to ask questions about their data. Query results from this data can then be brought into visualization tools or moved into spreadsheets for further analysis. All modern organizations, big or small, deal with data in some way, and each of these steps can become daunting if data sizes are large and data sources are disparate.

I once worked at a small nonprofit, and we faced the same types of data issues as any large corporation. Our donor database was implemented using a relational database hosted on a single machine. We also had a Web-based system for online donations, which collected names and addresses, and this information was stored in a separate relational database. We made extra money by selling books and CDs, the inventory

---

3. www.economist.com/node/12381449

of which constituted a third source of data. Volunteers who came to our events often signed up for our email list; the signup sheet was on paper, and if we were lucky it was entered eventually into a spreadsheet somewhere.

Answering a question such as "Were any of our online donors at last night's fundraising event?" or "Which of our donors who live nearby are on our email list?" was a huge challenge, simply because the data we needed to access was sharded across many silos. Even when we could easily run queries over these separate data stores, it wasn't always clear if various records were referring to the same person. Are Mike Jones and Michael Jones the same person? This donor didn't list the state he is from; is it Pasadena, California, or Pasadena, Texas?

If a small nonprofit organization can have so much trouble with these problems, imagine what happens with larger organizations. In the enterprise world, the various databases and systems used to collect transactional data generated from users and purchases are known as **operational systems**. These systems are responsible for the day-to-day activity of dealing with customer and purchase data, financial transactions, and just about anything for which data state is important. These types of systems are often designed to ensure that their data is correct and up to date, but they are not necessarily ideal for data reporting and analysis.

Planning for Data Compliance and Security

Back in 2000, the Enron Corporation was riding high on investor confidence, with a 60 billion dollar market capitalization. Although Enron was becoming a Wall Street darling, the veneer of success was a charade. As Enron's profile grew, the business world, and especially journalists, began to realize that the company's financial reporting practices were not always clear to shareholders. In reality, the company was employing faulty accounting practices to hide the fact that the numbers just weren't adding up. In order to conceal and keep the stock price high, the company formed limited offshore partnerships to buy up debt from poorly performing units. Eventually, Enron's house of cards toppled, taking the consulting firm Arthur Andersen down with it.

As a result of the Enron scandal, it wasn't difficult for the United States Congress to pass the Sarbanes and Oxley Act (Sarbox, or SOX), which mandated an unprecedented level of regulation around financial reporting. Sarbox requires that U.S. companies implement a number of data compliance policies. SOX compliance is just one example of financial regulation that requires good control and understanding of data flow through an organization, forcing businesses to learn how to deal with data silos effectively. The impulse to merge organizational data from different sources into a single, unified repository can sometimes help with the need to maintain proper data governance strategies.

Enter the Data Warehouse

A **data warehouse**, often referred to using the more professional-sounding title "enterprise data warehouse," or EDW, is a type of system designed to be a repository of aggregated information, used primarily for reporting and analysis. Although the various operational data systems are dealing with real-time transactions, such as purchases and customer updates, a data warehousing solution is designed as a way to overcome the problems created by these data silos.

Data warehouses are often described as **subject oriented**, because the design of the data structures used is centered around asking questions about a particular subject or concept. In other words, an operational database is designed to make sure that a customer's contact information is correct and up to date. A data warehouse is concerned with questions such as, "Over a certain period of time, which customers have made in-store purchases and online purchases?"

Data warehouse tools are not meant to handle day-to-day updates of customer data. An operational database might be consistently updated at any time. Meanwhile, a data warehouse might be used to append a daily snapshot of data for analysis. As an example, think of an airline reservation system. As customers make changes to their plans, the reservation system is updated in real time accordingly. However, at the end of each business day, a process might be defined that appends a snapshot of this data into a warehouse application. Other data, perhaps from the airline's separate loyalty card database, might be appended into the data warehouse as well. The next day, queries can be run across this aggregated data to inform the airline about trends in frequent-flyer points over time.

Another basic requirement of a data warehouse is obviously to provide the ability to build reports and ask questions about data. In order to pull in data from many different sources and to quickly run queries, the data structure used in modern large-scale data warehousing software requires careful modeling. One of the simplest ways to represent data in a warehouse system is by using a **star schema**, so named because the diagram of this schema resembles the points of a star. A record of data in a star schema is somewhat **denormalized**, meaning that data is replicated in various tables. In its simplest form, a star schema represents data by using two types of tables: a fact table and one or more dimension tables. This schema is best illustrated with an example. Let's consider a single record of a customer transaction. In a star schema, this type of data might be represented by a single **fact table** containing records of the customer ID, a product ID, a cost, and a time of purchase. Within an organization, there's more to the data than just this basic information. Each customer will also have associated contact information, including an address, a phone number, and an email address. The product sold has other metadata associated with it, as well, including its supplier information. These additional types of data would be stored in **dimension tables**, with a key corresponding to the fact table information. The additional information found in the dimension tables completes the entire picture of data that encompasses the subject of a customer purchase. The use of star schemas, and more complex data-modeling structures like them, is meant to make querying as efficient as possible without the excessive joins that might be found in a standard relational database.

The design and implementation of this type of schema, as well as more complicated versions of this concept, goes well beyond the scope of this book. In practice, modeling of data for warehousing is a specialized skill that requires a great deal of training and domain knowledge. The main point here is that it takes a lot of effort to gather and process operational data into a form that satisfies the dimensional hierarchy of the data warehouse. Furthermore, these structures must be well planned, as there can be a significant cost to changes in the schemas used in data warehousing software.

Data Warehousing's Magic Words: Extract, Transform, and Load

Facilitating the movement, processing, and storage from operational databases into a data warehouse often involves a collection of tasks known as Extract, Transform, and Load or, more commonly, **ETL**. Like most of the terms in this chapter, this phrase belies the underlying complexity of the actual process.

ETL processes encompass more than just copying data from one place to another. Data must be extracted out of existing data stores. Once the raw data is available, it must be cleaned and validated, meaning that data must meet a standard of integrity. Erroneous data must be corrected or deleted. The application of business rules is important as well. Is there private customer information that must be obfuscated or deleted before moving it from one place to another? Once all of these possibly complex steps are taken, data is then loaded into tables in the data warehousing application. Generally, these processes are automated, but in large organizations a great deal of effort must be applied to ensure that data integrity is consistent across each step in an ETL pipeline.

Transforming and stuffing the data necessary to make business decisions often runs into a problem when data grows large. As we've noted before, moving data across the network can be slow, and as data sources grow, ETL processes can become increasingly complicated.

Data warehousing is also not necessarily a great tool for asking questions quickly. First of all, the entire ETL pipeline must be run before data can be queried. What happens when a new dimension of the table is required? Because data warehousing is so front heavy, changing the data model used may require a lot of effort. The ETL process doesn't lend itself to constant change. Data is pulled from a variety of sources—a large mainframe server, an online relational database, and even data created in spreadsheets from the accounting department. If these data sources are interrupted or changed, the automated ETL processes could fail.

Hadoop: The Elephant in the Warehouse

Traditional data warehousing technologies were born in a pre-Internet world. The growth of the Internet has resulted in the exponential growth of several generations' worth of Web, mobile, and sensor data. If the concepts of data warehousing seem to represent an ideal but unattainable goal, then new technologies in data analytics are often portrayed as disruptive to the concepts of the data warehouse.

The data warehouse concept represents the philosophy of spending a great deal of effort upfront in order to extract and merge data from various silos for effective analysis. Technologies like Hadoop tend to represent a different philosophy, embracing huge, unstructured datasets and processing data in an ad hoc fashion. Why bother with the seemingly impossible task of constantly extracting, normalizing, and structuring data when we can use tools like Hadoop's MapReduce framework to answer questions about huge amounts of data whenever the need arises? Why not simply dump unstructured data into Hadoop's distributed filesystem each day and write a custom MapReduce function whenever it's necessary to query the data?

There's an interesting culture clash between the traditional enterprise world of the data warehouse and the world of technologies symbolized by newer, open-source projects such as Hadoop. Users of each type are beginning to find ways in which these technologies complement each other. One thing that distributed processing technologies is starting to reveal is that perhaps data silos aren't such a bad thing after all.

Data Silos Can Be Good

Like many of the terms you hear in the enterprise data world, such as "business intelligence" or "ETL," the term "data silo" should be up for scrutiny. Data silos have a bad reputation because of all the previous challenges that we've discussed. As data sizes grow, the concept of providing a single repository for all this data is not always the most practical solution. In a world without any feasible way to handle the massive amounts of data being generated across an organization, the only practical solution has been to make a clean, streamlined copy of aggregated data and store it in a data warehouse.

Now even small organizations are beginning to have access to technology that can process large amounts of data on demand, and storage is getting even cheaper as well. This means that it is becoming economically feasible to simply keep data in whatever silo is the best fit for the use case and then run reporting tools. In this model, the focus is more on keeping data where it works best and finding ways to process it for analysis when the need arises. In other words, as one business-intelligence software developer once told me: "Data silos exist because they are useful."

The reality is that that data warehousing doesn't solve every data silo challenge effectively. Approaching every data problem from an ad hoc perspective by assuming Hadoop will be the answer to the challenge isn't practical for solving every use case either. Dumping raw, unstructured data from operational data stores into a distributed filesystem lacks some of the discipline imposed by good data warehousing design. Certainly, there are good reasons to use data warehousing technology, and until a single database system can be used for all aspects of an organization's data needs, data must be moved from system to system to be used effectively.

Similarly, managing the complexity of ad hoc systems requires a great deal of effort. Building custom systems that bridge together disparate data sources can be difficult and require a different sort of expertise.

Concentrate on the Data Challenge, Not the Technology

I believe that the most important solution to problems caused by data silos isn't actually technological. The most important goal is to understand the scope of questions that you aim to answer and choose the most effective solution.

Data warehousing is not always the right solution to overcoming the challenges of data silos, and neither is a distributed processing system such as Hadoop. In fact, both require a great deal of investment and skill to use effectively. In practice, many cross-organizational data questions can be answered without the need for a data warehouse. However, investing in a data warehousing solution does make sense if the same questions are being asked over and over, and regular reporting and compliance needs must be met.

A distributed processing system combined with a fast, ad hoc analytics database might be the best solution when faced with the need to process data quickly in the face of changing requirements.

For security and compliance challenges, such as those posed by Sarbox, data warehousing can be a good solution. If data is automatically transformed and loaded into a data warehouse that can only be directly accessed by a few, then it is easier to ensure that the data are correct during audits. Building automated ETL processes for this purpose, as well as the strict modeling of data that goes along with it, can help enforce the stringency necessary to fulfill good compliance practices.

Empower Employees to Ask Their Own Questions

The concept of the data warehouse is often tied to hierarchical models of organizational structure. Executives, the decision makers and captains of the ship, are expected to have a high-level view of an organization's data, and employees down the tree are merely tasked with data collection. The organization's leaders are expected to use this high-level information for decision making and analysis.

This view contrasts with models that aim to build in data analysis as a fundamental aspect of the organization's structure. Industries that are being "eaten by software," as Marc Andreessen puts it, should be able to make decisions backed by metrics whenever possible, whether the CEO is involved or not.

Trying to come up with a definition for "data-driven organization" is very similar to the problem of trying to define "business intelligence"—it's a simple term that describes a goal that can be very difficult to reach in practice. For some, the concept of a **data-driven organization** is an ideal state in which every single decision is carefully prefaced by metrics. In practice, organizations that use data to become successful seem to operate in much the same way that researchers use the scientific method: Someone in the organization uses data to test a hypothesis from the observations and insights that come from interactions with customers and others outside the organization.

This concept means that everyone in the organization has access to the data tools necessary to be able to get answers to data-related questions. This doesn't mean that just anyone in your company should be able to peruse the private financial or medical records of customers. What it does mean is that the people in your organization are given access to tools that help them find out the answers to questions quickly and are expected to back up their ideas with metrics when appropriate. It also means sharing organizational data freely to help inform, inspire, and empower employees to come up with their own innovative ideas for solving problems.

Invest in Technology That Bridges Data Silos

Embracing the concept that data silos are actually beneficial allows system architects to rethink their approaches. If the data warehouse is seen less as a be-all and end-all solution to data analysis, and distributed computing tools such as Hadoop are seen as useful for processing tasks, this allows administrators to focus on investing in technologies that bridge the gaps between these systems.

Visualization tools, such as Tableau and QlikView, are beginning to provide access not only to traditional relational database systems through traditional ODBC drivers but also to new data tools such as Google's BigQuery and Cloudera's Impala. Similarly, users of business productivity tools, such as Microsoft Excel, should be able to run queries by using connectors to underlying data warehousing software.

Convergence: The End of the Data Silo

Many of the technologies and jargon of traditional data warehousing were developed before the wide-scale adoption of the Internet. Large, single-machine data warehouse appliances are common in the enterprise market and often bring with them large price tags and expensive support contracts. Building a distributed data processing system on a cluster of machines using open-source technologies such as Hadoop provides a different type of challenge, requiring expertise and infrastructure maintenance. Essentially, dealing with either of these system designs requires specialized training and various trade-offs.

In practice, data warehousing and distributed computing technologies such as Hadoop have overlapping use cases. For example, creating a MapReduce workflow can often be a more performant way to solve a complicated ETL transformation step when moving data from a customer database to a data warehouse. There's been a gradual movement, from both commercial and open-source projects, towards combining aspects of popular distributed data projects with features found in data warehouses and analytical databases. For example, the Spark project, an open-source distributed computing system, is designed to be a very fast in-memory analytics platform. One of the most interesting projects built with Spark is Shark, a data warehouse application that is compatible with Hadoop's Hive. As a result of this combination, Spark and Shark together provide both a warehousing capability and fast analytics capabilities. Traditional data warehousing products are also getting into the act, with industry stalwarts such as Oracle and SAP incorporating Hadoop into their offerings.

A major theme of this book is to reduce costs and infrastructure needs by considering the use of cloud computing solutions whenever possible. Some companies are building data warehousing systems completely in the cloud. Amazon's Redshift is an example of a product that attempts to take advantage of an all-cloud architecture. One of Redshift's key design principles is that data can be loaded from other Amazon cloud data sources, such as DynamoDB and Elastic MapReduce. Other companies are following suit as well, launching completely managed Hadoop Hive installations on virtual clusters. Cloud-based data warehousing leads to a secondary advantage; as more and more application development is done on the Web, having a data warehouse completely in the cloud makes it easier for browser-based visualization and reporting tools to access the underlying source data.

Technology now exists to collect, process, and store data on a large scale. Data can be processed with tools such as MapReduce, and aggregate analytics tools are getting faster and faster as well. All of this can eventually take place using cloud utility computing systems, with Web-based visualization and business productivity tools providing an interface to the data. With all of these components in place, the ability to address many of the technical problems that result from data silos is available. Perhaps common storage and standardized interoperability between cloud-based systems will make transformation between data sources a much more trivial process. These technological developments, combined with a cultural change in organizational attitudes toward empowering employees to become data experts, means that discussion about the challenges caused by data silos will likely become less and less important.

Will Luhn's Business Intelligence System Become Reality?

The business intelligence system that Luhn envisioned was not merely a tool to ask questions about organizational data. Luhn's ultimate goal was to create a technology to identify patterns of interest within the stream of business data and then push relevant information based on these models to those who needed it—at just the right time. Luhn said that such a system would ensure that new information pertinent or useful to certain action points would be selectively disseminated to those points without any delay.

One might argue that some aspects of the business intelligence system that Luhn envisioned are already available, thanks to a technology that was born near the end of his life: the Internet. Many Web applications are able to use crowdsourced data to present users with ratings, advice, and targeted advertising. Predictive analytics are being used to build recommendation engines for users, pushing data to mobile devices depending on the user's location or time of day. Some aspects of the business intelligence system that Luhn envisioned are being developed today, but at a scale far beyond what his original paper conveyed.

Summary

Even in small organizations, important data can be found in various formats, managed by a variety of applications, and stored on different machines or in the cloud. The result, a siloing of data, makes it difficult to ask questions that require a variety of data sources to find the answer.

An organization's data often becomes stored in many disparate places for practical reasons. Operational data stores may be optimized for the constant transactional duties of customer-facing applications. Meanwhile, tasks involving aggregate queries and data interoperability are best suited for specialized analytics systems. Analysts may be most productive using tools such as spreadsheets. Compliance, security, and user privacy are all valid reasons for keeping data in separate locations, accessible only to specific people. Much of an organization's useful data lives in unstructured formats such as email, user comments, or social media posts.

There are many conceptual approaches to solving the data challenges created by silos. Data warehousing refers to the strategy of structuring and storing data generated by operational databases into a central repository. Since data from a variety of sources may not have the same structure, data warehousing challenges often require a process for data extraction, transformation, and loading (ETL).

The Internet, mobile applications, social media, email, and other communication technologies have all led to an increase of data sources that an organization may want to collect and analyze. Another approach is to ask questions about disparate datasets using technology that is designed for distributed processing, such as MapReduce.

Although these contrasting philosophies have strengths and weaknesses, the real solutions to data silo problems are organizational rather than technological. Understanding the types of data challenges you face before looking at technology is a key first step. In some cases, it's possible that data can be queried without a data warehousing solution at all, enabling users to skip a traditional ETL process. When investing in technology, it often makes sense for organizations to concentrate on technology that bridges different sources of data rather than technology that merges and moves data into a central repository.

Many projects are combining the large-scale processing of distributed systems such as Hadoop (to improve data processing) with more traditional analytic database or data warehousing technology, using those techniques to speed up the queries. With so much data already "in the cloud," there are unique advantages to using data applications as a service. Visualization and reporting tools are also being built to connect directly to data sources besides those of the traditional data warehouse.

III

Asking Questions about Your Data

## 5

Using Hadoop, Hive, and Shark to Ask Questions about Large Datasets

The concept of data warehousing has long been in the domain of large enterprises. A huge industry has developed to attack the problem of quickly asking questions about data from across an entire organization. Data warehouse practices encompass the design of complicated ETL pipelines and the art of processing data from transactional databases using OLAP cubes and star schemas. This mature field is being challenged by new approaches to dealing with data warehousing issues: approaches that, in some cases, can be more scalable and performant as well as cheaper.

The Hadoop project provides an open-source platform for distributing data processing tasks across clusters of low-cost commodity servers. Hadoop's implementation of the MapReduce framework provides the ability to run batch-processing jobs on large datasets. Asking questions about data is often an exploratory, iterative process in which analysts expect fast results. Writing new custom MapReduce code for query after query is far too slow and cumbersome to use in practice.

In this chapter, we'll take a look at Apache Hive, an open-source project that helps users explore data managed by Hadoop by writing queries in a familiar, SQL-like syntax. We'll also discuss some trends in interactive query for large datasets, including the Spark and Shark projects.

What Is a Data Warehouse?

The world of enterprise data analytics is a spawning ground for poorly-defined jargon. The kaleidoscope of terms that make up the world of data warehousing are among the most confusing. **Data warehousing** is a problematic term, as it can refer to a large number of things, including the process of organizing company data or the physical hardware used for storage. Some data warehouses are used for canonical storage of organizational data, whereas others are used as temporary databases simply to be used for analytics. There is not one particular tool—or class of tools—that solves the problem of aggregating all the data in a company, and every company has unique problems that make a general solution difficult. Nonetheless, there exists a huge industry of solution providers and the requisite tech media to discuss the pros and cons of various attempts at providing solutions.

Although the term "data warehouse" might mean different things in different contexts, the goal of providing a single unified place for organizational data is a common use case. Organizations need ways to ask questions about large datasets that are affordable and timely and often need to be able to deal with data from a variety of sources, each with different schemas and growth patterns. A common source of data comes from **operational data stores,** which are often relational databases that live on the frontlines of the organization, collecting and processing customer data at all times. These databases are optimized to handle transactions such as the creation and updating of individual records but not to run large queries over the entire database. Operational data stores are often the canonical source of data for an organization, a source of truth that changes from moment to moment. Moving snapshots of this data to a data warehouse can provide insight into sales and advertising trends. Operational data isn't the only source organizations are interested in analyzing. There is an ever-growing amount of unstructured organizational data, such as the text from social media, blog posts, and emails.

Analysts need to understand how data from all of these different sources is related. For example, you might want to explore possible statistical relationships between signals in social media and sales of a particular item. One way to accomplish this goal is to pipe all organizational data into a central relational database such as MySQL, Microsoft SQL Server, Oracle, or any of the available commercial or open-source products. This secondary data store can be maintained indefinitely as an organization data record. In other cases, it might be used simply as a means to analyze data that has been aggregated.

The process of taking data from the operational databases and converting it into a form useful for aggregation in a data warehouse is often called **ETL**, which stands for "extract, transform, and load." Some data needs to be **normalized**, meaning variables and some data types require conversion into other types. Building ETL pipelines can be a complicated task, and there are many products available that are specialized for this purpose.

There are a few drawbacks to this "traditional" approach to data analytics. The first is simply cost. The market for many commercial data warehousing solutions is often large enterprise customers, and can be expensive for many smaller organizations. Once data is aggregated, analysts want to be able to ask questions about data in the warehouse. However, relational databases are usually not the fastest way to query when data sizes grow. When data sizes are relatively small, aggregate queries run on well-tuned relational databases with proper indexing can be screamingly fast. However, no matter how powerful the machine, relational databases by nature are ultimately challenging to deal with as data sizes grow very large. Running complicated aggregate queries over large tables is not a great use case for a relational database. Joining the results from two large, normalized tables may take a great deal of time.

In the classic model of disruption, organizations are finding that they can solve some of their data challenges without the need for complicated ETL, star schemas, and other conventions of enterprise data warehousing. Companies that deal with massive amounts of data, such as Facebook, recognized that the existing data warehouse solutions available were not able to cope, neither technologically or economically, with the huge amounts of data being generated by Internet applications. With data sizes approaching petabytes of data, Facebook had to turn to a data processing model that could scale. The Apache Hadoop project was just this platform. Hadoop provides an open-source implementation of MapReduce, a data processing framework that can scale horizontally as data sizes increase. Even better, Hadoop makes it possible to use clusters of low-cost servers.

Apache Hadoop has long been the media darling of open-source data processing, and for good reason. Hadoop, along with the Hadoop Distributed File System (HDFS), provides a framework for splitting data processing tasks across a collection of different machines. With a vanilla Hadoop installation, MapReduce is provided as an interface. In order to create a MapReduce job to process data, it's possible to write MapReduce workflows using a scripting language such as BASH or Python (see Chapter 8, "Putting It Together: MapReduce Data Pipelines"), using a library such as Cascading, or using the workflow language Pig (see Chapter 9, "Building Data Transformation Workflows with Pig and Cascading").

A MapReduce job is a great way to facilitate batch processing of unstructured data. For example, MapReduce can be used to convert the values in a huge collection of raw text files from one data type to another.

Relational databases are useful tools for asking questions about structured datasets. Can you use a MapReduce job to ask a similar question? You definitely can, but it is not as easy to write the code for interactive query jobs when in an interactive environment. Running a query over data is a different process than that of defining batch-processing jobs. With a data processing job, there's no expectation of instantaneous results. Data analysis lends itself to ad hoc exploration: As soon as a query is complete, you may want to run more follow-up queries immediately. Even experienced developers would find it cumbersome to write out a new script for every iteration of a query. Additionally, the act of querying is often done by analysts and decision makers who may not be specialists at writing code or managing Hadoop instances.

Relational databases also tend to support standard versions of the Structured Query Language, or SQL, which is well known and easy to learn. SQL supports common database functions such as selecting the results of mathematical operations, joining query results from different tables, and grouping results together by a particular value. SQL is very expressive, but the biggest advantage for providing access to SQL is that the language is well understood by a large number of people, meaning that analysts can use it without needing to know how to write code.

Apache Hive: Interactive Querying for Hadoop

In order to apply the ability to run SQL-like queries using Hadoop's MapReduce framework, Facebook needed to build software that could both manage database-like structures and translate queries into multistage MapReduce jobs. Facebook's solution was to create a data warehousing tool known as Hive. On the surface, Hive looks a bit like typical data warehousing solutions based on relational databases. However, it provides a number of advantages that especially apply to the challenges that Facebook was encountering. First of all, Hive is able to use the underlying Hadoop framework to more or less scale indefinitely as data sizes grow. Hive is also extensible; because it is based on Hadoop, you can simply write new user-defined functions (or UDFs) using the same MapReduce framework used by Hive.

Use Cases for Hive

As happens time and time again, the use cases for Apache Hive overlap those appropriate for other technology solutions. When is it best to use Hive? For some users, Hive can be an inexpensive and flexible alternative to commercial data warehousing solutions. Depending on the use case, Hive can make it possible to skip building complicated ETL pipelines for data processing, which simplifies data analysis tremendously. Thanks to the underlying Hadoop framework, Hive is also able to scale well as data sizes grow large.

Despite the ability to scale across many machines and the presence of an SQL-like query language, Hive is not meant to be used as the database backend of a high-traffic system (sometimes known as an "operational" data store). MapReduce is a powerful processing concept, but it's designed to provide a flexible and programmable interface to batch processing rather than raw speed. In many cases, Hive queries can be "fast enough," returning results over large datasets on the order of minutes. For already structured data, Hive can return results fast enough to enable users to skip the ETL steps necessary to build the star schemas for traditional data warehouses. If the solution to your data challenge requires even faster query results, it might make sense to consider investing in the overhead of more traditional data warehousing software or to add an analytical database to your data processing pipeline (see Chapter 6, "Building a Data Dashboard with Google BigQuery").

There's another reason why you might choose to go with the traditional data warehouse over Hive: to take advantage of the robust sets of features available from the more mature commercial market. For example, commercial data warehouses are often built on top of hardware that provides features such as data disaster recovery. Hive provides a much simpler set of features, and tasks such as data replication might require more manual work.

At its core, Hive is neither a database nor a traditional data warehouse (although it combines some features from both). Hive is really a tool for making some of the advantages of the MapReduce framework available to address challenges that normally could only be handled by complex ETL and data warehouse tools. Hive can be a very flexible choice for aggregating organizational data, providing relatively low cost at the expense of raw speed. This makes Hive the right choice for integration with existing Hadoop installations. When data grows to extreme levels, such as the petabyte scales experienced by Facebook, then distributed solutions such as Hive might be the only viable way to provide economically feasible data warehouse functionality.

Hive in Practice

Although Hive's query language is meant to be familiar to users of relational databases, there are many differences that stem from Hive's underlying Hadoop infrastructure. In order to understand how Hive works, let's take a quick look at some of the basic concepts behind Hadoop and MapReduce.

The Hadoop ecosystem contains a soup of terminology that can be confusing to beginners. Hadoop itself is a framework for distributing data processing jobs across many machines. Hadoop's MapReduce model for processing data is a three-step process. In the first step, called the **map phase**, data is split into many shards, each of which is identified by a particular key. The next phase, the **shuffle sort**, aggregates data shards containing the same key on the same node in the cluster, allowing for data processing to take place close to the actual data. Finally, in the **reduce phase**, the shuffled data from individual nodes is crunched on local machines and output to produce a final result.

The MapReduce framework is a simple concept overall, but applying this processing model to complex tasks can be tricky. A task such as a count of individual words in terabytes of individual files might require just a single MapReduce job. However, a complex aggregate query result from two tables, including mathematical operations and joins of two different types of data, may require multiple MapReduce steps to accomplish.

The Hadoop Distributed File System (HDFS) provides an abstract interface for distributing data files across a cluster of machines. Users don't have to know exactly which data is available on a particular node in the Hadoop cluster. Moving data to a location at which it will be processed is an expensive task, requiring data to be sent over a network and potentially creating a performance bottleneck. Instead of moving data from storage nodes to processing nodes, HDFS helps nodes process data that is on a particular machine. This design choice makes Hadoop efficient for large data processing jobs. HDFS also provides fault tolerance through replications: If a node in the Hadoop cluster goes down, the data will still be available somewhere else in the cluster.

HDFS is designed to facilitate batch processing of huge amounts of data, but it's not meant to be a database by any means. This means that in order for Hive to keep track of data sources, it must provide a database-like structure on top of files initially contained in HDFS. In order to keep track of this database structure, Hive uses a database of its own, known as the metastore.

The Hive Metastore

When data is loaded from HDFS into Hive, it is necessary to describe the schema of the data. Hive keeps track of the schema, location, and other data about various inputs to its tables by using a relational database called the **metastore**.

By default, Hive provides its own embedded metastore (powered by the relational database Apache Derby). This default database makes it easy to start using Hive without having to do much work, but it has some limitations. The embedded metastore can only be used with one Hive session at a time, so multiple users will not be able to work together. When using Hive in production with multiple users and large datasets, the best solution to this problem is to set up an external relational database, such as MySQL, to act as the metastore.

Loading Data into Hive

With Hive, "loading" is a bit of a loaded term. Hive is relatively data agnostic, with the ability to support queries over a range of source formats, including raw text files, Hadoop Sequence files (the key–value format used for intermediate MapReduce data processing), and specialized columnar formats.

Hive's basic unit of data is the table. A table in Hive acts much like a table in a relational database: a two-dimensional collection of columns of different datatypes, with rows containing records. Also like relational databases, Hive tables can be organized into distinct "databases," which act as namespaces to hold specific table names. In other words, two different databases can have the same table names; they won't clash.

Like relational databases, Hive supports a number of primitive data types for each field, including various forms of integers, Booleans, floating-point decimals, and strings. Hive also supports arrays and structs of values, Unix timestamp values, and a number of mathematical functions as basic data types.

Hive has two main concepts of how data is controlled: managed and external. This distinction determines whether Hive is responsible for deleting source data when tables are dropped. A common use case for Hive is to operate over data that is also being used by other applications, such as custom MapReduce code. In this case, you want Hive to be able to access the data in place. Also, if you want to drop a table, Hive will only delete its own references to it, not the actual data itself. External tables can be configured by using the EXTERNAL modifier when creating new tables.

Hive natively supports several file formats. Besides text, Hive can also use Hadoop's SequenceFile format, which is the native key–value format used to keep track of intermediate data in a MapReduce flow. For better performance, Hive can read files in a format called Record Columnar File (RCFile). We'll take a look at how to create RCFile tables later in this chapter. Listing 5.1 provides examples of creating Hive tables.

Listing 5.1 **Creating Hive tables using data from local and HDFS sources**

```
/* Create a Hive-managed table. Deleting this table will remove
   both the table metadata and the data itself. */
CREATE TABLE employee_ids (name STRING, id INT);
LOAD DATA INPATH '/users/ids.csv' INTO TABLE employee_ids;
```

```
/* Create an external table. Deleting this table will leave the
   data intact but remove the table's metadata. */
CREATE EXTERNAL TABLE employee_ids (name STRING, id INT)
  LOCATION '/external/employee_ids';
LOAD DATA INPATH '/users/ids.csv' INTO TABLE employee_ids;
```

Querying Data: HiveQL

Now that we've created tables using Hive to keep track of our input files, we can start asking questions about the data. Hive provides an SQL-like language known as HiveQL, which enables functionality (such as GROUP BY, JOINs, and HAVING) familiar to users of standard SQL.

HiveQL can't express every type of query that is possible with standard SQL. The differences between standard SQL and HiveQL mostly stem from the differences between the design of relational databases and the MapReduce framework. As Hive is not meant to do appends to existing datasets, transactions are not supported, nor are materialized views. However, Hive is able to take advantage of some of the unique benefits of MapReduce. One of the most useful is the multiple insertion feature, which enables Hive queries to produce multiple output tables from a single query (rather than just one, which is the normal result of an SQL query). This is more efficient than running separate queries, as Hive will only scan the source table once during a multiple insertion. An example of a multiple-insertion query can be seen in Listing 5.2.

Listing 5.2   **Using a multiple-insertion query in Hive**

```
FROM bookstore
INSERT OVERWRITE TABLE book
SELECT author, SUM(revenue) AS total
WHERE category='book' GROUP BY author
INSERT OVERWRITE TABLE comics
SELECT author, SUM(revenue) AS total
WHERE category='comic' GROUP BY author;
```

Another difference between the standard SQL of a relational database and HiveQL is the absence of inequality JOINs. The MapReduce model is not well-designed to compare keys that do not match. Therefore, it is only possible with Hive to run JOIN queries between two tables when a particular key equals another.

These examples merely scratch the surface of what is possible with Hive. For practical explorations of asking questions about datasets, it's possible to run Hadoop and Hive on a single machine, using either the local filesystem or a local Hadoop filesystem for testing. Scaling the system up to use an external MySQL database to act as a remote Hive metastore is slightly more work (mostly due to configuring proper permissions on the MySQL database).

The ease of setting up Hive on a small installation makes it a tempting choice for small datasets, but if your data sizes are such that a single server will suffice, then it is always a better option to use a relational database to ask questions about your data. On its own, Hive can speed up the process of asking questions about very large datasets thanks to providing an SQL-like interface on top of the MapReduce paradigm.

Optimizing Hive Query Performance

The MapReduce framework is designed to spread data processing tasks across many machines, making large-scale data solutions economically feasible through parallelism. Although MapReduce is a great model for transforming a huge batch of raw files in a timely manner, query performance can be slow. Using Hive's EXPLAIN statement, you can see that queries can often require multiple MapReduce steps, each of which is further slowed by many disk-access events.

The first step in improving performance is to restrict the amount of data necessary to provide a query result. An initial way to do this is to use Hive's partitioning function. When data is partitioned, Hive will only look at the partition requested rather than all the data in the entire table. It is also possible to build indexes on columns in Hive. Proper indexing is often crucial for optimizing the speed of Hive queries.

Another optimization is to use a file format that is most efficient for the types of queries that you are interested in running. When Hadoop stores intermediate processing files in HDFS, it natively uses a format called Sequence Files, which features a key–value structure in which each key points to a single row of data. When using raw text files or sequence files with Hive, the entire row of data must be accessed every time a query is run. These file types are not the best format for running fast queries that only require a few columns of data. However, a format called RCFile makes it possible for Hive to only access the columns necessary to provide the query result.

One simple way to create an RCFile from original flat data is to populate a new RCFile table using a SELECT statement. First, load data into Hive using the original text format. Then create a new, empty Hive table that is stored in RCFile format. Finally, run a Hive query that populates the RCFile table. Listing 5.3 demonstrates the steps involved, as well as the HiveQL query performance difference between these two file types.

Listing 5.3 Convert a text table to an RCFile table

```
/* Create a table for the original text format file */
CREATE TABLE text_table(
  name string,
);

/* Load data from HDFS into the table */
LOAD DATA INPATH '/names.txt' INTO TABLE text_table;

/* SELECT everything and write results into
   the new RCFile Hive table */
```

```
CREATE TABLE rcfile_table(
  name string,
) STORED AS RCFILE;
```

Using Additional Data Sources with Hive

Hive doesn't just open up a world of relational queries to users. An attractive feature of Hive is its ability to access and even write to other types of data sources.

There are many key–value data stores, but one that is well known to users of Hadoop is HBase. HBase is a great solution when you have lots of data coming into the system and have a need to quickly retrieve data by key. Hive can be configured to use HBase as a data source. For more information on when to use nonrelational and key–value data stores, see Chapter 3, "Building a NoSQL-Based Web App to Collect Crowd-Sourced Data."

Another useful way to interact with Hive is through drivers. Hive is an open-source project, and there are available JDBC and ODBC drivers that can be used as an interface to external programs. Finally, Hive can interact directly with data coming from Thrift servers (for more about Thrift, see Chapter 2, "Hosting and Sharing Terabytes of Raw Data").

Shark: Queries at the Speed of RAM

Apache Hive is essentially a system to translate SQL-like queries into Hadoop MapReduce jobs. MapReduce is meant to be used as a batch process, intended more for flexibility than raw speed. This isn't the optimal underlying design for interactive queries, in which user results are iterative. One of the design goals of Hadoop—that data is sharded across disks on many machines and processing happens on the same nodes—means that data tends to be read and written to disk quite often. In terms of performance, disk I/O is often one of the main bottlenecks for data processing tasks. Hive queries can often result in a multistage MapReduce process, meaning that in the course of a single query there can be plenty of disk reads and writes.

Recognizing that Hadoop isn't the optimal tool for every data use case, some developers have been rethinking the underlying technology for use cases such as distributed processing. An exciting new development in the open-source data world is Spark, a project created at the UC Berkeley AMPLab. Spark is a distributed processing framework like Hadoop, but it attempts to use system memory to improve performance. Spark's core data model is based on objects called Resilient Distributed Datasets, or RDDs. An **RDD** lives in system memory and is available without the need for disk access. Spark is currently on the list of Apache Incubator projects, which is a step toward it eventually becoming an officially supported Apache project like Hadoop and Hive, and it is mature enough that it is being used in production by several well-known technology companies.

It's not enough to provide just a distributed in-memory environment; we need practical tools like Hive to make the platform more accessible. Of course, a distributed data warehousing solution built using Spark absolutely must be named after an animal; it's almost a hard and fast rule of distributed data applications. The codebase of Hive was extended to run on the Spark platform, and the result is called **Shark**.

Because it is based on Hive, Shark is inherently easy for the data application developer to use. Shark works well with existing Hadoop and Hive instances, and just like Hive it can access HBase tables as well. In fact, it's easy to get a Shark instance running. Some users have even reported success accessing Shark queries from external applications such as Tableau, using existing tools such as the Hive ODBC driver.

Shark is an excellent choice for many ad hoc queries for which Hive would normally be used, but like other in-memory data technologies, performance is dependent on the amount of available memory in the cluster. However, even when Shark must access a disk, some users have reported that query performance still beats a similar Hive installation. However, another drawback to using very new technologies such as Shark in production is that they lack the tool ecosystems and developer communities of more mature projects.

From a practical standpoint, for long-running MapReduce jobs that process more data than fits in available memory, Hadoop is still the right tool. Using Shark and Hadoop in conjunction might provide the best of both worlds: A disk-based batch-processing tool for transforming large amounts of data and an in-memory query engine for analysis.

Another open-source implementation of a fast query engine on top of Hadoop is Impala. Impala is very different from Hive or Shark, but it covers similar use cases. Unlike Hive or Shark, Impala shares many of the same design characteristics of Google BigQuery, which we will discuss in Chapter 6, "Building a Data Dashboard with Google BigQuery."

Data Warehousing in the Cloud

Throughout this chapter, we've discussed using Hive in the context of an existing Hadoop installation. Large-scale data analytics and cloud computing have grown together. By necessity, an entire industry of compute clouds and virtual servers for hire has appeared.

Although completely managed Hadoop systems are becoming available, distributed systems inherently require some type of administration. Some products are taking the virtual, distributed data warehouse idea a step further, providing a fully managed solution. One technology that has become popular in this space is Amazon's Redshift. Redshift isn't a Hadoop-based product like Hive, but because it is based on PostgreSQL, it has more in common with relational data warehouses.

From a practical standpoint, there's a lot of great reasons to consider using cloud-based solutions for data warehousing. As more and more applications move to the Web, data is already being hosted in the cloud. More importantly, as there are no upfront infrastructure costs and capacity can be scaled to need, the economic model for cloud data warehouse applications may be more affordable.

Summary

The relational database architecture of the traditional data warehouse concept is being challenged by new, disruptive open-source technologies. When data sizes grow very large, commercial data warehouse solutions can be economically prohibitive for many organizations. Some data challenges, like those involving completely unstructured data, do not lend themselves to the use of relational tables, star schemas, and complicated ETL processes inherent in the enterprise database world.

The Apache Hadoop project provides a framework for processing data using clusters of commodity hardware. Hadoop, along with the underlying Hadoop Distributed File System (HDFS), is able to scale horizontally as more and more data is added to the system. The processing model that Hadoop provides, MapReduce, is designed to enable data processing to take place as near as possible to the distributed data storage. This makes complex batch processing of data across the network possible—usually as a result of streaming MapReduce scripts, Apache Pig workflows, or complete applications using a high-level language such as Java.

Hadoop isn't just for data processing; it is possible to use MapReduce to find the answers to aggregate queries involving sums, grouping, joins, and other functions. However, the procedure of querying datasets often requires an iterative process. Query tasks can also require multiple MapReduce jobs to attain the result, and it can be cumbersome to iteratively develop code to define complex MapReduce workflows. The open-source Apache Hive project, originally started at Facebook, was created to provide an SQL-like interface for Hadoop in order to speed up the process of writing iterative queries over data stored in HDFS.

Hive is a project that applies some of the concepts from data warehousing to the Hadoop framework. Unlike traditional data warehousing applications built using relational databases, Hive defines tables and indexes for data available to the Hadoop Distributed File System (HDFS). This enables users of Hive to interrogate datasets through an SQL-like query language called HiveQL. Hive's query language does not support all the functions of standard SQL-92, but it does provide some features specific to the MapReduce paradigm, such as the ability to provide multiple table output for query results. Hive supports native data types based mostly around the datatypes available to Java: various types of integer formats, floating-point numbers, strings, and more. Hive also provides support for arrays, maps, and custom structs.

Hive can access a variety of formats natively, including text data, Hadoop Sequence Files, and the columnar RCFile format. Data files can be completely managed by Hive itself, or data can be referenced to external locations, making it possible for Hive to coexist with existing MapReduce applications and workflows. It is also possible to improve query result speed by applying partition and index information to Hive tables. Because Hive is an interface to Hadoop, it is possible to create user-defined functions that can be compiled and used in queries. Due to its popularity, there is a large eco-system of tools available for Hive, including command-line tools, the Hive Web inter-face, and various connectors such as JDBC drivers that can be used to provide access from external software.

Hive is not the only distributed data warehousing solution. The AmpLab Spark project extends the Hive codebase to operate over data using the Spark distributed processing engine. Shark's in-memory model enables queries to return results expo-nentially faster than a typical Hive query. Shark can be used in conjunction with exist-ing Hadoop clusters. Although Shark is relatively new, it is becoming more popular as a replacement for Hive when interactive ad hoc querying is necessary.

Hive is a popular choice for users who need to ask questions about datasets that are too large to be handled by relational databases or are relatively unstructured. Hive is also useful for datasets that are constantly growing, as it scales well across many machines, a situation in which other approaches may be economically challenging. In addition, Hive makes a great complementary tool to existing Hadoop installations, providing nondeveloper analysts access to data that would otherwise require compli-cated code to query.

6

Building a Data Dashboard
with Google BigQuery

The media success of Apache Hadoop has been both a blessing and a curse for those who have an interest in learning about new distributed data technologies. The hype, although well-deserved, has led to an emphasis on Hadoop as the be-all and end-all solution for anything related to "big data."

In reality, applications built to handle large-scale data problems often require a collection of different technologies, each optimized for a particular use case. Nonrelational databases are useful for managing data at scale, especially when the amount of data reads greatly exceeds the amount of writes. MapReduce frameworks are useful for transforming data from one form into another. Along with these use cases, analysts need to be able to ask questions about the entire set of data, ideally using an iterative process. Neither MapReduce frameworks nor nonrelational databases are ideal for running queries over huge datasets quickly. In order to deal with aggregate queries, we need to look at another potential solution: an analytical database.

This chapter focuses on the concept of analytical databases: in particular, Google BigQuery, a technology that is very different from, and often complementary to, many of the other technologies covered in the rest of this book. BigQuery, which is a hosted service accessed through an API, allows developers to run queries over large datasets and obtain results very quickly. We'll take a look at how this technology can be useful for quickly building online data dashboards. We'll also take a look at how to make practical decisions about when to use tools like BigQuery versus MapReduce for similar use cases.

Analytical Databases

The process of asking questions about large amounts of data requires many steps. Data collection itself takes effort; as we've seen in previous chapters, the process of storing and sharing lots of data can be a great challenge. Transformations, processing, and normalization must take place before we can start analyzing our datasets. Once the data is in the shape that we want, we may want to merge it with other datasets to provide additional context for our questions. Finally, after these steps are complete, we are ready to start asking questions about our large datasets by running queries against them. The answers to our questions can sometimes create more questions, so we need to come up with a solution for iteratively querying our data. In the world of traditional relational databases, large, aggregate queries over huge tables are not particularly fast without additional indexing or the use of additional techniques for shaping the data into a different form. Nonrelational databases are also not designed for this purpose. What we need is another type of technology optimized for the purpose of asking questions and retrieving the result quickly.

When working with business data in large organizations, a common pattern is to use one type of system for keeping track of day-to-day data and other types of systems optimized to analyze the data. For customer-facing applications, which handle data such as financial transactions, Web content, or personal information, relational databases are often used. The main goals of these systems are to provide high consistency for data. If one of many millions of customers updates their address via a Web form, it is important that this transaction is recorded accurately and immediately. Data integrity is obviously very important in this context. Because large organizations depend on multiple databases for customer data updates, many invest in tools to provide transaction consistency across systems.

The workhorse databases that bravely face the outside world are often described as "online transactional processing" or **OLTP** systems. There is no canonical software design that typifies an OLTP system, as the "transaction" might mean any number of things to different people. Sometimes this term refers to the technical database term "transaction," or it can mean that the database is handling inserts that describe the customer transactions of some type. In any case, a good way to think about OLTP systems is that they are designed to be good for handling data that might constantly be updated as operational data. In practice, an OLTP system is usually some type of relational database, which is great for ensuring consistency and enforcing that data fits a particular schema. As we mentioned earlier, the relational model isn't always the best design for those applications that require running aggregate database queries quickly (see Chapter 3, "Building a NoSQL-Based Web App to Collect Crowd-Sourced Data," for more information about the role of relational and nonrelational databases).

Our crucial frontline databases are optimized to make sure our customers' data is in good shape, but they are not designed to make the analyst's job easier. Analysts need to be able to ask questions about their data and use the resulting information to help shape the strategy of the organization. Speed is a major concern because waiting minutes or hours for a query result to complete can be the difference between being able to make a quick decision and missing a deadline.

The need to perform fast queries on data stored in relational databases is sometimes solved using techniques that use an online analytical processing, or **OLAP,** system. While the term OLAP looks confusingly similar to its cousin OLTP, it means something very different. OLAP systems use techniques for shaping data originating from existing operational data into a format that makes it fast to query. A common goal of OLAP systems is to shape data in a way that avoids excessive JOIN queries, which are typically slow over large datasets in relational databases. In order to do this, some data is pulled, or extracted, into a new schema in the OLAP system. This entire process is complex and time consuming, but once it is done, it enables analysts to run faster queries over data at the expense of flexibility. Once a new type of query is required, the process of building new OLAP schemas may sometimes need to be repeated.

The OLAP concept has proven useful and has spawned an industry of large enterprise vendors, including stalwarts such as Oracle and Microsoft. However, some technologies take a different approach. One class of software, broadly known as analytical databases, dispenses with the relational model. Using innovations in on-disk storage and the use of distributed memory, analytical databases combine the flexibility of SQL with the speed of traditional OLAP systems.

Dremel: Spreading the Wealth

In 2003, Google released a paper describing their MapReduce framework for processing data. This paper was a milestone in the movement toward greater accessibility of large-scale data processing. MapReduce is a general algorithm for distributing the processing of data over clusters of readily available commodity machines. The MapReduce concept, in conjunction with a scalable distributed filesystem called GFS, helped to enable Google to index the public Internet. Constant drops in hardware costs along with Google's success in the search industry inspired computer scientists to spend more time thinking about using distributed systems of commodity hardware for data processing. Engineers at Yahoo! added capabilities inspired by the MapReduce paper to process data collected by the Apache Nutch Web crawler. Ultimately, the work on Nutch spawned the Hadoop project, which has since become the shining star of the open-source Big Data world. Hadoop is a horizontally scalable, fault-tolerant framework that enables developers to write their own MapReduce applications.

One of the biggest advantages of the MapReduce concept is that a variety of large data processing tasks can be completed in an acceptably short time and using hardware that is relatively inexpensive. Depending on the type of job, tasks that were previously impossible to run on single machines could be completed in hours or even minutes.

The Hadoop project has gained quite a lot of media attention, and for good reason. One of the drawbacks to this attention has been that some people new to the field of data analytics might even consider Hadoop and MapReduce to be synonymous with Big Data. Despite the success of the Hadoop community, some algorithms simply don't transfer well to being expressed as distributed MapReduce jobs. Although Hadoop is the open-source champion of batch processing, the MapReduce concept is not necessarily the best approach to dealing with ad hoc query tasks.

Questioning data is often an iterative process. The answers from one question might inspire a new question. Although MapReduce, along with tools such as Apache

Hive, makes ad hoc queries on large data sets possible, these technologies aren't always fast enough to match the iterative behavior and processes of data analysts.

After a number of years using MapReduce, developers at Google started to rethink the process of running aggregate queries over large datasets. An iterative query experience requires the ability to write and run queries quickly. In 2010, Google released a research paper that illustrated a technology known as Dremel. With Dremel, engineers could formulate queries using an SQL-like syntax, speeding up the process of iterative analysis without dealing with the overhead of defining raw MapReduce jobs. More importantly, Dremel used a novel technical design that could return query results over terabyte-scale datasets in seconds.

How Dremel and MapReduce Differ

In practice, data processing applications are often built using a collection of complementary technologies. As data flows through various pipelines, specialized resources are used for the steps of collection, processing, and analysis. Systems that enable batch processing of data, such as MapReduce, and those that provide ad hoc analytical processing, represented by Dremel, are complementary.

In Chapter 5, we looked at Apache Hive, a project that provides an SQL-like interface for defining MapReduce jobs that return the results of queries. Hive enables users to concentrate on thinking about data questions rather than the underlying MapReduce jobs that produce query results. Superficially, Dremel looks a bit like Apache Hive, as Dremel also features an SQL-like interface for defining queries.

MapReduce is a flexible design. The MapReduce model enables a great variety of different tasks to be implemented as is evident through the large ecosystem of software available for frameworks such as Hadoop. Dealing with unstructured data is possible by defining custom workflows to process that data.

Dremel requires data to conform to a schema. Several data types are available, including basic strings, numeric formats, and Booleans. Data in Dremel may be stored as flat records or in a nested and repeated format in which individual fields in a record can have child records of their own.

Hadoop stores data at rest in a distributed filesystem called the Hadoop Distributed Filesystem, or **HDFS**. Dremel stores data on disk in a columnar format. Storing data in columns instead of rows means that only the minimum data necessary needs to be read from disk during a query. Imagine a data table that contains information about a person's address. One way to represent this data would be to store first name, last name, street, city, zip code, and other elements in individual fields. If your query requires you to find out how many people named "Michael" live in each zip code, Dremel only needs to inspect the data in the first name and zip code columns. Use of columnar datastores is not a technique exclusive to Dremel; we'll take a look at several other technologies that use a columnar data structure later on.

Imagine an SQL-like query that operates over an entire table of data. The query may do several things, including grouping, joining, and ordering. Queries that may take many steps with MapReduce frameworks generally store their intermediate results to disk. Unlike MapReduce, Dremel does its best to not use a disk at all. For aggregate queries that require a full table scan of data, BigQuery does all of its work using available system memory, which makes for speedy query performance. For more information on how developers are using in-memory data systems such as Redis and MemSQL to increase data throughput, see Chapter 3.

The use cases for batch processing with MapReduce frameworks and the iterative querying tasks solved by BigQuery are complementary. In fact, a system that uses even more specialized software systems such as a key–value store for high-volume data collection (see Chapter 3), a MapReduce framework for normalization or processing, or an analytical database for the ability to question the collected data quickly may be even more common for a commercial application.

BigQuery: Data Analytics as a Service

Dremel is an internal Google tool, so how can it be used as a practical data solution for everyone else? Similar to the way in which Amazon released their key–value datastore DynamoDB, Google has provided the technology used by Dremel to outside developers via an application programming interface (API). This service is known as Google BigQuery.

Commonly used applications such as Web mail, social networking, and music are becoming available as cloud services to be consumed through an interface such as a Web browser or a mobile device. Instead of relying on desktop hardware for processing power, the application space is being re-envisioned through standards-based protocols. Although there are many pitfalls to overcome, the advantages to this model include device independence, the potential for lowering costs, and new opportunities for social collaboration.

For data scientists, offloading hardware responsibilities to service providers is becoming more common. The move to hosted services is not just a result of taking advantage of the latent processing capabilities of cloud environments. Using a cloud service also allows analysts and software engineers to more easily collaborate on tasks without having to manage hardware. As we've seen in other chapters, when data sizes are large, using cloud-based services can sometimes be the only way to economically solve a data challenge.

As we've seen in example after example in this book, a common theme of working with data at scale has been innovative rethinking about technology. Nonrelational databases, such as key–value datastores, were created to address the difficulty of scaling the relational model to Web-scale data.

BigQuery is not a database in the traditional sense, and it exhibits characteristics different from those of a traditional relational database. Although it is possible for BigQuery to store data, it is an append-only system. Individual records cannot be updated; it's only possible to append data to existing data tables. Also, unlike a standard relational database, the system doesn't support the complete range of standard

SQL commands. Creating and updating tables and adding data to existing tables is accomplished via API calls rather than SQL commands.

As with a relational database, data in BigQuery is structured into tables. These tables are organized into groups known as datasets. In turn, each dataset belongs to a project. Because the service is completely hosted, BigQuery's billing model is associated with the project level. The BigQuery service also enables project owners to share datasets with users outside of the project. In this case, users from other BigQuery projects could run queries on the public datasets that you create; they would cover the costs of the query they run on your public dataset, and your project would be billed only for storage of the data. BigQuery also supports a notion of access control lists, or ACLs. Access to your datasets can be scoped down into whatever granularity is appropriate: private to one person, shared only with the members of a domain, or a combination of sharing permissions.

BigQuery's Query Language

Asking questions about the data stored in a relational database almost always means that you will be writing queries in SQL, using syntax that is similar to an established standard such as SQL-92. BigQuery uses an SQL-like syntax, but it doesn't support all, or even most, of the functions available in SQL-92. Some of the differences are due to the fact that BigQuery is a query engine, not a transactional database, so it lacks the SQL syntax necessary to create or update individual records.

One of BigQuery's primary use cases is to provide fast aggregate query results over large tables of data. Many times, a GROUP BY clause is used together with an ORDER BY clause to produce a count of TOP results. This type of query is so common that Big-Query provides a shortcut method called TOP for this purpose. Let's look at one of BigQuery's current sample tables, called "wikipedia," which contains over 300 million rows of Wikipedia revision history information. Listing 6.1 provides an example of using the TOP method to produce an ordered list of the top five most revised pages that contain the term "data."

Listing 6.1 BigQuery's TOP function

```
/* BigQuery TOP() function: Combines the functionality
   of GROUP BY, LIMIT and ORDER BY
*/
SELECT
  TOP(title, 5),
  COUNT(*)
FROM
  [publicdata:samples.wikipedia]
WHERE
  title CONTAINS "data";
```

BigQuery also supports data structures that have nested and repeated fields. This means that a particular field may define a new row containing a set of child attributes—for example, a `person` field might contain a list of records that define a playlist.

Each time a query is run, BigQuery creates a new table to hold the results. If you explicitly name the table, it will persist indefinitely (otherwise, the table is considered "temporary" and is only stored for a short time).

Building a Custom Big Data Dashboard

In Chapter 4, "Strategies for Dealing with Data Silos," we took a look at strategies for breaking down data silos. One of these strategies is to help empower employees to ask their own questions about your organization's data. Unless you are very lucky, it's likely that not everyone in your organization is a data scientist; therefore, it is sometimes necessary to provide or build tools to help less technical users access analytical information. When datasets become very large, common analysis tools such as R and Excel may not be able to easily handle the job, forcing your IT department to spend time either processing data or managing distributed data processing infrastructure. Every organization is different; big or small, each has specific data-reporting needs. This can sometimes make generalized organizational analytics tools hard products to provide; inevitably, many customizations are required. Furthermore, organizations rely on a variety of software for data reporting, including Excel, R, and Tableau, often in conjunction with custom-written code. When trying to evaluate what to build or buy (see Chapter 13, "When to Build, When to Buy, When to Outsource"), it pays to understand which tools members of your organization are already familiar with; however, a common pattern in large organizations is that there is often a need for custom data-reporting tools.

The Dremel-based infrastructure that powers BigQuery is something that data developers will never access directly; every BigQuery feature is made available via a programmatic interface. Although a BigQuery command-line tool (called bq), and a BigQuery Web UI are available, both are applications that make calls to the BigQuery API service. Providing data analytics as a service enables a kind of development flexibility not found in most distributed data software. Although hosted and completely managed Hadoop services are becoming more available, an out-of-the-box Hadoop installation requires your organization to manage hardware and software updates and hire experienced staff to keep it all running. Hosted systems free up developers to concentrate on building applications without having to spend quite so much time managing infrastructure. There are, of course, trade-offs and challenges that arise when incorporating a data analysis API into your application-development process. To illustrate the process of developing our own large-scale data analysis tool, we will take a look at how to build a simple data dashboard using the BigQuery API.

When it comes to processing data in batches, Hadoop is an excellent choice; however, like many other distributed systems, it inherently requires some amount of infrastructure management. Hadoop's APIs are designed for building MapReduce-based applications, but connecting these applications to a browser-based client requires another layer of framework code. In contrast, the BigQuery API makes it a good choice for building or integrating into existing data dashboards. Because there is no infrastructure to manage, developers can focus primarily on building client-side tools.

To illustrate the process of using a browser-based client to connect to the BigQuery API, we will use JavaScript along with some helpful libraries. The Google API Client Library for JavaScript provides methods for making calls to the BigQuery API and some helper methods for authorizing access to BigQuery. Our simple application does three things: asks the user to authorize access to the BigQuery API, runs a query, and returns the results to a browser in order to display a visualization.

Authorizing Access to the BigQuery API

The BigQuery API is a Web-based service; it is accessed via an HTTP request that makes a call to a URL available on the public Internet. Web services need to have both fine-grained permissions and a mechanism to ensure proper authorization of their use. BigQuery supports a variety of sharing options for each dataset. A dataset may be made available to a single user or a group of users, or even made public to anyone with access to the API. When a user tries to access our dashboard, how does the BigQuery API know if that user has permission to access a particular table or dataset?

One solution to this problem might be to give each user a password to access the BigQuery API. When our dashboard needs to make a call to BigQuery, the application can ask the user to either supply the password or share an already stored password. Unfortunately, requiring passwords is not a very secure way to provide access to BigQuery. How do we know the application in the middle—that is, our dashboard—will store our precious password securely? There is no way for us to guarantee the security of what happens with our application.

When building an online application, we ideally want to allow the application to use external APIs on a user's behalf without that user having to share the password for that service. In this case, we want our data dashboard application to access BigQuery without users sharing their Google account passwords. Instead, we would like to give the application access to the user's BigQuery data for only a limited time.

Fortunately, there is a way to provide this level of access. The **OAuth** protocol defines a standard for accessing network resources without having to share your user password. Instead, a special access token is created by the service provider (in this case, Google), and the token is scoped to allow access only to a specific network resource—such as a user's BigQuery tables. In a typical browser-based flow, the application (in our case, our dashboard) will make a call to the BigQuery API asking for authorization. The BigQuery API will redirect the user to a Web page that it controls, from which it provides a form that asks the user to authorize access to the API.

Not every application is Web-based, of course. Some applications are designed to run on the desktop or on embedded devices or left to whir away on servers. What if the application doesn't have access to a browser window? Apart from the browser-based authorization flow, the OAuth protocol defines a variety of flows to access Web services using these other methods.

One of the criticisms of the original OAuth specification is that it was too complex for client-side developers to implement. The latest iteration of the protocol, OAuth 2.0, simplifies the requirements to address this concern. OAuth 2.0 is gaining traction and is being implemented to allow access to services from Facebook, Foursquare, Google, and many others.[1]

In order for our application to be authorized to use the BigQuery API, we need to register it with Google. Service providers that offer OAuth all provide some way to register known applications that request access to available APIs. Google provides something called the Cloud Console, which enables teams of developers to collaborate on projects. We will need to use the console to create two values that will allow our application to use OAuth. The first is simply a developer project ID. We will also need to generate a client ID, which uniquely identifies the application to Google.

Our application will also need to know the *scope* of data access that will be granted by the user. In this case, we want the dashboard application to provide access only to the BigQuery service and no other Google services (such as the Maps API or the Google Drive API). The scope is simply a string value that identifies which service the application may access. A scope can also limit the way the BigQuery API is used, such as providing only read-only access to tables and projects. See the Google BigQuery documentation (https://developers.google.com/bigquery/) for more information about available scopes.

When generating a client ID, Google needs to know where to send the user after the authorization step. This location is called the callback URL, and for the Google API Client Library for JavaScript, the default location for callbacks is http://your_application_url/oauth2callback. If you are testing this sample using a Web server on a local machine, then the callback URL will likely be something such as http://localhost:8000/oauth2callback, depending on which port your local Web server uses.

Once we have made all of this information available to our data dashboard application, it will be able to initiate an OAuth user flow. When the OAuth flow begins, your application will redirect the browser window to a Web page hosted by Google. This Web page will identify itself as the authorization screen for the BigQuery API. If the user is not logged in to his Google account, the page will request that the user authenticate himself by providing a username and password. Note that this password is for the service provider (in this case, Google) and not the application itself, so it is not shared with the data dashboard in any way. If the user has permission to access the BigQuery API, then he will be asked to allow the application to "view and manage your data in Google BigQuery." This will provide an access token to the application, allowing it to make calls to the BigQuery API on the user's behalf. Once this permission is granted, the application will redirect the user back to the application, which is now allowed to make calls to the BigQuery API on behalf of the user. This same flow might be familiar to users of apps that depend on Twitter or Facebook logins.

---

1. http://oauth.net/2/

Let's add the project ID, our new client ID, and the BigQuery scope as variables in our application. Listing 6.2 demonstrates how to define an authorization flow, using the Google API Client Library for JavaScript.

Listing 6.2   **Adding the project id, client id, and scope information**

```html
<html>
  <head>
    <script src="https://apis.google.com/js/client.js"></script>
    <script
     src="https://ajax.googleapis.com/ajax/libs/jquery/1.7.2/jquery.min.js">
    </script>
    <script>
      // Your project ID and client ID
      var project_id = 'XXXXX123456';
      var client_id = 'XXXXX123456.apps.googleusercontent.com';

      var config = {
        'client_id': client_id,
        'scope': 'https://www.googleapis.com/auth/bigquery'
      };

      function auth() {
        gapi.auth.authorize(config, function() {
            gapi.client.load('bigquery', 'v2');
            $('#client_initiated').html('BigQuery client initiated');
        });
      }
    </script>
  </head>

  <body>
    <h2>BigQuery + JavaScript Example</h2>
    <button id="auth_button" onclick="auth();">Authorize</button>
  </body>
</html>
```

Running a Query and Retrieving the Result

Now that we have registered our application with Google and set up the parameters we need for authorization, we can start making calls to the BigQuery API. But what exactly does this mean? Essentially, all interaction with BigQuery takes place via a REST-based API. Messages are sent to BigQuery in JSON format, and results and job metadata are also returned as JSON objects.

BigQuery's API is jobs based, meaning that data-intensive operations such as queries, loading data, and exporting require that an API call be made to insert that job into the system. The API response will return a unique job ID that the application can use to check on the status of the job. To run a query, the application first inserts a job configuration containing a query string. Next, the application starts a polling loop, checking for the status of the query job. When the job status is complete, you can go ahead and retrieve the query result. This is also called an asynchronous query.

For query jobs, BigQuery supports a convenient API method that wraps the job insertion, the polling loop, and the result retrieval step into a single call. Because this API method will block until a result is returned (or an error is thrown), the API method takes an additional timeout parameter. Our example in Listing 6.3 uses this convenient method to query a result.

Listing 6.3   **Simple BigQuery query example in JavaScript**

```
function runQuery() {
  var request = gapi.client.bigquery.jobs.query({
    'projectId': project_id,
    'timeoutMs': '30000',
    'query': 'SELECT TOP(repository_language, 5) as \
            language, COUNT(*) as count FROM \
            [publicdata:samples.github_timeline] \
            WHERE repository_language != "";'
  });
  request.execute(function(response) {
    console.log(response);
    $('#results')
      .html(JSON.stringify(response.result.rows, null));
  });
}
```

Caching Query Results

BigQuery returns query results very quickly, usually on the order of seconds. For responsive Web-based applications, users expect delays of far less. To provide a satisfying interactive user experience, our application should make an effort to return a result to the user even faster whenever possible.

By default, the BigQuery API will make a best effort to remember the results of a query result if the underlying table hasn't changed. The results are saved on a per-user basis, meaning that the cached query result run under the account of one user won't affect the result of another. Although this can speed up the results of a repeated query, it still requires a round-trip call to the API to retrieve the result. It's more efficient to store query results locally, using browser-based storage.

There are a variety of ways to store local data using HTML5 APIs, each of which has various strengths and weaknesses. In this example, we will use the simplest and most well-supported method: Web Storage. Once we retrieve a query result, we will create a key based on a hash of the query itself. Then we will store the result data

locally on the client machine. This way, if the user requests a particular query that
has already been retrieved, we can access the locally cached copy for a very quick user
experience. Listing 6.4 provides an example of using the HTML Web Storage API to
cache results locally. Note that this example does not include any cache expiration or
sophisticated string hashing.

Listing 6.4 **Simple BigQuery query example in JavaScript**

```
// A simple hashing function
String.prototype.hash = function(){
  var hash = 0, i, char;
  if (this.length == 0) return hash;
  for (i = 0, l = this.length; i < l; i++) {
    char  = this.charCodeAt(i);
    hash  = ((hash<<5)-hash)+char;
    hash |= 0;
  }
  return hash;
};

function runQuery() {
  var query = $('#query').val();
  var results;

  // Attempt to retrieve our cached query result
  cachedResult = localStorage[query.hash()];

  if (!cachedResult) {
    var request = gapi.client.bigquery.jobs.query({
      'projectId': project_id,
      'timeoutMs': '30000',
      'query': query
    );

  request.execute(function(response) {
    results = response;
    localStorage[query.hash()] = JSON.stringify(results);
    drawTable(results);
  });

  // If the cached result exists, return the cached value
  } else {
    results = JSON.parse(cachedResult);
    drawTable(results);
  }
}
```

Adding Visualization

We've already demonstrated how to use BigQuery for processing a query: initiating a query job via API call and retrieving the result. At this point, our dashboard simply retrieves a JSON object. Sure, a lot of people consider a raw JSON object a beautiful thing, but it may be a bit more useful to display this resulting data in a format that is easier to interpret. Let's add a visualization to our dashboard.

Because BigQuery is accessed via an online API, there are many existing visualization software tools, both commercial and open-source, that can connect natively to the service. In this case, let's create a simple table using Google Charts, a service for creating client-side graphs. Using Google Chart Tools simply requires adding a few lines of JavaScript to our existing application code. Listing 6.5 demonstrates how to use the Google Chart Tools library to display BigQuery results in a tabular format.

Listing 6.5   **Visualizing BigQuery results using the Google Charts API**

```
<!-- Include the Google Charts Tool libraries  -->
  <script type='text/javascript'
      src='https://www.google.com/jsapi'></script>
  <script type='text/javascript'>
    google.load('visualization', '1', {packages:['table']});
  </script>


    <script>
    // drawTable takes a BigQuery result object
    // and draws a Google Charts Table
    function drawTable(queryResults) {

      var data = new google.visualization.DataTable();

      // Retrieve column names from BigQuery result schema
      $.each(queryResults.schema.fields, function(i, item) {
        data.addColumn('string', item.name);
      });

      // Push each row of data into a data table
      $.each(queryResults.rows, function(i, item) {
        var rows = new Array();
        for (var i=0;i<item.f.length;i++) {
          rows.push(item.f[i].v)
        }
        data.addRows([rows]);
      });
```

```
        // Draw the Google Charts Table
        var table =
          new google.visualization.Table(document.getElementById('results'));
        table.draw(data, {showRowNumber: true});

      }

  </script>

  <body>
    <h2>BigQuery + JavaScript Example</h2>
    <button id="auth_button" onclick="auth();">Authorize</button>
    <hr>
    <div><input id="query" type></input></div>
    <button id="query_button" onclick="runQuery();">Run Query</button>
    <hr>
    <div id="results"></div>
  </body>
```

The Future of Analytical Query Engines

The Hadoop project was inspired by the design concepts described by Google's publicly available MapReduce and Google File System research papers. Similarly, ideas
from Google's paper on the technology behind Dremel have formed the basis of several open-source projects that aim to speed up query processing over large datasets.

One of these projects is Cloudera's open-source **Impala**, which aims to provide
fast, interactive queries over data stored in HDFS or HBase. Like Dremel, Impala
uses a columnar data format for structuring data at rest. Impala also skips Hadoop's
MapReduce framework entirely, using an in-memory processing engine to ensure that
queries run fast.

There are other projects that use in-memory data objects to produce very fast query
results over large datasets. The AMPLab **Shark** project is a data warehouse system
based on Apache Hive. Like Impala, Shark is able to use data from existing HDFS and
HBase sources. Shark uses a completely in-memory model that returns query results
many times faster than Hive in some benchmarks (see Chapter 5, "Using Hadoop,
Hive, and Shark to Ask Questions About Large Datasets," for more information on
Shark and the related project, Spark).

With so many potential choices for analytical databases, it can become difficult to
decide which tool is the best fit for a particular challenge. One of the potential benefits of Impala and Shark is to improve the speed of queries over data that is already
in a Hadoop environment. In contrast, tools such as Google BigQuery are excellent
choices for projects that lack existing distributed infrastructure.

One of the most interesting things about Google BigQuery is that it is a pointer
toward what other data processing tools may look like in the future. There are many

examples of applications in the data-science domain, from machine learning to data collection, that are being developed entirely as services in the cloud. At the same time, desktop and mobile applications are increasingly being developed as Web applications; the aggregate data generated by these applications is already in the cloud. This combination of trends will result in more fully hosted and managed cloud-based analytics services.

Summary

Gaining insight from massive and growing datasets, such as those generated by large organizations, requires specialized technologies for each step in the data analysis process. Once organizational data is cleaned, merged, and shaped into the form desired, the process of asking questions about data is often an iterative one. MapReduce frameworks, such as the open-source Apache Hadoop project, are flexible platforms for the economical processing of large amounts of data using a collection of commodity machines. Although it is often the best choice for large batch-processing operations, MapReduce is not always the ideal solution for quickly running iterative queries over large datasets. MapReduce can require a great deal of disk I/O, a great deal of administration, and multiple steps to return the result of a single query. Waiting for results to complete makes iterative, ad hoc analysis difficult.

Analytical databases are a specialized class of technologies designed for ad hoc querying over large datasets. These systems often have features meant for raw query speed, such as storing data in columnar formats, using in-memory processing, and providing access via SQL-like query languages.

Google BigQuery is an analytical database designed to run SQL-like queries over very large datasets with results returned in seconds. Unlike some analytical databases, BigQuery is completely hosted and accessed via a REST API. This enables developers to focus on building applications that ask questions about data, rather than building the infrastructure itself. Although this model presents some unique challenges, including the process of loading data into the cloud, it removes the overhead of administering a cluster of computers.

The design of BigQuery differs fundamentally from relational databases and MapReduce frameworks. Data is stored not in rows but in a columnar format, allowing data in the columns specified by the query to be accessed when necessary. BigQuery supports both flat and nested data structures. Query results are returned as JSON objects, and very large results can be materialized into a new table.

Because BigQuery uses a REST-based API, it is useful for building interactive tools such as online dashboards. Applications built with the BigQuery API require users to authorize access to their data using a protocol called OAuth that prevents users from having to share their passwords.

Although a hosted, in-memory analytical database such as BigQuery is an excellent choice for building or incorporating large-scale data analysis into applications, it's not the best tool for every data processing need. For long-running batch-processing tasks that don't fit into available system memory, MapReduce is the correct approach. For applications that require running fast, ad hoc queries over data already contained in HDFS or HBase, applications such as Cloudera's Impala or the AMPLab Shark project might be a better fit. The concepts from Google's research paper on their Dremel technology have inspired a great deal of innovation in the world of analytical database technology, and the number of distributed ad hoc analytics technologies is growing.

## 7

Visualization Strategies for Exploring Large Datasets

There is no such thing as information overload.
There is only bad design.
—Edward Tufte

According to Bit.ly's Hillary Mason, data scientists generally do "three fundamentally different things: math, code... and communicate."[1] Although some of the technologies available in the data toolbox primarily focus on engineering whereas other technologies focus on mathematical analysis, the visual representation of information requires a combination of both of these skills along with an extra helping of communication skill. One could say that a goal of data visualization is to communicate abstract concepts that emerge from the world of math and metrics using the more human language of spatial representation.

The current practice of data visualization has a rich cultural history backed by many decades of pioneering and practice that dates to long before the digital age. Aesthetic considerations are important to mastering the communication of visual information, so this is not a field that one can be expected to master in a short amount of time. Although the field offers a great deal of time-tested best practices, innovations are still being developed thanks to constantly improving interactive digital technology and the practice of analysts sharing more and more datasets on the Web. The use of techniques borrowed from fields such as user-experience design is helping visualization researchers understand how to best communicate data narratives.

Although the world of data visualization is rich enough to fill a library of books, this chapter will touch on some practical considerations for dealing with large datasets. We'll also take a look at popular open-source software that is often used for building compelling visualizations for both desktop and Web.

---

1. www.hilarymason.com/blog/getting-started-with-data-science/

Cautionary Tales: Translating Data into Narrative

Although many people may associate the name "John Snow" with the character from the *Game of Thrones* fantasy novels, students of epidemiology may be more likely than most to associate this name with a 19th century physician who unraveled the mystery behind a deadly 1854 cholera outbreak near Broad Street in London.

The cholera outbreaks in the city during the 1850s claimed the lives of tens of thousands of people. At the time, the prevailing medical consensus was that the vehicle for cholera transmission was a miasma, or "bad air," perhaps originating from pollution. Complicating matters were ideas that people from lower economic classes were more naturally susceptible to disease (a result of a supposed "moral depravity" of the poor[2]) and that these poor residents tended to create more pollution due to overcrowding and lack of resources.

John Snow's investigations into the cholera outbreaks eventually led him to believe that the miasma theory for cholera transmission was faulty. Snow used a variety of techniques to study the tragedy, including working with Reverend Henry Whitehead, a local expert on the behavior of people who lived in the London outbreak zone. One of Snow's tools to convince others that the outbreak was due to an infected water supply from a particular pump was to create a map plotting the deaths. Without having any knowledge of the germ theory of disease transmission (which was not well regarded at the time), Snow came to the conclusion that the epicenter of the outbreak was a pump central to the deadly cases he plotted. This was only part of the story; Snow then needed to convince local authorities as well as fellow scientists of his theory—and he did so with the help of a type of visualization now known as a *dot-distribution map* (see Figure 7.1). His resulting Broad Street pump cholera map is an oft-cited milestone in the development of using cartography for understanding and, more importantly, communicating the impact of medical outbreaks.[3]

The well-known information visualization pioneer and author Edward Tufte makes the claim that an 1869 work by Charles Joseph Minard "may well be the best statistical graphic ever drawn,"[4] and it's difficult to disagree with this assessment. Minard's chart, titled *Carte figurative des pertes successives en hommes de l'Armée Française dans la campagne de Russie 1812–1813*[5], tells the statistical story of Napoleon's disastrous foray into Russia during the campaign of 1812 (see Figure 7.2). Not only is the work aesthetically appealing, but it packs an amazing amount of information into a single chart. Minard's work is an example of a **flow map**, which combines aspects of area charts and maps. The representation of the numbers of troops using dynamically sized bars begins with a thick, light-colored bar depicting the massive and confident army of nearly half a

---

2. Johnson, Steven. *The Ghost Map*. New York: Riverhead, 2006.

3. www.ncgia.ucsb.edu/pubs/snow/snow.html

4. Tufte, Edward R. *The Visual Display of Quantitative Information*. New York: Graphics Press, 1983, p. 40.

5. www.datavis.ca/gallery/minbib.php

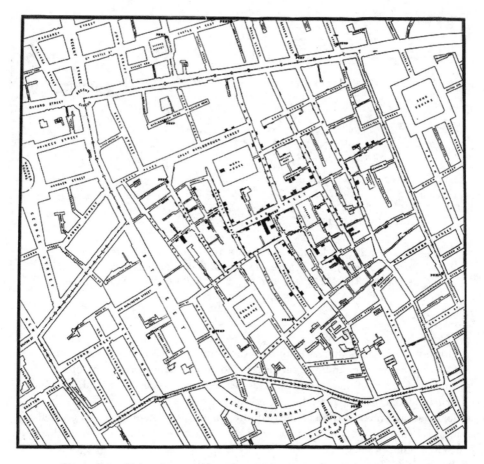

Figure 7.1   19th-century epidemiology pioneer John Snow's famous dot-distribution map communicating the impact of an 1854 cholera outbreak near London's Broad Street

million troops tromping into Russia. A timeline is included, as well as a line graph visualization of the temperature over time. Famously, as the winter temperatures decreased over time, Napoleon's troops began to succumb to the cold, lack of supplies, and other logistical disasters. Minard depicts the dwindling size of the army during the retreat using a black, increasingly narrowing line, closely mirroring the drop in the temperature over time. Although this information visualization is widely known to be a masterpiece, Minard's graphic also tells only one side of the story—nearly as many Russian troops, as well as a great deal more civilians, perished as well, making this conflict one of the most deadly in history.

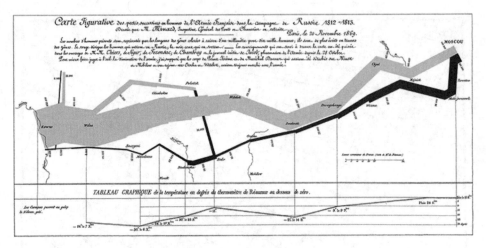

Figure 7.2   Charles Joseph Minard's 1869 work *Carte figurative des pertes successives en hommes de l'Armée Française dans la campagne de Russie 1812-1813,* described by Edward Tufte as the best statistical graphic ever drawn

Both of these stories illustrate not only the power that visualizations can provide but also the complexity and care that it takes to condense numerical data into a compelling work. Each of these data visualizations took a great deal of multidimensional information and made it accessible. In a simple two-dimensional space, ideas about time, space, and metrics were condensed into a narrative. The impact of a great visualization is that it not only tells a great story but also can be used to convince others of a particular point of view.

Both of these masterpieces of historical visualization are inspiring, and the ability to create visual representations of data is more accessible than ever. Many people are familiar with the graphing features of common business productivity tools such as Microsoft Excel. Excel has excellent capabilities for creating charts and graphs, but the push-button aspect of tools such as Excel means that it is very easy to generate charts and graphs that are not particularly compelling or which tell a misleading story. Because spatial representations of data can be so powerful, a good data scientist must take great care to understand what types of depictions best support his or her narrative.

An overarching goal of information visualization is to communicate abstract concepts using spatial features. Aesthetics are important, in much the same way that the way one speaks or writes when telling a story can affect the recipient's experience. However, one pitfall of data visualization is not being familiar with which types of data can be presented using which type of visual representation.

Human Scale versus Machine Scale

Many of the examples in this book discuss how to deal with the challenges of very large datasets. Relatively new open-source technologies, including nonrelational databases and distributed processing frameworks such as Hadoop, have made collecting and processing large amounts of data more accessible than ever. The ability of humans to comprehend large amounts of spatial data, however, has not evolved accordingly.

Interactivity

Before the invention of the digital display, charts were bound to paper. Thankfully, visualizations are no longer shackled to a static substrate. Over the past few decades, the development of new interfaces has increased the speed with which researchers have developed innovative visualization techniques. Using methodology borrowed from the world of user experience and cognitive science, data visualization researchers are increasingly able to quantify the effectiveness of their work. As a result, new types of visual data representations are being developed all the time. An example of fairly recent visualization innovation includes the **Streamgraph**,[6] a comparative, flowing area graph developed as an improved way to compare large, changing datasets over time. Similarly, Edward Tufte's **Sparklines** visualization[7] concept (developed in the late 1990s) embedded short, intense line-graph metrics of a single changing metric within surrounding text. This type of visualization has become a common feature of online financial publications.

Interactive visualizations enable researchers with very large, multifaceted datasets to allow end users to select the slices of data that are relevant for answering a particular data question. A well-known example of online, interactive visualizations is the pioneering work of Hans Rosling who, through his Gapminder Foundation, led the development of a software tool known as Trendalyzer. Trendalyzer enables users to compare a variety of economic metrics of the countries of the world (such as average income and birth weight) through a *bubble chart* visualization. Along with this representation, the tool adds an element of time, giving users the ability to play back changes in country metrics as they change over time.

In summary, interactive visualizations provide yet another strategy for providing visual representations of large datasets. By allowing users to select facets of the data to explore, it's sometimes possible to reduce the worrisome problems of clutter and visual overload that can render visualizations useless.

---

6. Byron, Lee, and Martin Wattenberg. "Stacked Graphs—Geometry & Aesthetics." *IEEE Transactions on Visualization and Computer Graphics* 14, no. 6 (November/December 2008): 1245–1252.

7. www.bissantz.com/sparklines/

Building Applications for Data Interactivity

In practice, the ability to ask ad hoc questions about datasets is an important goal for data analysts. The ability to generate plots and visualizations quickly is useful for exploring data interactively as well as sharing insights about the data with others.

There is an enormous number of tools, both commercial and open-source, for creating graphs and visualizations for both general data visualization and niche industries. Products from companies such as Tableau and Qlikview focus on providing interactivity with a variety of data sources. Other commercial data products, such as Splunk, incorporate visualization into their data analytics workflow.

For those who are either exploring data sets interactively or building their own Web-based applications, a commercial solution isn't always the most flexible choice. In some cases, writing the code to provide a custom visualization is a more practical solution.

Interactive Visualizations with R and ggplot2

R is currently the most popular open-source scientific and numerical analysis language. R features an intuitive design inspired by other functional languages as well as a massive community of users who contribute modules for solving an incredible range of analysis challenges. A seemingly underappreciated strength of the language contributing to R's impact is its rich set of functions and installable libraries available for plotting and graphics.

Let's retell the story taken from a well-cited and interesting 2002 paper by Shaughnessy and Pfannkuch entitled "How Faithful is Old Faithful?" This paper is an excellent foray into the world of statistical analysis. Furthermore, the Old Faithful eruption dataset used in the paper is one of many available public datasets in the core R distribution for testing.

A scatterplot is an excellent visualization tool for looking for possible correlations, and because it is also a great type of plot to explore two-dimensional numerical data, R makes it tremendously easy to create one: It's a matter of simply typing plot(). Listing 7.1 shows how to do this and how to save an R plot as a PNG file, useful for publications. For an example of the output, see Figure 7.3.

Listing 7.1 **Simple example of the plotting functions of R**

```
# Show the first three lines of the faithful dataset

head(faithful,3)

  eruptions waiting
1     3.600      79
2     1.800      54
3     3.333      74
```

```
# Produce a scatterplot of the Old Faithful dataset
plot(faithful)

# Saving the plot as a PNG file using R
# save a 500 X 500 plot
png(filename="old_faithful.png", width=500, height=500, pointsize=16)
plot(faithful)
# This command closes the file
dev.off()
```

This example produces useful visualizations, but without additional work the standard R graphics package produces results that are definitely a bit barebones. It's possible to make core R graphics more aesthetically pleasing, but many people prefer to look to other libraries for this purpose. For far more complex and aesthetically pleasing visualizations, a popular choice is the ggplot2 library (see Listing 7.2). ggplot2 tends to be slightly more verbose to use with simple visualizations such as the scatterplot example, but when it's used to create more complex data visualizations, it's definitely well suited to the task. The core idea behind ggplot2 is that the data itself and how it

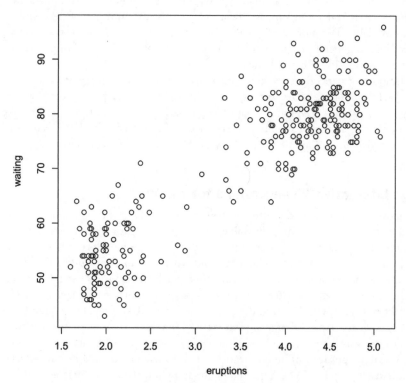

Figure 7.3   A scatterplot depicting number of eruptions versus waiting time of "Old Faithful," using R's sample faithful dataset

is presented are kept separate. Once data is loaded into a ggplot object, *aesthetic* functions are used to describe how that data will be presented.

Listing 7.2   **Using the ggplot2 library to create a scatterplot**

```
# Load the ggplot library
library(ggplot2)
# Create a ggplot object, mapping eruptions and wait time using an
# aesthetic
geyser_plot <- ggplot(faithful, aes(eruptions, waiting))
# Instruct ggplot to construct a dot plotgeyser_plot + geom_point()
```

matplotlib: 2-D Charts with Python

For many developers, Python is the general-purpose language of choice. The sparse, simple syntax and overall design philosophy mean that Python scripts are very readable and accessible. The sheer number of Python developers also ensures that there is an enormous number of libraries available for data analysis work. The award-winning iPython interactive shell is widely used by data analysts, and the iPython notebook provides a Web-based interface for this powerful tool. Similarly, Python data analysis libraries, such as SciPy and Pandas, are starting to rival R in terms of the number of features available. For more on how Python is helping to make interactive data analysis accessible to general purpose programmers, see Chapter 12, "Building Analytics Workflows Using Python and Pandas."

An important part of the Python data analysis tool chain is matplotlib, a powerful and actively-supported 2-D graphing and plotting library. matplotlib, developed primarily by the late John D. Hunter, can generate a variety of charts and graphs. Apart from sporting a familiar, Pythonic, object-oriented interface, matplotlib can also be used in a procedural mode that resembles the interface of the commercial application MatLab.

D3.js: Interactive Visualizations for the Web

If matplotlib's self-described motto (borrowed from PERL) is that it "tries to make easy things easy and hard things possible," then D3.js might be described as a toolkit for making even impossible visualization needs possible. The Internet has obviously become an amazing tool for sharing data, and when it comes to toolkits for building interactive visualizations, very few options can touch the D3.js (D3 stands for data-driven documents) library. D3.js is the successor to another popular JavaScript visualization library, protovis. The lead developer for D3.js, Mike Bostock, currently works for the New York Times, designing interactive data visualizations that sometimes stand alone as stories in their own right. The use of D3.js and tools like it to create interactive visualizations for online publications is an excellent example of **data-driven journalism**, a growing field that attempts to apply journalistic principles to data analysis in order to tell a story. Although some may argue that the Internet has had a negative economic impact on the field of journalism, Web-based interactive toolkits such as D3.js are evidence that the role of the online journalist may actually be evolving and may incorporate some techniques normally ascribed to data scientists.

Visualizations depend on graphics, and the open standard for vector-based graphics files on the Web is the powerful, but seemingly underappreciated, XML-based *Scalable Vector Graphics* format, or SVG. At its core, D3.js is a library for creating and transforming SVG objects, with a focus on methods that help build common visualization elements from underlying data sources. Despite a great deal of online documentation and online tutorials from the data visualization community, newcomers can sometimes find D3.js's conventions maddeningly complex. Although some of the design and structure of D3.js is similar to the popular JavaScript framework jQuery, the conventions used to actually define and create SVG manipulations may appear unfamiliar. Part of the reason for that seems to be a lack of widespread understanding of how SVG graphics work. Before we take a brief look at D3.js, let's examine an SVG file by viewing its XML source.

Listing 7.3 is a simple XML file created using the open-source vector-graphics tool Inkscape. The code describes a square object that is 100 by 100 pixels in size and which is located at the coordinates of 57 (*x*-axis) and 195 (*y*-axis). One common point of initial confusion when using SVG graphics is that the origin of the coordinate system is in the top-left corner, with the *y*-axis extending toward the bottom-left corner. When opened in a Web browser, this file will appear as a blue square (with a 1 pixel black border) as expected, sitting perfectly still at a location of 57, 195.

Listing 7.3   SVG: A simple blue square with a black border

```
<?xml version="1.0" encoding="UTF-8" standalone="no"?>
<!DOCTYPE svg PUBLIC "-//W3C//DTD SVG 1.1//EN"
"http://www.w3.org/Graphics/SVG/1.1/DTD/svg11.dtd">
<svg xmlns="http://www.w3.org/2000/svg" version="1.1">
    <rect
      width="100"
      height="100"
      x="57"
      y="195"
      id="my_square"
      style="fill:#0000ff;stroke:#000000;stroke-width:1px;" />
  </svg>
```

Recall that D3.js is a tool for SVG graphics. With this in mind, let's create the exact same square programmatically. In Listing 7.4, we create a simple Web page, use the D3.js library to create a new SVG object, and then "append" the blue square to this object. Save this as something like d3test.html, and open the file in your Web browser to see the square.

Listing 7.4   **D3.js: Drawing the blue square programmatically**

```
<html>
<head>
<!-- Include a recent version of the d3.js library -->
<script src="http://d3js.org/d3.v3.min.js" charset="utf-8"></script>
</head>
<body>

<script>
// Create a new SVG object, and append it
// to the <body> element of the page.
var svgObject = d3.select("body")
                  .append("svg");

// Now, add some size, color, and position information
// to the SVG object we've created. In this example,
// we will create a blue square with a black border,
// just like the one in the pure SVG example.
var blueSquare = svgObject.append("rect")
                    .attr("x", 57)
                    .attr("y", 195)
                    .attr("width", 100)
                    .attr("height", 100)
                    .attr("fill", "#0000ff")
                    .attr("stroke","#000000")
                    .attr("stroke-width","1px");
</script>
svg</body>
</html>
```

In Listing 7.4, the code for creating a blue square seems to be a bit more complex than the simple, raw XML we used in the SVG example in Listing 7.3. However, creating shapes is not the real point of D3.js; we want to take the next step and manipulate shapes into patterns for the visualization of data.

Building on what we learned in the previous example, we will now create a simple bar chart using D3.js that displays the relative ages of all United States presidents at the time of inauguration. This example, although very simple, illustrates some of the useful features that make D3.js so powerful. Listing 7.5 presents the code.

We start by defining our sample dataset using a simple JavaScript array called usaPresidentAges. We will also create an svgObject for our base graphic as we did in the blue-square example. The d3.scale.linear function helps us define a dynamic range for the width of our chart.

One of the great features of D3.js is the ability to iterate over values in a dataset and apply a function to assign values to parts of the visualization. The .data(usaPresidentAges) method iterates through each of the values in our president age array, applying a function to each value that increases (in this case, returning the width of the bar pertaining to the age of the president).

Listing 7.5   **D3.js: Creating a simple bar chart with D3.js**

```
<html>
<head>
<script src="http://d3js.org/d3.v3.min.js" charset="utf-8"></script>
</head>
<body>

<script>
// Let's add some data to our example!
// This array is a list of the ages, at
// inaguration, from Ford to Obama.
var usaPresidentAges = [57, 61, 57, 57, 58, 57, 61,
                        54, 68, 51, 49, 64, 50, 48,
                        65, 52, 56, 46, 54, 49, 50,
                        47, 55, 55, 54, 42, 51, 56,
                        55, 51, 54, 51, 60, 62, 43,
                        55, 56, 61, 52, 69, 64, 46,
                        54, 47];

// Set the total height of the bar chart
//
var height = 15 * usaPresidentAges.length;
var width = 600;

// Create a new SVG object, and append it
// to the <body> element of the page.
var svgObject = d3.select("body")
                .append("svg")
                .attr("width", width)
                .attr("height", height);

// Create
var x = d3.scale.linear()
        .domain([0, d3.max(usaPresidentAges)])
        .range([0, 420]);

//
svgObject.selectAll("rect")
                .data(usaPresidentAges)
                .enter().append("rect")
                .attr("y", function(d, i) { return i * 20; })
                .attr("width", x)
                .attr("height", 20)
```

```
                    .style("fill","#CCCCCC")
                    .style("stroke", "#FFF");
</script>
</body>
</html>
```

These examples merely scratch the surface of what can be created with D3.js. Data visualization experts have used it to build an amazing variety of compelling narratives. Although newcomers to Web-based data visualization may find the learning curve of D3.js to be daunting, it's currently an important technology for those interested in communicating interactive data insights to online users.

Summary

A primary goal of the visual representation of data is to communicate abstract ideas about numeric concepts into spatial representations that viewers can easily understand. Not only does this field require analytical expertise, but notions of aesthetics are important as well.

Although the tools for working with larger datasets have become more accessible, the ability of humans to comprehend information presented in spatial formats has not. Therefore, a common challenge for creating data visualizations is to understand how to best produce subsets of data to expose to users. Data-transformation processes are often required to cluster, or aggregate, data from very large datasets. Visualizations are no longer bound to the medium of paper. Digital publishing provides data scientists with the opportunity to produce interactive visualizations that enable users to select their own slices of data to explore.

A very useful feature of the statistics language R is its feature-rich plotting and graphics capability. Many scientific publications currently publish data visualizations generated directly using R, and the additional ggplot2 library is very popular as well. The Python programming language is also growing in use by the data community. matplotlib is a popular 2-D plotting and charts library for Python and is often used in conjunction with other Python data analysis libraries such as SciPy and Pandas. matplotlib is also well integrated with the iPython interactive shell, making it easy to collaborate and share data analysis and visualizations with other researchers.

The Internet has become an amazing medium for publishing interactive data visualizations, especially for growing fields such as data-driven journalism. One of the most popular and useful tools for building Web-based visualizations is the D3.js library, which provides an interface for manipulating and transforming SVG graphics files. D3.js is very well designed and feature complete, and a large number of open-source plug-ins extends its utility.

IV

Building Data Pipelines

## 8

Putting It Together:
MapReduce Data Pipelines

It's kind of fun to do the impossible.
—Walt Disney

Human brains aren't very good at keeping track of millions of separate data points, but we know that there is lots of data out there, just waiting to be collected, analyzed, and visualized. To cope with the complexity, we create metaphors to wrap our heads around the problem. Do we need to store millions of records until we figure out what to do with them? Let's file them away in a *data warehouse*. Do we need to analyze a billion data points? Let's *crunch* it down into something more manageable.

No longer should we be satisfied with just storing data and chipping away little bits of it to study. Now that distributed computational tools are becoming more accessible and cheaper to use, it's more and more common to think about data as a dynamic entity, flowing from a source to a destination. In order to really gain value from our data, it needs to be transformed from one state to another and sometimes literally moved from one physical location to another. It's often useful to think about looking at the state of data while it is moving from one state to another. In order to get data from here to there, just like transporting water, we need to build pipelines.

What Is a Data Pipeline?

At my local corner store, there is usually only one person working at any given time. This person runs the register, stocks items, and helps people find things. Overall, the number of people who come into this clerk's store is fairly manageable, and the clerk doesn't usually get overwhelmed (unless there is a run on beer at 1:55 a.m.). If I were to ask the shopkeeper to keep track of how many customers came in that day, I am pretty sure that not only would this task would be manageable, but I could even get an accurate answer.

The corner store is convenient, but sometimes I want to buy my shampoo and potato chips in gigantic sizes that will last me half the year. Have you ever shopped in one of those massive warehouse clubs, the ones that sell wholesale-sized pallets of toilet paper and ketchup by the kilogram? One of the things that has always amazed me about these huge stores is the number of checkout lines available to handle the flow of customers. Thousands and thousands of shoppers might be purchasing items each hour, all day long. On any given weekend, there might be twenty or more checkout lines open, each with dozens of customers waiting in line.

The checkout lines in a warehouse club are built to handle volume; the staff running the registers are not there to help you find items. Unlike the corner store clerk, the job of the register staff is specialized; it's to help the huge number of customers check out quickly.

There are other specialized tasks to be performed in our warehouse club. In order to be able to move pallets of two-liter maple syrup bottles to the sales floor, some employees must specialize in driving forklifts. Other employees are there simply to provide information to shoppers.

Now imagine that, as you pay for your extra-large pallet of liquid detergent, you ask a person at the checkout counter about the total number of customers that pass through all checkout lines for the entire day. It would be difficult for them to give you a real answer. Although the person at the register might easily be able to keep a running tally of the customers making their way through a single line, it would be difficult for them to know what is going on in the other checkout lines. The individuals at each register don't normally communicate with each other very much, as they are too busy with their own customers. Instead, we would need to deploy a different member of the staff whose job it is to go from register to register and aggregate the individual customer counts.

The Right Tool for the Job

The point here is that as customer volume grows to orders of magnitude beyond what a small convenience store is used to, it becomes necessary to build specialized solutions. Massive-scale data problems work like this too. We can solve data challenges by distributing problems across many machines and using specialized software to solve discreet problems along the way. A data pipeline is what facilitates the movement of our data from one state of utility to another.

Traditionally, developers depended on single-node databases to do everything. A single machine would be used to collect data, store it permanently, and run queries when we needed to ask a question. As data sizes grow, it becomes impossible to economically scale a single machine to meet the demand. The only practical solution is to distribute our needs across a collection of machines networked together in a cluster.

Collecting, processing, and analyzing large amounts of data sometimes requires using a variety of disparate technologies. For example, software specialized for efficient data collection may not be optimized for data analysis. This is a lot like the story of the warehouse club versus the tiny convenience store. The optimal technology necessary to ask huge, aggregate questions about massive datasets may be different from the software used to ensure that data can be collected rapidly from thousands of users.

Furthermore, the data itself may need to be structured differently for different applications. A data-pipeline strategy is necessary to convert data from one format to another, depending on the need.

One of my favorite things about emerging open-source technologies in data is the potential to create systems that combine different tools to deal with massive amounts of data. Much of the value of large Internet companies is based on their ability to build efficient systems for large-scale data processing pipelines, and this technology is very quickly becoming more accessible.

Data Pipelines with Hadoop Streaming

One of the hallmarks of large-scale data processing technologies is the use of multiple machines in parallel to tackle data challenges. Using a cluster of inexpensive machines (or even a collection of virtual machines in the cloud) allows us to solve data problems that would be thought of as impossible just a few years ago. Not all problems can be easily solved by distributing them across a collection of machines, but many data collection and transformation tasks are well suited to this approach. Taking large amounts of unstructured data collected from a variety of sources, transforming it into something more structured, and then analyzing it is a very common use case. While there are many strategies for how to distribute a computational problem, a good general purpose approach is known as *MapReduce*. MapReduce can be a great way to facilitate large-scale data transformations in a reasonable amount of time, and many people are using it as the fundamental part of their data-pipeline work.

MapReduce and Data Transformation

MapReduce, apart from being a catchy term, is a software framework originally created at Google for running applications distributed across a number of machines. In short, the idea behind MapReduce is to take a problem and split it up into small chunks, each of which can be processed independently on a number of machines. Once each of these chunks are processed, the resulting data can be grouped in a way that enables batches of machines to process them and return a result. The coordination of splitting up, or sharding, the data into discreet chunks is called the **map phase**. To keep track of each mapped task, the sharded data is assigned a key. Each of the independent machines solves its subproblem and returns the result. A shuffle step sorts the resulting data by its assigned key into groups. Finally, a reducer step takes each group of results and further processes it into the final result.

If your source data is naturally broken up into a number of relatively small pieces (think about a large collection of scraped Web pages), then the MapReduce approach may likely be an excellent solution to your analysis problem. Compare this to the procedure of processing the data contained in a single, very large document. In that case, the most efficient way to break the data up into small pieces may not be obvious.

Tasks that require very little work to distribute across a number of machines are known as **embarrassingly parallel** problems—probably because this type of problem provides you with an embarrassment of data riches. Or it might mean that you tell your boss, "I'm embarrassed to say this, but all I really had to do to earn my paycheck was to process your 200GB dataset by writing a 20-line Python script."

The overall concept behind MapReduce is fairly simple, but the logistics of coordinating all the shards, shuffling, and subprocesses can become very complex, especially when data sizes get large. First of all, imagine having to build a system that keeps track of the mappings of shards of data being processed. Likewise, dealing with the coordination of separate machines passing messages from one to another is daunting. The shuffle phase of MapReduce can be fairly tricky as well; when you are dealing with millions of independently processed shards of data, the process of efficiently sorting them all into their respective reducer steps can take quite a long time. Because of these challenges, building your own custom MapReduce framework is not a practical idea. Instead, it's better to avoid reinventing the wheel; use an available framework.

There are many open-source frameworks that provide MapReduce functionality, but the most popular is undoubtedly Apache Hadoop. Hadoop handles the complexities of coordinating MapReduce jobs along with providing tools such as a distributed filesystem for storing data across multiple machines.

Hadoop is written primarily in the Java programming language. Many MapReduce applications are created directly with Hadoop in Java. Although interacting directly with the Hadoop Java APIs can be performant, the framework itself can be a bit complex for the uninitiated. Furthermore, some developers may prefer to use a different language, such as Python.

Fortunately, it's possible to build components of our data pipeline in almost any language we want using the Hadoop streaming utility. **Hadoop streaming** allows developers to use arbitrary applications as the mapper and reducer, provided that they can read and write from the standard data pipeline streams—better known as standard input (stdin) and standard output (stdout). Even if you are not familiar with the concept of stdin or stdout, if you have ever typed a single command on the command line, you have used them.

Let's take a look at how to build simple single-step and multiple-step data pipelines using the Hadoop streaming API. Our examples use scripts written in Python to transform data stored in a Hadoop HDFS filesystem via a MapReduce job. We will start with unstructured source-text documents, extract structured data, and save the result in new files suitable for loading into an aggregate analysis or visualization tool.

The Simplest Pipeline: stdin to stdout

Before we take a look at how to start building large, distributed pipelines for transforming large amounts of data, let's take a look back at a familiar standard for pipeline programming: the Unix command line. One of the fundamental control structures found on the Unix command line are pipes. Unix **pipes** work with data in much the same way real pipes deal with water and transport video game plumbers: Something goes in one side and comes out the other side. The output of one Unix program can be piped into the input of another. Arbitrary-length chains of applications can be connected together, with data flowing out from one and into another.

Unless you explicitly state otherwise, stdin normally refers to data piped in from another application, whereas stdout is generally output to the terminal screen as text output. For example, if you type a command such as ls (which produces a list of files in the current directory) the stdout will be sent to the terminal.

By connecting two applications together with the pipe operator (|) we can run very powerful computations with just a few commands. In the example in Listing 8.1, we demonstrate piping the output of ls to the word count utility wc to produce a count of the lines that ls produces. Similarly, we can run a trivial data transformation by piping the text output of echo to a sed string-substitution command.

Listing 8.1 Examples of a Unix command-line pipe to redirect stdout

```
# How many files are in the current directory?
# Pipe the result of ls to wc (word count)
> ls | wc -l
10


# Display text to stdout (terminal)
> echo "Here's some test data"
Here's some test data


# Use a pipe to redirect output to another program,
# in this case a text replace with the sed program
> echo "Here's some test data" | sed 's/Here/There/'
There's some test data
```

Simple, right? The Unix pipeline examples in Listing 8.1 take advantage of built-in command-line tools. We can run useful data analysis processes with these tools alone. Remember: Sometimes the best way to deal with a data challenge is to use the simplest solution.

For more complex or custom tasks, we will probably want to use a more expressive way to process data. A great solution is to use a general-purpose language such as Python. Python's core libraries feature easy-to-use system modules for scripting tasks. Let's take a look at a slightly more complex example. Let's write our own Python scripts that can manipulate data provided from standard input. In Listing 8.2, *input_filter.py* takes string input from stdin, filters out any characters that are not spaces or in a lowercase ASCII format, and outputs the resulting filtered string to stdout. Another Python script, *output_unique.py* (Listing 8.3), splits the resulting string and produces only the unique words in the string.

By piping the output of *input_filter.py* to *output_unique.py*, we can produce a list of unique terms. Something much like this simple example could be the first step in producing a search index for individual phrases or records.

Listing 8.2 **Example of custom Python scripts for manipulating data from stdin:**
              input_filter.py

```
#!/usr/bin/python
import string
import sys

legal_characters = string.ascii_lowercase + ' '
for line in sys.stdin:
  line = line.lower()
  print ''.join(c for c in line if c in legal_characters)
```

Listing 8.3 **Example of custom Python scripts for manipulating data from stdin:**
              output_unique.py

```
#!/usr/bin/python
import string
import sys

for line in sys.stdin:
  terms = line.split()
  unique_terms = list(set(terms))
  print sorted(unique_terms)

#Pipe the input and output
> echo 'best test is 2 demo... & demo again!' | \
    python input_filter.py | python output_unique.py
['again', 'best', 'demo', 'is', 'test']
```

Now we are starting to get somewhere; this simple Python example gives us some hints for how to transform unstructured source data into something with more clarity. However, if we ran this script over many gigabytes or terabytes of source files on a single server it would take forever. Well, not literally forever, but it probably would not run fast enough for you to be able to convince anyone to give you a raise.

If we could run these simple scripts at the same time on many files at once, using a large number of machines, the transformation task would be much faster. This type of process is known as **parallelization**. Providing automatic parallelization is how Apache Hadoop and the MapReduce framework come to our aid. The power of using Hadoop to process large datasets comes from the ability to deploy it on a cluster of machines and let the framework handle the complexities of managing parallel tasks for you.

There are many ways to deploy Hadoop using physical hardware, using a collection of virtual machines, and even by purchasing access to an already running cluster complete with administrative software. Because there are a large variety of ways to deploy

Hadoop, we are not going to go into detail here about how to install and administrate a multinode cluster. However, even if you don't currently have access to a cluster, it is possible to run versions of streaming applications on a single machine using Hadoop in a *single node* or local mode. It is even possible to simulate a distributed environment in which various Hadoop daemons are run in separate Java processes (this is called pseudo-distributed mode). One of my favorite things about the Hadoop streaming framework is that you can test your scripts on small sets of data much like we did previously; by piping the output of the mapper into the reducer, you can sanity check your application before scaling up.

A One-Step MapReduce Transformation

Programming tutorials often introduce new languages by demonstrating how to display "hello world." This usually takes just a few lines of code, if that, and is often quite useless in the overall scheme of things.

The "hello world" of MapReduce implementations is definitely the *word count*, an example that takes a collection of input documents and produces an overall word count for each unique word in the corpus.

Instead of counting words, let's do something very similar but perhaps more interesting. We will use publicly available American birth statistics data to count the number of births in any given year. The United States requires that information about all births be recorded. This task falls to the U.S. National Vital Statistics System, which makes basic information about every birth recorded in the United States available. Using raw data provided by the NVSS, we will run a simple MapReduce job that counts the total number of births per month for a single year.

This task will take a slight bit of processing because our NVSS source data files are a bit raw. The Center for Disease Control provides each year's worth of NVSS data as a huge text file, with information about one birth on each line. The uncompressed data file containing information for babies born in 2010 is nearly three gigabytes and contains information for over four million births.

Let's take a look at a single year: 2010. According to the user guide for the 2010 NVSS dataset,[1] each birth is recorded as a single, ugly, 755-character line (see Listing 8.4 for an example of a single NVSS birth record). An individual record contains all kinds of coded information about the birth, such as birthday, weight, and whether or not the child was a twin. It also contains risk factors involved in the pregnancy, such as information about maternal smoking. Although some of the information requires the user guide to decipher, one piece of information that is easy to pick out of the raw file is the year and month of the birth. Let's start by extracting this value out of each birth record as part of our MapReduce job.

---

1. ftp://ftp.cdc.gov/pub/Health_Statistics/NCHS/Dataset_Documentation/DVS/natality/UserGuide2010.pdf

Listing 8.4   **A single NVSS birth record**

```
# Note the year and month of the birth. Other information
# is more obfuscated.
# Easy to process... but hideous.
      S       201001       7          2              2
30105                                        2  011     06   1  123
3405   1   06  01          2   2                                    0321
1006   314           2000                             2    222
2 2              2     2  2            122222
11      3   094      1
M 04  200940   39072        3941
083                              22        2
2  2 2
110 110 00    0000000      00
000000000 000000   000       00000000000000000000011              101
1   111            1 0     1     1  1
111111              11        1
1   1 1
```

Extracting Relevant Information from Raw NVSS Data: Map Phase

The first step in constructing our MapReduce job is to break down our source data into smaller chunks that can in turn be processed in the future. This is the job of our map phase. Our mapper function will be applied to every separate birth in parallel—meaning that multiple birth records will be processed at the same time, depending on the size of our compute cluster.

The result of our map function will be a key–value pair, representing a shard of processed data. In this case, we will simply read each record (one per line), determine the month and year of the birth, and then assign a count of "1" to the record. The key will be a string representing the month and year, and the value will be 1. At the end, the map phase will result in thousands of shards containing the same month and date key.

Our map phase is provided by our *mapper.py* script, as shown in Listing 8.5. The resulting processed key–value pairs will be emitted as strings, with the key and value separated by a tab character. By default, Hadoop's streaming API will treat anything up to the first tab character as the "key" and the rest of the data on a line of standard input is treated as the value.

Listing 8.5   **A mapper that outputs the month and a count of "1" for each birth record: mapper.py**

```
#!/usr/bin/python
import sys

def read_stdin_generator(file):
  for record in file:
    yield record
```

```
def main():
  data = read_stdin_generator(sys.stdin)
  for record in data:
    # Extract the year and month string from each line
    year = record[14:18]
    month = record[18:20]
    # Print year-month (our key) along with
    # separated  to stdout
    print '%s-%s\t%d' % (year, month, 1)

if __name__ == "__main__":
  main()
```

Counting Births per Month: The Reducer Phase

In a MapReduce job, the **reducer** step takes the aggregate of a collection of keys from the mapper step. Prior to the reducer step, some form of sorting is required in which the many key–value pairs generated are aggregated before being passed to the reducer functions. With millions or even billions of individual shards, this shuffling of data can be quite resource intensive. Much of the "special sauce" of the MapReduce framework takes place in this sorting step.

In our simple example, the reducer phase is defined by the *reducer.py* script, which accepts the output of the *mapper.py* script and aggregates the result. The *reducer.py* script takes each of the key–value pairs generated in the previous step and groups them by key. Next, the sum of all the births from each distinct month is calculated. Recall that the value for every unique month–year key was 1, so this reducer step is simply producing the sum of each key. See Listing 8.6 for the reducer code.

Listing 8.6   **A reducer.py script featuring Python iterators for counting values**

```
#!/usr/bin/python

import sys
from itertools import groupby
from operator import itemgetter

def read_stdin_generator(data):
  for record in data:
    yield record.rstrip().split('\t')


def main():
  birth_data = read_stdin_generator(sys.stdin)
  for month, group in groupby(birth_data, itemgetter(0)):
    births = sum(int(count) for month, count in group)
    print "%s:%d" % (month, births)
```

```python
if __name__ == "__main__":
  main()
```

Testing the MapReduce Pipeline Locally

Because the Hadoop streaming API enables us to use any script that accepts input through stdin, we can easily test our MapReduce scripts on a single machine before farming them out to our Hadoop cluster. It is useful in these situations to try your MapReduce job on a small sample of your source data in order to sanity check the workflow. In the example that follows, I've simply used the Unix head command to slice off the first hundred thousand records into a new, smaller file called *birth_data_ sample.txt*.

In order to use our mapper and reducer scripts with Hadoop streaming, we will also need to make sure that they will be treated as executable files. Use the chmod command to let the system know that the scripts should be treated as executable (see Listing 8.7).

We are ready to test our pipeline. The output of the mapper script will be piped into the reducer script as input. Between the mapper and the reducer step, we will sort the values by key. This simulates the shuffle sorting that is handled for us on a Hadoop cluster.

Listing 8.7   Running our mapper.py and reducer.py scripts locally on test data

```
# Create a small, 75 MB sample of the 2012 birth dataset
> head -n 100000 VS2010NATL.DETAILUS.PUB  > birth_data_sample.txt

# Make sure that the mapper.py and reducer.py scripts are executable
> chmod +x mapper.py
> chmod +x reducer.py

# First, test the mapper alone
> cat birth_data_sample.txt | mapper.py

2010-09 1
2010-10 1
2010-08 1
2010-07 1
2010-10 1
# etc...

# Now pipe the sorted results of the mapper into the reducer step
> cat birth_data_sample.txt | ./mapper.py | sort | ./reducer.py

2010-01:8701
2010-02:8155
2010-03:8976
2010-04:8521
```

2010-05:8546
2010-06:8917
2010-07:9384
2010-08:9452
2010-09:9734
2010-10:7792
2010-11:5885
2010-12:5937

Running Our MapReduce Job on a Hadoop Cluster

It looks like our mapper and reducer scripts are providing a reasonable result. Now we can start running this code on our cluster. To do this, our first step will be to move our large source-data file off of our local disk and onto a filesystem that every node on our Hadoop cluster will be able to access.

Hadoop was initially named after the toy elephant of creator Doug Cutting's son. Many tools in the Hadoop ecosystem are named similarly (such as Zookeeper, Mahout, and Pig). A notable exception to this feral naming convention is Hadoop's distributed filesystem, which is surprisingly known as the Hadoop Distributed File System (HDFS). Although the naming is uninspiring, HDFS is a crucial component of Hadoop. HDFS enables our data to be stored and accessed by all the machines in the network, by breaking data up into chunks and distributing them throughout the nodes in our cluster.

Why is a distributed filesystem important to our processing task? Moving data can be a bottleneck because, as we noted in Chapter 2, the network is slow. Rather than shipping a large chunk of data from a central location to a node for processing, a distributed filesystem like HDFS allows our cluster to process data where it lives. Some shards of our data will live on a node. Hadoop helps facilitate this data distribution so that we can worry about our data problem rather than the technology itself.

Let's place our data in Hadoop by using the `copyFromLocal` filesystem shell command. Once we have copied our source data into HDFS, we can use the `hadoop jar` command to invoke the Hadoop streaming API. This is done by using Hadoop's streaming *.jar file, normally found in the contrib directory of the Hadoop installation. In Listing 8.8, we specify the names of our scripts using the `mapper` and `reducer` flags. The `file` flag lets Hadoop know that our mapper and reducer scripts live on the local disk rather than in HDFS. We will also specify the source data (which can be a single file or an entire HDFS directory of files) and an output location for our resulting data. When we run this command, a normal MapReduce job will be initiated on the cluster, using the mapper and reducer scripts that we tested previously.

Listing 8.8 **Moving our data into HDFS and invoking a streaming MapReduce job**

```
# Copying the source data into HDFS
> hadoop dfs -mkdir /user/hduser/data
> hadoop dfs -copyFromLocal \
  VS2010NATL.DETAILUS.PUB /user/hduser/data/VS2010NATL.DETAILUS.PUB
```

```
# Kick off the streaming MapReduce job using local mapper
# and reducer scripts. Note: Filepaths may differ from
# your implementation.
>hadoop jar $HADOOP_PATH/contrib/streaming/hadoop-*streaming*.jar \
-file $HOME/mapper.py -mapper $HOME/mapper.py \
-file $HOME/reducer.py -reducer $HOME/reducer.py \
-input /user/hduser/VS2010NATL.DETAILUS.PUB \
-output /user/hduser/output
```

Managing Complexity: Python MapReduce Frameworks for Hadoop

The Hadoop streaming API can be a great way to write custom MapReduce jobs, especially for single-step tasks. Once you start writing a lot of Hadoop streaming scripts, you quickly start to realize that there are many scenarios in which a few simple map and reduce steps will not be enough. Complex data transformations require additional steps that must be pipelined into the input of another.

The monthly-birth-count example shown previously is very simple. It demonstrates a single processing step. What happens if you want to run two mappers at once and then use a single reducer step to join the output? Building this type of processing pipeline is definitely possible, but the code can become unwieldy fast.

Fortunately, there are many open-source frameworks built on top of Hadoop's streaming utility that help to address these challenges. These frameworks not only help in managing the complexity of MapReduce jobs with useful features, but also can simplify the amount of code needed to craft our processing pipelines.

One of these frameworks is an open-source Python module known as **mrjob**, which was created by Yelp to help speed up the process of building and running MapReduce tasks on Hadoop clusters. Using mrjob is a natural progression from writing Hadoop streaming API jobs directly in Bash or Python. Just like a vanilla Hadoop streaming script, mrjob can be used both locally for testing and with an existing Hadoop cluster. Because Yelp does quite a lot of work in Amazon's EC2 environment, mrjob is especially well suited to running jobs with Amazon's Elastic MapReduce service.

Rewriting Our Hadoop Streaming Example Using mrjob

mrjob can be built and installed like any other Python module. In order to use it, extend the MRJob class with a custom class defining a series of processing steps. For one-step MapReduce jobs, simply define a mapper and reducer function within your class and call the MRJob.run method, as in Listing 8.9. Like our previous Hadoop streaming scripts, our mrjob script will read data from stdin and output data to stdout.

Listing 8.9   **A simple one-step MapReduce counter using mrjob**

```
from mrjob.job import MRJob

class MRBirthCounter(MRJob):
  # The mapper will read records from stdin
  def mapper(self, key, record):
    yield record[14:20], 1

  def reducer(self, month, births):
    # The reducer function yields a sum of the
    # counts of each month's births.
    yield month, sum(births)

if __name__ == '__main__':
    MRBirthCounter.run()
```

Underneath the hood, the *mrjob_simple_example.py* script uses the same Hadoop streaming API that we used earlier, meaning that it is still possible to test our code by piping from stdin.

After we've tested our mrjob script on a local machine, let's run it on a Hadoop cluster (Listing 8.10). This step is as easy as running the script like a normal Python application, as long as we've set the HADOOP_HOME environment variable on the machine in which our script lives. In order to do this, we will need to use the -r flag to specify that we want to run the script on our Hadoop cluster, as opposed to running locally.

Listing 8.10   **Testing and running mrjob_simple_example.py**

```
# Run the mrjob script on our small sample data
> python mrjob_simple_example.py < birth_data_sample.txt

"201001"    8701
"201002"    8155
"201003"    8976
# etc...

# Run the mrjob script on an existing Hadoop cluster
# Ensure HADOOP_HOME environment variable is set
# (This setting may differ from your implementation)
> export HADOOP_HOME=/usr/local/hadoop-0.20.2/

# Specify that mrjob use Hadoop on the command line
> python mrjob_simple_example.py \
    -r hadoop hdfs:///user/hduser/data/VS2010NATL.DETAILUS.PUB
```

Building a Multistep Pipeline

Although some large data processing tasks can be accomplished using a single MapReduce step, a common pattern is to run a job that takes multiple steps. In other cases, two separate sources will use two mapper functions to emit data containing the same key. Then a single reducer phase will combine the data based on the matching key into a combined output.

To illustrate this type of pipeline, let's extend our original birth count example by adding another step. Let's count only the female births that happened per month in 2010. Before determining the number of births per month, let's filter each record by gender. To do this, let's add a new mapper function called filter_births_by_gender. This mapper will emit a value only if the birth record is female. The key emitted will simply be an F, and the value will be the month and year of the birth. The output of this mapper will be fed into another mapper function called counter_mapper, which will assign a 1 to the month–year key (just as we did in the single-step example). Finally, the output from this mapper function will be fed into our original reducer, sum_births, which will emit the total number of female births per month.

To specify the order in which we want the mappers to run, we will overload the MrJob.steps method to return an array containing each individual map and reduce phase in order. See Listing 8.11 for the code for each of these steps.

Listing 8.11   **A two-step MapReduce mrjob script**

```
mrjob_multistep_example.py

from mrjob.job import MRJob

class MRFemaleBirthCounter(MRJob):

  def filter_births_by_gender(self, key, record):
    if record[435] == 'F':
      year = record[14:18]
      month = record[18:20]
      birth_month = '%s-%s' % (month, year)
      yield 'Female', birth_month

  def counter_mapper(self, gender, month):
    yield '%s %s' % (gender,month), 1

  def sum_births(self, month, births):
      yield month, sum(births)

  def steps(self):
    return [self.mr(mapper=self.filter_births_by_gender),
            self.mr(mapper=self.counter_mapper,
                    reducer=self.sum_births)]
```

```
if __name__ == '__main__':
    MRFemaleBirthCounter.run()
```

It's time to test our script using the slice of test data we created earlier. Multistep MapReduce jobs introduce more complexity than single-step jobs, with more opportunity for something to go wrong. Fortunately, a cool feature of mrjob is the ability to specify a particular step to run using the step-num flag on the command line. This is a useful way to perform a quick sanity check on a section of our pipeline. As shown in Listing 8.12, we can specify that we want the script to send the output of the first mapper step (zero-based) to stdout. Just as before, we can run the entire pipeline on our test data.

Listing 8.12   **Testing the mrjob_multistep_example.py script locally**

```
# Test the output of the mapper from the first step
> python mrjob_multistep_example.py --mapper \
    --step-num=0 < birth_data_big.txt


"F"     "10-2010"
"F"     "11-2010"
"F"     "09-2010"
"F"     "10-2010"
# etc...


# Test the output of the entire pipeline
> python mrjob_multistep_example.py < birth_data_sample.txt


"Female 01-2010"    4285
"Female 02-2010"    4002
"Female 03-2010"    4365
"Female 04-2010"    4144
```

Running mrjob Scripts on Elastic MapReduce

One of the core principles of this book is that data processing solutions should avoid managing hardware and infrastructure whenever it is practical and affordable. A great feature of mrjob is the ability to easily run MapReduce jobs using Amazon's Elastic MapReduce (EMR) service.

In order to take advantage of EMR integration, first create an Amazon Web Services account and sign up for the Elastic MapReduce service. Once these are created, you will also note (but don't share!) the Access Key ID and the corresponding Secret Access Key (under the Security Credentials section of the AWS accounts page).

With these Access- and Secret-Key values, set the AWS_ACCESS_KEY_ID and AWS_SECRET_ACCESS_KEY environment variables on the machine on which your mrjob script is hosted. It is also possible to add many of these values to an *mrjobs.conf* configuration file stored in the user's home directory. Once this is set up, kick off your MapReduce job by running your mrjob script with the -r flag set to emr. It is also possible to specify the number and type of EC2 instances to use for your MapReduce job. See Listing 8.13 for an example.

Listing 8.13   **Using mrjobs with Elastic MapReduce**

```
# Set the Access Key ID and Secret Access Key Environment Variables
> export AWS_ACCESS_KEY_ID=XXXACCESSKEYHEREXXX
> export AWS_SECRET_ACCESS_KEY=XXXSECRETKEYHEREXXX

# Start an Elastic MapReduce job with 4 small instances
> python your_mr_job_sub_class.py -r emr \
  --ec2_instance_type c1.small --num-ec2-instances 4
```

Alternative Python-Based MapReduce Frameworks

mrjob is not the only Python-based MapReduce framework for Hadoop streaming. Another popular framework is **Dumbo**. Dumbo is similar to mrjob in many ways, and for simple MapReduce tasks, the structure of a Dumbo script is fairly similar to one using mrjob. In my opinion, one of the strongest differentiators is in mrjob's EMR integration. Because Yelp runs a lot of data processing tasks in the Amazon cloud, kicking off a job on Elastic MapReduce is a bit easier using mrjob than it is when using Dumbo. To its credit, Dumbo is probably a bit easier to use if you need to work with some type of custom data-input format.

Both mrjob and Dumbo are wrappers for the Hadoop streaming API, but they don't attempt to provide direct access to all the classes and methods found in the lower-level Hadoop Java API. For even more fine-grained access to these functions, it might be worth taking a look at Pydoop. Pydoop's goal is to be a Python interface for Hadoop and HDFS itself. By sidestepping Hadoop's streaming API, it *may* be more performant to use Pydoop over frameworks such as mrjob or Dumbo. If you are analyzing terabyte datasets, a 2X boost in performance might mean huge savings in overall processing time.

Summary

Dealing with the collection, processing, and analysis of large amounts of data requires specialized tools for each step. To solve this problem, it is necessary to build data processing pipelines to transform data from one state to another. Hadoop helps to make distribution of our pipeline task across a large number of machines accessible—but writing custom MapReduce jobs using the standard Hadoop API can be challenging. Many common, large-scale data processing tasks can be addressed using the Hadoop streaming API. Hadoop streaming scripts are a great solution for single-step jobs or scaling existing Python processing scripts from a single machine to a distributed environment.

Python-based MapReduce frameworks for Hadoop streaming provide a great deal of utility for building more complex multistep pipelines while keeping code simple and manageable. Frameworks such as mrjob and Dumbo can not only be used locally and with existing Hadoop clusters but can also use cloud-based services such as Elastic MapReduce as a processing environment. Because of the overall advantages and useful features available in these frameworks, it is almost always a good idea to use these tools whenever building anything more complicated than a simple single-step streaming pipeline.

Hadoop streaming scripts and frameworks can be very useful for a large number of tasks, but as data workflows get even more complex, even streaming scripts can become hard to manage. Another consideration is performance; building tools using scripting languages that call the Hadoop streaming API may be easy to write but may ultimately be slower overall than tools that interact directly with the raw Hadoop API. In the next chapter, we take a look at some Hadoop-based tools designed to manage data workflows.

9

Building Data Transformation Workflows with Pig and Cascading

Collecting and processing large amounts of data can be a complicated task. Fortunately, many common data processing challenges can be broken down into smaller problems. Open-source software tools allow us to shard and distribute data transformation jobs across many machines, using strategies such as MapReduce.

Although frameworks like Hadoop help manage much of the complexity of taking large MapReduce processing tasks and farming them out to individual machines in a cluster, we still need to define exactly how the data will be processed. Do we want to alter the data in some way? Should we split it up or combine it with another source?

With large amounts of data coming from many different sources, chaining together multiple data processing tasks into a complex pipeline directly using MapReduce functions or streaming API scripts can quickly get out of hand. Sometimes a single data concept might require several MapReduce steps, resulting in hard-to-manage code. It's far more practical to abstract the problem even further, by defining workflows that in turn dictate underlying MapReduce operations.

Imagine how hard it would be to explain how your MapReduce job works to the average person on the street. Instead of defining how your mapper, reducer, and combiner steps work, you would probably just say, "Well, I took this big collection of data, joined each record with some data from somewhere else, and saved the results in a new set of files."

This chapter is all about using tools that help us work at a level of human-friendly abstraction. We will take a look at two very popular but very different open-source tools for managing the complexity of multistep data transformation pipelines: Pig and Cascading.

Large-Scale Data Workflows in Practice

Since the dawn of the information age, clueless managers have approached beleaguered software engineers with requests to take on impossible data processing tasks. Invariably, these requests involve data interoperability between incompatible systems. Someone from the upper ranks will say, "Why can't System X simply talk to System Y? All we need to do is take the gigabytes of data that we collect each day on our Web site, merge them with the gigabytes of data we store in our data warehouse, and send the results to our visualization tool. Oh, and we are going to need you to go ahead get it into us by 8 a.m. tomorrow."

In response, the engineers bring up the issues of incompatible formats, inconsistent data, the time it takes to process all those records, and how it's not their job, and finally they remind management that none of these problems would have happened if the company hadn't purchased that particular database.

If there's one thing that our woefully ignorant management and our oppressed worker bees may both be able to agree on, it is that there can be a great deal of value in combining large datasets in useful ways. The term "unlock" is often used to describe the process of processing, joining, and transforming data in order to discover a previously unknown fact or relationship. I think that this metaphor is misleading as it assumes that there is always a kind of buried treasure at the end of a data processing rainbow. Perhaps a better way of looking at our data is to imagine that it exists to help us answer questions and tell stories. Data needs to be transformed into a state in which the stories can be told more completely, and sometimes our questions need to be asked in the right language.

It's Complicated: Multistep MapReduce Transformations

In Chapter 8, we took a look at how easy it can be to build MapReduce-based data pipelines using Hadoop's Streaming API and Python MapReduce frameworks such as mrjob. For relatively simple processing tasks that require only a few MapReduce steps (such as the ubiquitous example of loading text from many files and counting the unique words within), it's easy to manually define mapper and reducer phases using a scripting language such as Python.

In practice, data pipelines can become very complex. For example, a common pipeline challenge that large companies face is the need to merge data from a variety of disparate databases in a timely manner. In some cases, records in the individual data sources may be linked by a particular key: for example, a common date or email address. Records may need to be filtered by a particular value, or certain values in certain records must be "normalized" and set to a common value. A large number of individual MapReduce steps might be needed to arrive at the desired result.

In these cases, maintaining MapReduce-based data-transformation code can be complicated. Passing around key–value pairs using streaming scripts is manageable for some tasks, but these scripts can become brittle if input or output parameters change. What if the requirements of your key–value mappings need to be updated? How many parts of your code must change? If your code depends on particular machine characteristics, such as the presence of a particular library or module, will the workflow break when ported from one cluster to another?

When we build data applications in this way, we are expressing our goals in a way that is a bit more computer than human. One of the core lessons of this book is to worry primarily about the data problem rather than the technology. The MapReduce paradigm is an abstraction that works well for machines. Computers are great at passing around and keeping track of thousands of individual chunks of data. However, on behalf of my fellow humans, thinking in terms of the individual steps of a MapReduce job is not our strongest skill. We likely don't want to worry about each step; we just want the machines to whir away and coordinate amongst themselves. We would much rather say "take this collection of data here, get rid of the values I don't care about, combine it with this other data, and put the result over here." This is why we need workflow software: tools that can take higher-level descriptions of data processing flows and translate them into distributed MapReduce steps that can be run on frameworks such as Hadoop.

Apache Pig: "Ixnay on the Omplexitycay"

When it comes to defining data workflows on Hadoop, the Apache Pig framework is often the tool of choice. The Apache Pig Web site claims that 40% of all Hadoop jobs run at Yahoo! are Pig jobs. Pig provides two components: a high-level and simple-to-learn language for expressing workflows and a platform to turn these workflows into MapReduce jobs. Pig was originally developed at Yahoo!, but it was migrated to the Apache foundation in 2007.

Pig's syntax is known as **Pig Latin.** Unlike the Pig Latin sketches from classic Three Stooges shorts, Apache's Pig Latin is not very useful for obfuscating messages. In fact, Pig's syntax is incredibly clear. Common verbs such as LOAD, FILTER, JOIN, and GROUP are used to define steps in a data workflow.

In some ways, Pig's workflow syntax is somewhat analogous to the use of SQL for managing and querying relational databases, and there is a bit of overlap with the types of results that can be produced from SQL queries and Pig statements. However, comparing Pig Latin's syntax to that of SQL is not really a fair comparison; the two tools occupy very different problem domains. SQL allows query writers to declare generally what type of operation should take place (such as a SELECT or a JOIN) but not the implementation details of these actions. Pig allows workflow writers to choose a particular implementation of each workflow step. SQL generally aims to provide a single query result from a query, perhaps joining the results of queries from several tables into a single result set. Pig provides a means to split data streams into multiple parts, filter, and save the results in multiple locations, making it excellent for extracting and transforming data.

Distributed frameworks such as Hadoop essentially take large data problems, split these problems into smaller tasks, and attempt to solve many of the tasks at the same time (in parallel). Pig provides an abstraction that allows users of Hadoop to express parallel MapReduce tasks as a series of high-level, step-by-step tasks. Pig can be thought of as having a *procedural model,* which tends to match the mental model of how we think about data workflows. This allows users to express the details without worrying about how the sausage gets made, so to speak.

Although a plain MapReduce job passes data around as a series of key–value pairs, Pig abstracts data workflows by approaching individual records as **tuples**, or an ordered list of fields. A collection of Pig tuples is referred to as a **bag**. Once source data is split up into a collection of tuples and loaded into a bag, it becomes known as a "relation." This abstraction makes it easy to write procedural commands. In other words, Pig allows you to think of a data transformation at a very human level. "Take this bag of data, process it, and place the results in this other bag."

Hadoop is designed to be used across a distributed network of many machines. When testing data-workflow scripts, running across a live cluster can create an additional level of complexity. Like other Hadoop-based tools, it's possible to run Pig on a single machine, or in local mode. It's always a good idea to test data transformation scripts locally before attempting a larger deployment as Pig will run the same way whether run locally or on a cluster.

Pig aims eventually to be supported by a number of frameworks, but for now installing Pig requires a recent version of Java and at least a single machine running Hadoop. For writing and testing Pig scripts on a workstation, it is possible to run Hadoop in "local" mode.

Running Pig Using the Interactive Grunt Shell

Pig commands can be run using the built-in interactive shell called *Grunt.* Grunt is useful for testing the individual steps in a Pig workflow and for displaying the results of each step at different points in the process. The Grunt shell can be invoked by typing pig on the command line, but by default the shell will assume that you want to run jobs on your Hadoop cluster and that your input data is in HDFS. To run Grunt on a local machine using input files on the local filesystem, use the -x flag (see Listing 9.1).

To demonstrate the basics of using Pig, let's first create a workflow that joins data from two CSV files by means of a particular key. Our examples use the diagnostic command DUMP to show the result of our workflow at given intervals. Although useful for debugging, it's not a good idea to use the DUMP command in a production script as it will reduce performance and prevent certain types of optimizations from being used. Also, when testing workflow scripts locally, don't forget to start with small samples of data rather than a full, massive dataset.

Pig loads data using the **PigStorage** module. By default, PigStorage considers separate fields in a record as delimited by a tab separator. In order to load data with a different delimiter (such as a comma), pass the desired delimiter character to PigStorage during loading.

Listing 9.1   **Load and run Pig commands using the grunt shell**

```
# users.csv
# Information about individual users
# user_id, user_name, date_joined, state
1,Michael Manoochehri,2010-03-12,California
7,Paul Pigstun,2010-03-12,Washington
19,Haddie Doop,2010-03-12,Maine
41,Bar FooData,2010-03-12,New York
# etc...


# webpurchases.csv
# List of online purchases by user id
# user_id, item_name, date, price
1,Item 2,2012-01-14,2.99
7,Item 3,2012-01-01,1.99
19,Item 2,2012-01-03,2.99
19,Item 3,2012-02-20,1.99
41,Item 2,2012-01-14,2.99
# etc...


# Start Pig interactive shell in "local" mode
> pig -x local

grunt> USERS = LOAD 'users.csv' USING PigStorage(',') AS
        (user_id:chararray, user_name:chararray, date_joined:chararray,
        state:chararray);
grunt> WEBPURCHASES = LOAD 'webpurchases.csv' USING PigStorage(',') AS
        (user_id:chararray, item:chararray, date:chararray, price:double);
grunt> WEB_BUYERS = JOIN USERS BY user_id, WEBPURCHASES BY user_id;
grunt> DUMP WEB_BUYERS;

(1,Michael Manoochehri,2010-03-12,California,1,Item 2,2012-01-14,2.99)
(7,Paul Pigstun,2010-03-12,Washington,7,Item 3,2012-01-01,1.99)
(19,Haddie Doop,2010-03-12,Maine,19,Item 2,2012-01-03,2.99)
(19,Haddie Doop,2010-03-12,Maine,19,Item 1,2012-01-14,4.99)
(19,Haddie Doop,2010-03-12,Maine,19,Item 2,2012-01-09,2.99)
(19,Haddie Doop,2010-03-12,Maine,19,Item 3,2012-02-20,1.99)
(41,Bar FooData,2010-03-12,New York,41,Item 2,2012-01-14,2.99)
# etc...
```

Filtering and Optimizing Data Workflows

When working with large datasets, a common requirement is to split out a smaller set of records based on a particular parameter. Pig provides a FILTER clause that can be used to either select or remove records. Listing 9.2 shows an example of using Pig to return records that match a particular date string.

Listing 9.2   Filtering and transformation steps in a Pig Workflow

```
# Filtering by field value
grunt> WEBPURCHASES = LOAD 'webpurchases.csv' USING PigStorage(',') AS
        (user_id:chararray, item:chararray, date:chararray, price:double);
grunt> DUMP  WEBPURCHASES;

(1,Item 2,2012-01-14,2.99)
(7,Item 3,2012-01-01,1.99)
(19,Item 2,2012-01-03,2.99)
(19,Item 1,2012-01-14,4.99)
(19,Item 2,2012-01-09,2.99)
# etc ...

grunt> JAN_03_2012_PURCHASES = FILTER WEBPURCHASES BY date == '2012-01-03';
grunt> DUMP JAN_03_2012_PURCHASES;

(19,Item 2,2012-01-03,2.99)
```

Running a Pig Script in Batch Mode

Now that we've tested our basic workflow using the Grunt tool, let's place our Pig Latin statements into a script that we can run from the command line. Remember to remove diagnostic operators such as DUMP from your script when running in production, as it will slow down the execution of the script. Store the commands in a text file, and run the script using the pig command (see Listing 9.3).

Listing 9.3   Run a Pig script with a Hadoop cluster (and data in HDFS)

```
# Pig commands in a file called "my_workflow.pig"

# Move the local files into HDFS
> hadoop dfs -put users.csv
> hadoop dfs -put webpurchases.csv

> pig my_workflow.pig
```

Cascading: Building Robust Data-Workflow Applications

Scripting a workflow using Pig is one approach to building a complex data workflow—but actually building, testing, and shipping a robust software product is another thing altogether. Although Pig has many features that allow it to be integrated into existing applications and even unit-tested, it may make more sense to express workflows using a language that can use a more robust development environment such as Java.

Hadoop itself is written in Java. The standard Hadoop Java API exposes the ability to define classes and interfaces for every detail in a MapReduce environment. This is fine for some applications, but, as we have seen already, developing an application by managing MapReduce steps can become unwieldy. In other words, the raw Hadoop Java API doesn't match the level of abstraction provided by a tool like Pig.

Although there are many data API frameworks built to improve the utility of developing Hadoop MapReduce applications, one of the most powerful and popular open-source frameworks is Cascading. Originally developed by Chris Wensel, Cascading provides a well-thought-out programming interface and is a great introduction to thinking about data in terms of streams. Cascading is a great addition to Hadoop's standard MapReduce interface, and it has resulted in a large ecosystem of tools built on top of it. In fact, I can't imagine many situations in which any type of Java-based Hadoop workflow—whether simple or complex—should be built without Cascading.

Thinking in Terms of Sources and Sinks

Thanks to humanity's great need for water, a metaphor we are all familiar with is flow. Water can flow from a reservoir source, and the flow can be split into multiple destinations. One of these streams may end up in a bathtub, whereas another might be sent to be converted into steam to make coffee. The underlying details of how individual water molecules flow is not really a concern to many of us. As long as individual pipes are able to connect, most of us don't think much about how the process of "flowing" really works. Water goes in one end of a pipe and comes out the other.

If you've ever used Unix command-line tools, you might already be familiar with the "pipe" paradigm. In a Unix pipe, the output of one process becomes the input of another. These operations may be chained together one after another. Even better, as long as each component in the pipeline completes the specific tasks as expected, the user doesn't have to worry much about the individual commands.

In Chapter 8, we introduced the Hadoop streaming API, which extends the concepts of software pipelines as an abstraction for defining distributed MapReduce algorithms. The output data of the mapper functions become the input data of reducer functions.

Cascading provides yet another layer of abstraction on top of MapReduce, to help us think of data as more like streams of water and less as individual MapReduce steps. Although Hadoop provides a layer of abstraction to easily manage distributed applications over a cluster of machines, Cascading provides an abstract model of processing data on a Hadoop framework.

In the Cascading model, data inputs (or *sources*) and outputs (known as *sinks*) are fed into the application through *taps*. These taps are connected together by *pipes*, which can be combined, split, and even run through filters. Finally, any number of flows can be assembled together. When flows are linked together, the result is a *cascade*.

Another characteristic of Cascading is that it provides a separation between defining the pipelines and the data itself. This allows developers to make changes by modifying code slightly. If one data source needs to be replaced by another, simply change the tap connected to that source.

A note of caution: Like water, data can be polluted. Your records may contain strange formatting, unwanted characters, and unescaped strings. Before using your data, you might need to run it through a filter. Cascading extends the pipeline concept with the idea of filtering.

Building a Cascading Application

It's possible to develop and test Cascading applications on a local workstation that has Hadoop installed. Although it's possible to manually add Cascading's libraries to your application's build path, the most recent Cascading JAR files and necessary dependencies are all available at the Conjars Web site.[1] Conjars also provides cut-and-paste directives for adding Cascading to existing projects managed by tools such as Maven or Ivy. You may also need to add dependencies for libraries that Cascading depends on, such as the SLF4J logging library and the latest Hadoop-core Java library from Apache.

The most trivial use of Cascading is to move data from a source to a sink without any filtering or data transformation. Using Cascading for this type of data flow is unnecessary (and overkill) for anything other than demonstrating how to use Cascading's excellent abstraction model (see Listing 9.4).

First, we create two taps: one for input from a local file and the other for final output. We then create a `Pipe` object to link the source tap to the sink tap. Our flow object will combine all of these parts together. There are a number of tap classes to choose from, including ones specifically designed for both local and HDFS filesystems. In this example, we will use the `tap.hadoop.Hfs` class, which will expect local files when run on a single-node Hadoop environment in local mode. When deployed to a live Hadoop cluster, an Hfs tap will expect data to be in the HDFS filesystem.

As with the Hadoop streaming and Pig scripts we looked at before, it's a good idea to test our Cascading workflow locally and on some small data before we move the resulting JAR file to our Hadoop cluster.

Listing 9.4 **A very simple Cascading application: Copy from a source to a sink**

```
import java.util.Properties;

import cascading.flow.FlowDef;
import cascading.flow.hadoop.HadoopFlowConnector;
import cascading.pipe.Pipe;
import cascading.property.AppProps;
import cascading.scheme.hadoop.TextDelimited;
import cascading.tap.Tap;
import cascading.tap.hadoop.Hfs;
```

---

1. http://conjars.org/

```
public class CascadingCopyPipe {

  public static void main(String[] args) {
    String input = args[0];
    String output = args[1];

    Properties properties = new Properties();
    AppProps.setApplicationJarClass(properties, CascadingCopyPipe.class);
    HadoopFlowConnector flowConnector =
        new HadoopFlowConnector(properties);

    Tap inTap = new Hfs(new TextDelimited(true, ","), input);

    Tap outTap = new Hfs(new TextDelimited(true, ","), output);

    Pipe copyPipe = new Pipe("Copy Pipeline");

    FlowDef flowDef = FlowDef.flowDef()
      .addSource(copyPipe, inTap)
      .addTailSink(copyPipe, outTap);

    flowConnector.connect(flowDef).complete();
  }
}
```

Creating a Cascade: A Simple JOIN Example

In order to build more workflows, we need to be able to connect various pipes of data together. Cascading's abstraction model provides several types of *pipe assemblies* that can be used to filter, group, and join data streams.

Just as with water pipes, it is possible for Cascading to split data streams into two separate pipes, or merge various pipes of data into one. In order to connect two data streams into one, we can chain pipes together using a Cascading *CoGroup* process.

Using a CoGroup, we can merge two streams using either a common key or a set of common tuple values. This operation should be familiar to users of SQL, as it is very similar to a simple JOIN. Cascading CoGroup flows require that the values being grouped together have the same type. Listing 9.5 presents a CoGroup example.

Listing 9.5   **Using** CoGroup() **to join two streams on a value**

```
import java.util.Properties;

import cascading.flow.FlowDef;
import cascading.flow.hadoop.HadoopFlowConnector;
import cascading.pipe.CoGroup;
import cascading.pipe.Pipe;
import cascading.pipe.joiner.InnerJoin;
```

```
import cascading.property.AppProps;
import cascading.scheme.hadoop.TextDelimited;
import cascading.tap.Tap;
import cascading.tap.hadoop.Hfs;
import cascading.tuple.Fields;

public class CascadingSimpleJoinPipe {

  public static void main(String[] args) {
    // Collect input fields from parameters
    String websales = args[0];      // Web sales input
    String users = args[1];         // User information
    String output_dir = args[2];    // The output directory

    // Create a flow connector for this class
    Properties properties = new Properties();
    AppProps.setApplicationJarClass(properties,
                              CascadingSimpleJoinPipe.class);
    HadoopFlowConnector flowConnector = new HadoopFlowConnector(properties);

    // The input tap for our Web sales information
    Fields websalesFields = new Fields("user_id", "item",
                                "date_purchase", "price");
    Tap websalesTap = new Hfs(new TextDelimited(websalesFields,","),
                                          websales);
    Pipe salesPipe = new Pipe("Websales Pipe");

    // The input tap for our user info
    Fields userFields = new Fields("user_id", "name",
                                "date_joined", "state");
    Tap usersTap = new Hfs(new TextDelimited(userFields,","), users);
    Pipe usersPipe = new Pipe("Users Pipe");

    // Join the two streams on the field "user_id"
    Fields joinOn = new Fields("user_id");
    Fields outputFields = new Fields("user_id", "item",
                                "date_purchase","price",
                                "user_id1", "name",
                                "date_joined", "state");

    // This pipe takes the information about our streams above
    // and joins the stream via the CoGroup Class
    Pipe joinPipe = new CoGroup(salesPipe, joinOn,
                              usersPipe, joinOn,
                              outputFields,new InnerJoin());

    // An output tap (comma delimited CSV file)
    // and the pipe that will feed it
```

```
    Tap outputTap = new Hfs(new TextDelimited(true,","), output_dir);
    Pipe outputPipe = new Pipe("output pipe", joinPipe);

    // The Flow definition hooks it all together
    FlowDef flowDef = FlowDef.flowDef()
        .addSource(salesPipe, websalesTap)
        .addSource(usersPipe, usersTap)
        .addTailSink(outputPipe, outputTap);

    flowConnector.connect(flowDef).complete();
  }
}
```

Deploying a Cascading Application on a Hadoop Cluster

Once your application is working as expected on small amounts of local test data, you can deploy the same packaged JAR file to a Hadoop cluster with no code modifications. Remember to add the Cascading JAR files to your application's lib directory and to make sure your source data is available in HDFS. Then move your application to a node on your Hadoop cluster, and launch it using the `hadoop jar` command. Listing 9.6 shows an example of running a Cascading application on a Hadoop cluster.

Listing 9.6   **Running your Cascading application on a Hadoop cluster**

```
# Make sure your source data is available in HDFS
$> hadoop dfs -put websales.csv /user/hduser/websales.csv
$> hadoop dfs -put user_info.csv /user/hduser/ user_info.csv

# Run the hadoop jar command
$> hadoop jar mycascading.jar /user/hduser/websales.csv \
          /user/hduser/users_info.csv output_directory

INFO util.HadoopUtil: resolving application jar from found
main method on: CascadingSimpleJoinPipe
INFO planner.HadoopPlanner: using application jar:
/home/hduser/ mycascading.jar
INFO property.AppProps: using app.id: 35FEB5D0590D62AFA6D496F3F17C14B9
INFO mapred.FileInputFormat: Total input paths to process : 1
# etc...
```

If you are relatively new to Hadoop, and Cascading is your introduction to writing custom JAR files for the framework, take a moment to appreciate what is happening behind the scenes of the `hadoop jar` command. A Hadoop cluster comprises a collection of services that have specialized roles. Services known as JobTrackers are responsible for keeping track of and sending individual tasks to services on other machines. TaskTrackers are the cluster's workers; these services accept jobs from the

JobTrackers and execute various steps in the MapReduce framework. Many instances of these services run simultaneously on a collection of physical or virtual nodes in the cluster.

In order for your application to be executed in parallel, it must be accessible by every relevant node in the Hadoop cluster. One way to deploy your code is to provide a copy of your application and any necessary dependencies needed for it to run to every node. As you can imagine, this can be error prone, is time consuming, and, worst of all, is plain annoying.

When the `hadoop jar` command is invoked, your JAR file (along with other necessary dependencies specified via the `-libjars` flag) is copied automatically to all relevant nodes in the cluster. The lesson here is that tools like Hadoop, Pig, and Cascading are all different layers of abstraction that help us think about distributed systems in procedural ways.

When to Choose Pig versus Cascading

Like many open-source technologies used in the large-scale data-analytics world, it's not always clear when to choose Pig over Cascading or over another solution such as writing Hadoop streaming API scripts. Tools evolve independently from one another, so the use cases best served by Pig versus Cascading can sometimes overlap, making decisions about solutions difficult. I generally think of Pig as a workflow tool, whereas Cascading is better suited as a foundation for building your own workflow applications. Pig is often the fastest way to run a transformation job.

Analysts who have never written a line of Python or Java should have little trouble learning how to write their own Pig scripts. A one-time complex transforming job should certainly use Pig whenever possible; the small amount of code necessary to complete the task is hard to beat.

One of Cascading's biggest strengths is that it provides an abstraction model that allows for a great deal of modularity. Another advantage of using Cascading is that, as a Java Virtual Machine (JVM)-based API, it can use all of the rich tools and frameworks in the Java ecosystem.

Summary

Pig and Cascading are two very different open-source tools for building complex data workflows that run on Hadoop. Pig is a data processing platform that provides an easy-to-use syntax for defining procedural workflow steps. Cascading is a well-designed and popular data processing API for building robust workflow applications. Cascading simplifies data using a metaphor that equates data to water: sources, sinks, taps, and pipes. Data streams can *cascade*. Thus Cascading is useful for building, testing, and deploying robust data applications. Because Cascading uses the Java Virtual Machine, it has also become the basis for data-application APIs in other languages that run on the JVM.

V

Machine Learning for Large Datasets

10

Building a Data Classification System with Mahout

The real problem is not whether machines think but whether men do.
—B. F. Skinner

Computers essentially perform a fairly simple set of tasks over and over. Data goes in, algorithms are applied to that data, and results come out. In order to know what to do, computers have to be explicitly programmed by humans. Since the beginning of the digital computing age, scientists have pondered the possibility of computers reacting to changes in data without new programming, similar to how humans learn from changes in their environment. If a computer could modify its programming models as input changes, it could be used as a tool for helping us make decisions about the future. And as data sizes grow beyond what humans are capable of processing manually, it becomes almost necessary to apply computer input to decision-making tasks. When faced with an onslaught of data, can we find ways for computers to make useful decisions for humans? The answer to this question is a resounding "Sometimes," and the field concerned with the ability of computers to provide accurate predictive output based on new information is known as **machine learning**.

There is currently debate and confusion about which tools in the data space can be automated to provide predictive business value given adequate data. In light of this debate, there have been many cases in which machine learning has improved the usefulness of everyday actions. Machine learning touches on use cases that consumers of Internet services experience every day. From spam detection to product recommendation systems to online insurance pricing, machine learning challenges are being increasingly solved by using distributed computer systems.

Machine learning draws upon the rich academic histories of mathematics, statistics, and probability. There's no simple way to sum up the variety of use cases and approaches to solving machine learning challenges. Some research projects attempt to model computer systems to emulate human thought processes, whereas others use clever statistical techniques to help predict the probability for some actions to be taken. To be proficient in machine learning techniques requires that you be well versed in mathematics and statistics. However, there are several well-understood machine learning techniques that are practical and that lend themselves well to distributed data systems. This chapter provides an overview of some of the terms and concepts in this field and an introduction to popular open-source tools used in machine learning for large datasets.

Can Machines Predict the Future?

No, machines are not able to predict the future. Unfortunately, there seems to be widespread misconception among those newly dabbling in data science about the potential for predictive models to magically emerge from datasets. If you think that you can simply collect a huge amount of data and expect a machine to provide you with accurate visions of the future, then you might as well turn back now.

Wait—you're still here? Okay, since you haven't skipped this chapter after reading my warning, I'll tell you something a bit more optimistic. Machines can report to you about the probability that relates to an existing mathematical model. Using this probability, the machine can also take incoming, unknown data and classify, cluster, and even recommend an action based solely on the model. Finally, the machine can incorporate this new data into the model, improving the entire system. Do you think this is not as exciting as predicting the future? Computers are able to do things that help us make decisions based on information we already know. In fact, a computer can obviously do a lot of these types of tasks much better than a human can, and, in some cases, these approaches are the only way to solve large-scale data problems.

Finding ways in which computers can generate models without having to be explicitly programmed is known as **machine learning** (often abbreviated **ML**—not to be confused with *markup language*), a growing and vibrant research space. Computer machine learning models are part of yet another field that has grown up along with the rise of accessible distributed data processing systems such as Hadoop. It's one thing to build predictive models using a small amount of data on a desktop machine; it's altogether another to be able to deal with the volumes of data being generated by Web applications, huge e-commerce sites, online publications, and spambots. Machine learning tools will not relieve you of your need to understand the how and why of predictive analytics or statistics. However, when applied correctly, they can be very effective tools for gaining practical value from huge volumes of data.

Challenges of Machine Learning

This chapter began with a warning about trusting the effectiveness of machine learning. Like many other technologies featured in this book, complex machine learning tools are becoming more accessible to everyday analysts. There is quite a lot of debate in the data field about how this may affect data solutions. Some worry that increased accessibility will cause an increase in poorly applied machine learning techniques. Because of the complex nature of machine learning algorithms, the potential for misuse of a technique for a particular challenge is strong. Furthermore, within each class of machine learning solutions there are often many algorithmic variations. The machine learning field has many pitfalls, and fallacies abound. As more tools become turnkey and accessible to engineers, the opportunities to derive untenable results from them grow. It's very important to make sure that the machine learning algorithm you choose is a viable model for your specific data challenge. For example, the field of clustering algorithms features an enormous variety of models for grouping similar data points. A *k-means* clustering algorithm places data points discretely in a particular group, whereas its cousin the *fuzzy k-means* can result in data points in more than one group. The choice of one versus the other is dependent on how well it addresses the problem being solved. These algorithms are discussed in more detail later in the chapter.

Providing a significant sample size is also important to building statistical models for predictive purposes. In many cases, only a small dataset is necessary to train a machine model. For example, Bayesian classification techniques often don't require massive datasets to build adequate predictive models. In some cases, using larger and larger datasets to train machine learning systems may ultimately be a waste of time and resources. Never use a distributed-processing approach unless absolutely necessary.

Bias-variance trade-off is another fundamental place for potential pitfalls when considering using a machine learning approach. Imagine that we have created a linear regression model. Our data can be arranged on a two-dimensional axis. Our model attempts to describe the relationship between two variables and assumes that the error components of both are independent of one another. When trying to build a regression line, our linear model would attempt to fit a line through the data points. Not all of our data points will sit on this line (in fact, perhaps very few or none will). This model has a certain type of bias problem; most points won't touch the regression line. New data that is applied to this model will also not appear on the line. However, the *variance* of predicted values will likely be low. For each new value associated with the regression line, the distance from the line may be quite small. In other words, nearly every predicted value will not be exactly correct, but each will only be incorrect by a small amount.

A more complex model might incorporate a line that touches every point explicitly. However, this decrease in variance means that the model is tightly connected to the data itself. The bias of the model is very low; it matches the observed data incredibly well, but new values may not fit well into the model. Consider the effectiveness of the predictive models for the use cases you are faced with. In some cases, variance can be minimized by using a more highly biased model.

Bayesian Classification

If you have an email address, chances are that you are already participating in a massive, worldwide, cyberspace arms race. The battleground is your inbox, and the bad guys are fighting with spam. Without proper spam filtering, email systems would become useless messes full of unwanted advertising. Use cases like spam detection are almost impossible to handle without using some sort of machine learning approach. The data sizes are too large and the problems too critical to handle in other ways. But how do these systems work?

One of the most common approaches to classification is to use an algorithm called a *naïve Bayesian classifier*. In short, a Bayes model treats incoming data as having a set of features, each feature independent of one another. In the case of spam emails, these features may be the individual words of the email itself. Spam email will tend to feature sensational advertising terms and words in all caps. By applying a probabilistic score to each feature, the Bayes classifier can produce a very good sense of the type of the email. If a particular email scores highly on multiple features, it is very likely to be classified as spam. This model is also indicative of the rich history of machine learning. Thomas Bayes was a Presbyterian minister and mathematician who lived in England in the 1700s. Bayes' probabilistic innovations predated not only computer science but much of modern statistics.

Like many other machine learning applications, a simple Bayesian classifier has drawbacks, and certain assumptions need to be met for the algorithm to be effective. The Bayesian approach can sometimes produce poor results if the training data is not particularly well differentiated or when there are too few examples of one type of classification in the training model. As a result, there are many modifications to the simple Bayesian approach and many other classification algorithms. With this in mind, for many practical applications, the naïve Bayesian approach is not always the most accurate way to classify text, but it is effective and conceptually simple. It also doesn't require a large amount of data to get started and can often produce acceptable results for many applications.

Clustering

Michael Lewis's 2003 book, *Moneyball: The Art of Winning an Unfair Game,* told the story of a professional baseball general manager named Billy Beane who had to field a team that could compete against rosters with a far greater payroll. This forced Beane to turn to statistical methods make up for the gap in talent. The book popularized the use of a quantitative approach to sport as Beane searched for overlooked players that could statistically replicate the performance of more highly paid, established stars.

This frugal approach has also been used in realms outside of baseball. In the NBA, professional basketball players are often classified into positions based on physical attributes rather than statistical behavior. The five traditional positions in basketball are often related to height. Guards tend to be shorter, faster, and responsible for handling the ball, whereas centers are tall and responsible for staying near the basket. In 2012, Stanford student Muthu Alagappan wondered if these positions were not created due to a bias about height. In Alagappan's view, the game was much more dynamic, and the traditional positions were not based on actual player statistics. Using a proprietary algorithm, he lumped players into 13 buckets based on statistical performance in games. Guards were placed into new categories such as *defensive ball handler* and *shooting ball handler*. Recognizing that centers, normally the tallest players on the floor, were more than just tall, they were organized into positions such as *paint protector* and *scoring rebounder*. This type of understanding could help NBA teams take a Moneyball approach to the game. Usually, tall centers are the hardest players to find and are paid accordingly. Perhaps instead of choosing a more expensive center, a team could get the same results from a shorter, under-valued player who falls into one of these new categories.

Alagappan's analysis is an example of cluster analysis. Clustering problems are those in which groups are inherent in the data in which some individual data points are more similar to certain data points than to others. **Cluster analysis** sorts the data into groups. As menitoned earlier, one of the most popular and simple clustering algorithms is known as k-means. Besides having a catchy name, **k-means** clustering is a fast way to group data points into a pre-determined number of clusters. For example, imagine a set of points described by two variables. The k-means approach randomly chooses data points as the cluster center and then computes the average distance from this point to all other points in the system. From this data, new centers are chosen, and the process continues. The process is iterative and can continue until the sum-of-squares value is as small as possible. This results in a collection of clustered data points that can only fall into a single group. There are many variations of this approach, including **fuzzy k-means** clustering that allows data points to fall into multiple groups. The major drawback to k-means clustering is that one must know how many clusters should be created before applying the algorithm. In other words, this would not have been helpful in the NBA example given previously. Luckily, there are many other and many more complex clustering algorithms available.

Despite the complexity of the clustering-algorithm space, it's becoming easier and easier to implement over collected data without understanding exactly what is being produced. Much like using classification algorithms such as the Bayesian approach, it's important to understand what the clustering problem being considered is and what the data challenge is. Are you trying to find new categories of customer? Or are you trying to figure out how similar a particular data point is to others? Each of these problems requires a different approach, as well as a different clustering algorithm.

Recommendation Engines

One particular problem domain has captured the attention of machine learning experts, a problem into which they can pour all the global computer power at their disposal. What is this critical social problem? Why, it's movie ratings, of course! More specifically, the problem is that of being able to recommend movies based on a particular user's past viewing history.

In 2006, online movie service Netflix announced that it would hold a public competition to discover an algorithm that could beat its current recommendation engine. So valuable is this feature to Netflix that the prize offered was substantial: one million dollars to the team of researchers who could best the existing engine by a certain accuracy percentage. The Netflix contest also generated a great deal of controversy. Although Netflix attempted to anonymize the data used in the competition, researchers were able to identify the identities of individuals based on data from public movie-ratings sites.

Of the many classes of problems that can be usefully solved with machine learning tools, recommendation algorithms seem to be the most human. Every day, we depend on our social circles for advice on what to buy, watch, and vote on. With the ubiquity of online commerce, this problem space is becoming more valuable by the day.

There are many ways to build recommendation engines. One method is to take existing customer choices and use these to try to predict future choices. Another approach is to look at content itself. Are some movies inherently similar to others? Action movies must all share similar features; they are noisy, fast paced, and colorful. A computer may be able to identify traits in a particular type of media and build a classification system accordingly.

Apache Mahout: Scalable Machine Learning

Many technologies introduced in this book are related in some way to the Hadoop MapReduce framework. MapReduce is an algorithmic approach to breaking up large data problems—those that cannot be easily tackled by a single computer—into smaller ones that can be distributed across a number of separate machines.

Implementing the algorithms used in many machine learning tasks can be challenging enough, and it is even more difficult to parallelize these across a number of different machines. In 2006, a group of computer scientists from Stanford (including the founder of Coursera, Andrew Ng) published a paper called "Map-Reduce for Machine Learning on Multicore." This paper described how a MapReduce framework could be applied to a wide variety of machine learning problems, including clustering, Bayesian classification, and regression.

Meanwhile, open-source developers working on the Apache Lucene search index project (which was started by Hadoop creator Doug Cutting) began to explore adding machine learning features to the software. This work eventually grew into its own project, which became Apache Mahout. As Mahout came into its own, it grew to express MapReduce-related features similar to those explored in the paper by Andrew Ng and others.

Apache Mahout has become a very popular project, not least of all because it is designed to solve very practical machine learning problems. Mahout is essentially a set of Java libraries designed to make machine learning applications easier to build. Although one of the goals of the project is to be somewhat agnostic as to which platform it is used with, it is well integrated with Apache Hadoop, the most commonly used open-source MapReduce framework. Mahout also allows new users to get started with common use cases quickly. Like Apache Hive (which provides an SQL-like interface to querying data in Hadoop's distributed filesystem), Mahout translates machine learning tasks expressed in Java into MapReduce jobs.

Using Mahout to Classify Text

Mahout is distributed as a collection of Java libraries that are generally used with the Hadoop platform. However, in addition to providing Java libraries, Mahout comes with pre-built components that can be used on the command line. In order to illustrate how to use Mahout together with Hadoop to solve a machine learning task, we will take advantage of some of these useful tools.

The Leipzig Corpora Collection[1] is an effort to provide randomly collected sentences in a common format for multiple languages. The sentences are culled from either random public Web sites or news sources. The Corpora collection is available either as MySQL databases or text files. In this case, we will use the Leipzig collection's samples of Wikipedia sentences in both French and English. Using already categorized sentences, we will build a training model that can determine the language of new sentences by "learning" from the training data. In this example, we will create two separate directories, each of which will contain either English or French sample documents. Listing 10.1 shows an example of what our sample training data looks like.

As with many distributed processing tools, it's possible to run Mahout locally without Hadoop, which is useful for testing purposes. In order to run these examples locally, set the `MAHOUT_LOCAL` environment variable to `TRUE`.

Listing 10.1 Using Mahout for Bayesian Classification: input files

```
# For testing purposes, use Mahout locally without Hadoop
> export MAHOUT_LOCAL=TRUE

# English sample sentences
It is large, and somewhat like the mid-boss of a video game.
Not all democratic elections involve political campaigning.
...

# French sample sentences
Le prince la rassura et il paya son dû.
Sa superficie est de 3 310 hectares.
...
```

Now that we have set up our raw training data, let's use this information to train a classifier model. Once this training model is created, we will be able to use it to classify test data. In order to build a classifier, we will need to tell Mahout a number of things about our sample dataset.

First, we need to provide the location of the sample data. Next, we will place the original text files into a format that Mahout can process. The useful *seqdirectory* tool will take a list of files in a directory and create Hadoop sequence-format files that can be used for the next steps in the classification flow (see Listing 10.2).

---

1. http://corpora.uni-leipzig.de/download.html

Listing 10.2 **Creating sequence and vector files**

```
# Create sequence files
> ./bin/mahout seqdirectory -i language_samples -o language_seq

# Create vectors from sequence files
> ./bin/mahout seq2sparse -i language_seq -o language_vectors
-lnorm -nv -wt tfidf

# Split the vectors into two batches: a training output
# and a testing output
> ./bin/mahout split -i language_vectors/tfidf-vectors \
--trainingOutput training-vectors --testOutput test-vectors \
--randomSelectionPct 30 --overwrite --sequenceFiles -xm sequential
```

Now that we have provided a set of training and testing vector files, we can demonstrate how Mahout classifies our testing data into a particular language. First, we will create a training model based on the training vectors we created in the previous step. Next, we will check our test-data vectors to see if they are classified as expected. Listing 10.3 illustrates the command necessary to apply this training model to a directory of unclassified data.

Listing 10.3 **Bayesian classification based on training model**

```
# Run the training model using the training vectors
# created in the previous step
> ./bin/mahout trainnb -i training-vectors -el -li labelindex -o model -ow

# In this example, the test input featured 45 documents,
# 25 in English and 20 in French

# Run the testnb command on the vectors using the model just created
> ./bin/mahout testnb -i test-vectors -l labelindex -m model \
-ow -o language-testing -c


=======================================================
Summary
-------------------------------------------------------
Correctly Classified Instances        :     45   100%
Incorrectly Classified Instances      :      0    0%
Total Classified Instances            :     45


=======================================================
Confusion Matrix
-------------------------------------------------------
a       b        <--Classified as
25      0        |  25        a     = english
0       20       |  20        b     = french
```

```
============================================================
Statistics
------------------------------------------------------------
Kappa                                    0.9206
Accuracy                                   100%
Reliability                            66.6667%
Reliability (standard deviation)         0.5774
```

Running a simple Bayesian classifier using the included binaries in the Apache Mahout distribution is just the tip of the iceberg for the types of applications that are capable of being created with this software. Indeed, it is possible to build far more complicated machine learning projects using the underlying Java interface. Thanks to a vibrant developer and user community, new features are being added to Mahout's core libraries every day.

MLBase: Distributed Machine Learning Framework

Mahout is not the only distributed machine learning system, but its integration with Hadoop is a very compelling reason to consider it for building applications. One of the criticisms of MapReduce-based approaches to data analysis is that performance is not optimal. For some batch-processing jobs on data sizes that are much larger than available memory, MapReduce is still often the best way to solve a problem. Nevertheless, MapReduce is heavily reliant on disk access.

The AMPLab, a group of researchers from UC Berkeley, has been approaching data challenges by building new open-source software applications that have performance in mind from the start. One of the core projects, **Spark**, is an in-memory implementation for cluster computing. Spark aims to rethink distributed systems by avoiding disk access as much as possible. Spark also is built around the idea of reusable memory-based chunks of data that can be processed without having to resort to reads from disk. For machine learning tasks, this can be very beneficial, as some predictive or clustering models may change only incrementally as new data is added. In order to take advantage of the Spark distributed environment, the AMPLab has sponsored a project called MLbase. MLbase consists of several parts. The first component is a general-purpose machine learning library, called MLlib, that is similar to Mahout in many ways. It provides a low-level, Spark-compatible interface to machine learning algorithms. The MLI is an API layer that sits on top of MLlib, providing a higher-level interface to the underlying system. Perhaps the most exciting tool in this stack is the MLOptimizer, with attempts to choose the correct algorithm based on the data and task provided. The MLbase platform, although newer than the Mahout project, may prove to be a viable option for working with large-scale machine learning tasks.

Summary

Although machines can't yet match the learning ability of humans, it is possible to create systems that can modify their output based on new data. These systems are part of the large and growing field of machine learning tools. Machine learning encompasses a huge variety of use cases, from computer vision to text classification to biological modeling. For projects that collect large amounts of Web-scale data, machine learning techniques are often the only viable way to provide predictive value to customers. Common successful use cases for machine learning approaches include product-recommendation systems, demographic grouping, and sorting out spam from inboxes.

There are many potential pitfalls to applying machine learning techniques to large-scale data analysis problems. Sometimes there is little requirement to use entire datasets, as models and analysis with samples of data can often be just as effective. Overfitting a predictive model to existing data can produce false results. A similar concern is that of ignoring the trade-off between sample bias and sample variance. Using a more general, biased model when creating predictive models may provide greater predictive use at the expense of highly variant results. Creating models that tightly match existing data may prevent flexibility when new data is collected. In summary, it is important to thoroughly understand the problem space and to consider the trade-offs inherent in algorithmic approaches to solving machine learning problems.

Machine learning approaches have been effectively used for several classes of Internet-scale data-collection problems. Classification systems use models built from existing data to classify incoming data. A familiar implementation of a classification can be found in the spam-detection systems common in Web mail systems. Cluster analysis attempts to take unclassified data and form groups according to certain parameters. Cluster analysis can be used to create logical groupings of individuals, such as customer demographics, that are based on a statistical metric. Recommendation systems are also a very popular use of machine learning algorithms. Many Web services, from media to shopping to online-dating Web sites, use recommendation algorithms to provide value to customers.

Machine learning algorithms have been developed for many systems, but as data sizes grow, the need for heavy processing in a timely fashion can overwhelm a single machine. Apache Mahout is an open-source set of libraries that help scale machine learning tasks over clusters of machines, using distributed frameworks such as Apache Hadoop. Mahout focuses on a collection of well-understood use cases, including clustering, classification, and recommendation. Although Mahout is primarily a library used to build other software packages, it also provides a great deal of useful binary tools for running distributed machine learning tasks from the command line. Applications built using the Mahout library can be easily integrated with the rest of the Hadoop ecosystem.

Mahout is just one of several tools that can be used for distributed machine learning. Integration with the Hadoop ecosystem can be a compelling reason to use

Mahout. However, MapReduce-based frameworks can also create a performance bottleneck due to heavy disk access. The UC Berkeley AMPlab, which produces the in-memory Spark distributed-computing framework, also sponsors a project known as MLbase. The components of the MLbase project aim to make distributed machine learning as accessible as possible and could be a viable and performant alternative to Mahout for some use cases.

VI

Statistical Analysis for Massive Datasets

11

Using R with Large Datasets

The sexy job in the next 10 years will be statisticians.
—Hal Varian

The role of traditional systems administrators is changing. Before the growth of cloud-computing platforms and distributed data frameworks, sys admins were primarily concerned with maintaining server hardware. There is still a need for this type of work, but thanks to hardware virtualization, companies are beginning to build products that are managed and hosted in the cloud. Companies are purchasing compute time on clusters of virtual machines. The underlying hardware that supports these clusters is abstracted away from the customer. As the tooling around scalable data analysis becomes more mature, applications that process large amounts of data are becoming more dependent on distributed-software expertise rather than hardware-management skills. This trend has focused a lot of attention on the role of a new type of admin, known as a DevOps engineer: in other words, a systems administrator who focuses on complicated distributed-software systems rather than hardware.

Cloud and data technologies are disrupting many other traditional IT tasks as well. One job role that doesn't look to be in jeopardy anytime soon is that of the statistician. In fact, there is growing need for knowledge of statistical skills across many job functions related to data analysis. Because computer scientists are finding new ways of processing ever-increasing amounts of data, the need for making sense out of this data is in greater demand than ever before.

Solving statistical-analysis challenges can require an expressive language for defining numeric workflows. The open-source software most commonly used by statisticians is R. If you are new to the field of data analysis, you have likely heard about R, as it has become a de facto tool for a wide variety of computational analyses. Although programming languages such as Python and Julia are gaining in popularity for numeric computations, R is the reigning champion of the open-source statistics world. R has a huge user community and many available packages that cover the range of numeric and visualization tasks. R has so many users that the vast number of users alone is good reason to make it a compelling choice for many organizations. Certainly very few statisticians have been fired for using R.

On the other hand, R was originally designed to work in single-machine and single-threaded environments with limited memory. It can be a challenge to use R for even moderately sized datasets, and large dataset use is growing. In this chapter, we'll take a look at some patterns for working with very large data in R and when to use one solution over another.

Why Statistics Are Sexy

Thanks to recent innovations in open-source software, it is easier than ever to collect, store, and manipulate large amounts of data. This ease is sometimes at odds with the challenge of understanding what the data signifies. Simply being able to work with large amounts of data does not guarantee that supposed correlations or informal observations are statistically significant. This is where statistics comes into play. Statistics is a broad, quantitative subject with a rich and well-scrutinized history. Statisticians are concerned with crucial aspects of inference such as the validity of scientific observations, the reliability of data and methods, and the accuracy of mathematical models. Due to the growing amounts of data being generated by Internet-connected software, the need for statisticians is growing as well. Google's chief economist Hal Varian once famously stated that the "sexy job in the next 10 years will be statisticians." Those who can navigate the onslaught of dirty data and guide organizations toward meaning and validity will become valuable computational rock stars in the future.

Because the problem space is vast, statisticians need flexible computational tools to build workflows for asking questions about data. In a recent poll, statisticians have voted that their favorite software is R.[1] R is an open-source programming language specifically created to tackle statistics and data-analysis problems. The language is simple to learn. Because it is a well-used open-source language, R also features a kaleidoscope of graphical user interfaces. Furthermore, R is also used heavily in academic environments, which leads to many graduates on the job market already trained in its use.

Many of the tools in this book address the challenge of collecting and storing data at scale. These tasks often require a distributed computing environment in which many machines act in concert to solve a difficult data challenge. Unfortunately, R was originally designed to be run on a single-threaded, single-machine system. This design is generally at odds with trends to use distributed systems to collect and process ever-growing amounts of data.

People love to use the tools they know best. Organizations want to hire people with best-practice skills. Therefore, it makes a lot of practical sense to find ways to incorporate tools such as R into an organization's overall data processing pipeline. As usual, there are always alternatives to tools in the data space; certainly software such as Apache Mahout (see Chapter 10, "Building a Data Classification System with Mahout") and the ecosystem of data tooling around Python can be used to solve the same problems. However, due to the pervasiveness of its massive user community, finding ways to fit R into existing solutions may make data exploration more efficient for your organization.

---

1. www.kdnuggets.com/2012/05/top-analytics-data-mining-big-data-software.html

Limitations of R for Large Datasets

Modern workstations and laptops are incredibly powerful. Average laptops with their multicore designs and impressive processors put models just a few years older to shame. Of course, everyone is familiar with the mythos of Moore's law: The overall density of transistors on processors tends to double about every two years. The Internet is full of apples-to-oranges comparisons between archaic computing systems and modern workstations. The Apollo Guidance Computer, one of the first computers built using integrated circuits, was responsible for helping humans travel to the moon and back. But even the average smartphone has orders of magnitude more processing speed and memory than the Apollo capsule's brain (which makes one wonder why our smartphones are such underachievers).

Memory capacity has also grown in a similar fashion, and in-memory data systems are becoming more common as a solution to high-throughput data problems. Keeping data in memory and away from disk is a useful way to speed up processing tasks. R is also designed to run completely in memory. This is great news for moderately sized datasets. A modern laptop may have many gigabytes of memory available in its standard configuration, but even with all of this power at hand it's not uncommon to run into data sources that generate gigabytes of data per day. Using R to directly access this amount of data is nearly impossible on a single workstation.

R has a somewhat notorious reputation for confusing newcomers with unintuitive messages about when the interpreter runs out of memory. For systems based on a 32-bit architecture, the total memory available to R is about 4GB, and in practical use, this number is actually closer to 2GB. With every operation, copy, or added dataset, the amount of memory available is impacted. Other restrictions, such as limits on how much memory an application can use per user, may also bring down the amount of memory available to R. Huge datasets may also contain very large integer values, and a 32-bit build of R may not be able to express values greater than a few billion. You wouldn't be able to produce an integer sum expressing values such as the United States national debt with this limitation.

With these limitations in mind, one of the most important first steps in avoiding memory problems is to use a 64-bit machine whenever possible. Like most interpreted languages, R has a garbage collector that frees up memory when objects go out of scope. Another approach to avoiding such problems is to manually flush R's garbage collector immediately once a dataset is no longer needed. The R function gc is primarily used to print out information about the memory available to the R system, but it will also try to force the garbage collector to delete objects. Listing 11.1 provides a collection of functions useful for interrogating the state of memory and objects in R.

Listing 11.1   **Helpful functions for understanding memory usage in R**

```
# Use the sessionInfo function to report on what build of
# R you are using, as well as which packages are attached.

> sessionInfo()
R version 2.15.1 (2012-06-22)
```

```
Platform: i386-apple-darwin9.8.0/i386 (32-bit)
...

# The largest integer value supported using the .Machine variable
> .Machine$integer.max
[1] 2147483647


# The gc function reports on and runs the R
# interpretor's garbage collector. Set the optional
# verbose parameter to true (T) for more detailed output.
> gc(verbose=T)

Garbage collection 12 = 6+0+6 (level 2) ...
8.1 Mbytes of cons cells used (57%)
2.8 Mbytes of vectors used (40%)
         used (Mb) gc trigger (Mb) max used (Mb)
Ncells 300765  8.1     531268 14.2    407500 10.9
Vcells 360843  2.8     905753  7.0    786425  6.0


# The object.size function will report the number of bytes used
# by an R data object
> object.size(mtcars)
5336 bytes


# Pass an R function to system.time to produce a
# report on the time it takes to run
> system.time(airline_dataframe ← read.csv.ffdf(
            file="huge_file.csv",header=TRUE))
user   system elapsed
136.370   7.586 149.617
```

R Data Frames and Matrices

Working with large datasets requires some knowledge of the data structures that R supports. One of R's strengths is the great variety of data structures available for various tasks. Let's revisit some common ways we interact with data in R. When using R, what does the data look like?

On its own, R supports a collection of **atomic** data types, including familiar variable types such as integers, real numbers, and strings. A fundamental R data structure is a **vector**, which is a group of contiguous values of one type. In other words, a vector is much like a list of similar values, such as a collection of readings from a thermometer or scores from a sports league.

A **matrix** is like a vector, but it can have two dimensions. Like a vector, a matrix must contain the same type of atomic data types. A matrix might be used to represent data from applications such as coordinate systems or the hue and saturation values of a two-dimensional digital image or to support more complex operations such as those used in linear algebra.

Some data can't be easily expressed as a collection of similarly typed numbers. It is obviously useful to have heterogeneous data in an easily addressable form. Tabular data structures like this are so common that R provides a data structure known as a data frame. Technically, a **data frame** is a list of vectors of the same length. Unlike a matrix, the individual vectors that make up data frames can each contain a different data type. Listing 11.2 presents examples of matrix and data frame structures in R.

Listing 11.2   **Examples of matrix and data frame structures in R**

```
# Create an R matrix with 3 rows and 6 columns
> example_matrix <- matrix(1:18, nrow=3, ncol=6)
> example_matrix

     [,1] [,2] [,3] [,4] [,5] [,6]
[1,]    1    4    7   10   13   16
[2,]    2    5    8   11   14   17
[3,]    3    6    9   12   15   18

# Value of a single matrix coordinate
> example_matrix[2,5]
[1] 14

# List first 3 rows of the "mtcars" sample data frame
> head(mtcars, 3)
               mpg cyl disp  hp drat    wt  qsec vs am gear carb
Mazda RX4     21.0   6  160 110 3.90 2.620 16.46  0  1    4    4
Mazda RX4 Wag 21.0   6  160 110 3.90 2.875 17.02  0  1    4    4
Datsun 710    22.8   4  108  93 3.85 2.320 18.61  1  1    4    1
```

Strategies for Dealing with Large Datasets

The computational tools described throughout this book are often concerned with processing tasks involving large amounts of data. However, although these tools are becoming more and more accessible, it should go without saying that it's not always necessary, beneficial, or desirable to use an entire dataset.

In their paper "Critical Questions for Big Data,"[2] researchers danah boyd and Kate Crawford describe myths that data scientists often subscribe to when working with large amounts of data. One of their assertions, that "Bigger Data are Not

---

2. boyd, danah, and Kate Crawford. "Critical questions for big data: Provocations for a cultural, technological, and scholarly phenomenon." *Information, Communication & Society* 15 no. 5 (2012): 662–679.

Always Better Data," cites examples in which collecting more data is not a panacea for high-quality data. For example, imagine the results of a survey. Survey data can be notoriously difficult to work with. Some survey respondents lie, skip questions, and generally do everything possible to uncover edge cases in your otherwise expertly designed question list.

A great deal of work in the field of statistical analysis is dedicated to attempts to determine the probability that a set of observations is significantly different from a random collection of values. However, a common fallacy of large data analysis problems is that you require an entire corpus of data to make decisions or arrive at conclusions. Indeed, one of the cornerstones of statistical analysis is to provide quantitative evidence that whatever subset of data you are looking at from the possible entire corpus can produce a convincingly valid and significant probability-based conclusion if the subset is collected properly (random sampling).

The corollary to this argument is, of course: If you can access all the data in an entire dataset, then why wouldn't you? For one thing, the processing power can be expensive and the process time consuming. You probably don't need to use the entire dataset for statistical analysis if a sample will provide the same result. As datasets grow larger, increasing numbers of statistically significant relationships may appear when in fact there may be no real-world relationship.

Large Matrix Manipulation: bigmemory and biganalytics

Numbers, numbers everywhere. You've just collected a huge amount of numerical data, and you'd like to run a summary and plot correlations to understand what the data means. In some cases, your available amount of machine memory is much smaller than your dataset. The challenges that prevent R from using the entire available memory of the system can be daunting. **bigmemory** is an R library that attempts to apply an extra level of memory management to large datasets. In fact, bigmemory uses a clever interface that interacts with a speedy C++ framework for managing underlying data.

R matrices all must contain the same data type. If you are working with a numerical dataset that can still potentially fit within system memory, then the bigmemory package is a good choice. bigmemory provides a data type called big.matrix, which works very similarly to a standard R matrix. A **big.matrix** object can only contain numerical data. The bigmemory package has an interesting design that enables multiple R instances to access underlying C++-managed data simultaneously. By itself, different instances of R cannot access each other's data objects. With bigmemory, it is possible to define on-disk binary files that not only can be shared but can be quickly loaded into R upon startup of a new session.

A very interesting dataset often used to demonstrate the bigmemory package is the U.S. Department of Transportation's airline on-time statistics database, collected and hosted by RITA (the Research and Innovative Technology Administration). This dataset is a blast to work with, not only because it is large and freely available, but because it provides very detailed statistics about an often-frustrating U.S. airline industry. These files can be challenging to use with R, as an uncompressed CSV file of statistics from the year 2000 alone is about 500MB. On a 32-bit machine, memory is quickly exhausted as data is loaded into R matrices for further analysis.

This is where the bigmemory package comes in. The bigmemory read.big.matrix function enables R users to read very large datasets into big.matrix objects, from an on-disk source. When using the read.big.matrix function, non-numeric entries are skipped and replaced with "NA." Listing 11.3 compares the use of a big.matrix object to that of a standard R matrix for loading a single year of airline on-time data from a CSV file.

Listing 11.3 **Using bigmemory to read large amounts of data**

```
# Attempt to read CSV file of airline on-time data from 2000
> airline_data = read.csv("2000_airline.csv", sep=",")
*** error: can't allocate region

# Using the bigmemory big.matrix object
> airlinematrix <- read.big.matrix("2000_airline.csv",
                          type="integer", header=TRUE,
                          backingfile="2000_airline.bin",
                          descriptor="2000_airline.desc")

> summary(airlinematrix)
    Length       Class      Mode
 164808363 big.matrix        S4
```

Another useful feature of the bigmemory package is the ability to place data objects in shared memory. This means that multiple instances of R can use the same bigmemory object, further saving total system memory when necessary.

ff: Working with Data Frames Larger than Memory

Data frames are the workhorse data structures of the R language and a very productive way to work with tabular data using named rows and columns. An R data frame is more than just a collection of addressable cells; R keeps track of a number of properties internally using object metadata. This is one of the reasons the R interpreter requires more memory than the size of the dataset for calculations, slicing, and other operations. Even if you have many gigabytes of memory available, it is easy to find a massive dataset that does not fit into system RAM. What happens when your dataset is even larger than the available system memory?

The **ff** package attempts to overcome the memory limits of R by decoupling the underlying data from the R interpreter. ff uses the system disk to store large data objects. When running an R operation over this on-disk data, chunks of it are pulled into memory for manipulation. In essence, ff tries to keep the same R interface and data types that are used with smaller, memory-sized datasets. Like bigmemory, ff is able to store data objects as on-disk images that can be read across R sessions.

The ff library supports the standard R atomic data types, such as integer and double. It also provides a few package-specific data types, such as single bits, bytes, and "nibbles" (four bits of information). These efficient atomic structures provide a space and performance advantage when working with some types of data, such as genomics information. Listing 11.4 provides an example of using ff to help find the maximum and average delay times across all U.S. flights in 2000.

Listing 11.4   Using ff to create data frames from large datasets

```
# Create an "ff" data frame
> library(ff)
> airline_dataframe <- read.csv.ffdf(file="2000_airline.csv",
                                      header=TRUE)


# List the number of records in the dataset
> dim(airline_dataframe)
[1] 5683047      29


# Find the max and mean arrival delay for all U.S. flights in 2000,
# ignoring any NA values
> max(airline_dataframe$ArrDelay, na.rm=TRUE)
[1] 1441
> mean(airline_dataframe$ArrDelay, na.rm=TRUE)
[1] 10.28266
```

biglm: Linear Regression for Large Datasets

A common data challenge is to understand how variables are related to one another. Sometimes this type of analysis is used to create models that can help predict unknown variables under given conditions. Are sales of a product possibly related in some way to weather, season, or other factors? Can the ratings of a movie help predict what similar movies viewers might want to watch?

Regression analysis is a common technique for determining how variables might be related to each other. The term *regression* is linked to the work of Sir Francis Galton, a man who is credited with inventing our modern scientific concept of correlation. In a drearily named publication called "Regression towards mediocrity in hereditary stature,"[3] Galton noted that children born from abnormally tall parents tended to be close to an average height. Galton's observance of this tendency, commonly known as *regression to the mean*, has been a cornerstone of statistical analysis ever since.

When comparing values from two independent variables (the relationship between measurements of height and weight is a commonly cited example), you can use a

---

3. Galton, Francis. "Regression towards mediocrity in hereditary stature." *The Journal of the Anthropological Institute of Great Britain and Ireland* 15 (1886): 246–263.

technique called *simple linear regression*. A common method for finding a regression line is called the least-squares method. Imagine a comparison of a collection of two categories of values, one of which we call x and the other y. We can plot all of these values on a graph, with the x values on the horizontal axis, and the y values on the vertical. The least-squares method produces a regression line with the smallest values for the sum of the squares of the vertical distance from each data point to the line. Put simply, this type of regression line is fairly easy to calculate. Even better, R provides functions that take care of this and other regression calculations.

A note of caution: Linear regression is conceptually easy to understand, and there are plenty of software packages that are able to provide regression analysis even when it is not appropriate. For this reason, it's easy to misuse this technique and to misinterpret the results. There are plenty of cases in which linear regression is not a great fit for determining relationships between variables. First of all, linear regression tests assume that the scatterplot of the distribution of the values of the two variables is roughly linear in shape and that the individual distributions of the variables both follow a normal distribution with few outliers. Another assumption that linear regression techniques make is that the variables involved have a uniform variance and are relatively free of random values (such as those derived from erroneous measurements). In situations in which any of these assumptions are not met, linear regression may not be a valid way to approach the problem.

Caveats and cautions aside, what happens when you have a legitimate linear-regression challenge and you can't fit it into available system memory? This is where the **biglm** package comes in. The biglm package enables linear regression analysis over very large datasets. The **biganalytics** package, the sibling of bigmemory, contains a useful wrapper function that helps to build linear regression lines from big.matrix data. Listing 11.5 demonstrates an example of this using the airline on-time data seen in the bigmemory example.

Listing 11.5   **Using biglm with big.matrix objects**

```
library(bigmemory)
library(biganalytics)
library(biglm)


# Load our airline on-time data
airlinematrix <- read.big.matrix("2000_airline.csv",
                                 type="integer", header=TRUE,
                                 backingfile="2000_airline.bin",
                                 descriptor="2000_airline.desc")


# Use the biglm.big.matrix wrapper function to create a
# regression line comparing ArrDelay and DepDelay values
delay_lm <- biglm.big.matrix(ArrDelay~DepDelay,data=airlinematrix)
summary(delay_lm)
```

```
Large data regression model: biglm(formula = formula, data = data, ...)
Sample size =  5481303
               Coef   (95%    CI)    SE p
(Intercept) -0.3857 -0.4000 -0.3714 0.0072 0
DepDelay     0.9690  0.9686  0.9695 0.0002 0
```

RHadoop: Accessing Apache Hadoop from R

Solving large data challenges often requires a combination of disparate technologies working in concert. R is a well-supported tool for statistical analysis, and Hadoop is popular for distributed data processing tasks. Hadoop provides a framework for defining MapReduce jobs: tasks that split large data challenges into smaller pieces that can be processed on a number of machines. Both R and Hadoop have an established user base and are great choices for specific use cases. For more on using the Hadoop MapReduce framework for data processing, see Chapter 8, "Putting It Together: MapReduce Data Pipelines," and Chapter 9, "Building Data Transformation Workflows with Pig and Cascading."

A practical way to build a bridge between distributed computing systems, such as Hadoop, and R is to provide interfaces from the programming language to the MapReduce framework. The Hadoop Streaming API (see Chapter 8) is one example of this type of interface, allowing MapReduce jobs to be defined using languages other than Hadoop's native Java. A popular choice for connecting R with Hadoop is the aptly named **RHadoop** project. RHadoop contains several packages, the key ones being rmr, rhdfs, and rhbase, that enable R developers to interface with Hadoop using an idiomatic syntax.

The **rmr** package is a bridge between R and Hadoop's MapReduce functionality. It's not a direct interface to the Hadoop Streaming API but rather a way to define MapReduce in a concise, R-friendly syntax. The **rhdfs** and **rhbase** packages provide interfaces to HDFS (the Hadoop Distributed File System) and the HBase database respectively. These packages provide simple functions to read, write, and copy data via R. Like many other libraries used to access Hadoop, it's also possible to debug Hadoop scripts written using RHadoop locally without touching a Hadoop backend. This can be done by setting the backend parameter to local in the rmr.options function.

In order to build and install the RHadoop packages, several additional R packages, including Rcpp and RJSONIO, are required. To run the rmr package over an existing Hadoop installation, each node must have a copy of R as well as rmr installed. Finally, R requires that the HADOOP_CMD and HADOOP_STREAMING environment variables point to the Hadoop binary and the location of the Hadoop Streaming API JAR files respectively.

Let's take a look at an example of using R and Hadoop together with the rmr and rhdfs packages. Listing 11.6 demonstrates how to use rmr to run a MapReduce job on an underlying Hadoop cluster.

Listing 11.6   **Using rmr to create a MapReduce job in R**

```
library(rmr)

# rmr uses a Hadoop backend by default. Set backend to local
# for debugging without accessing Hadoop
rmr.options(backend = "local")

# The mapper function splits words on
# spaces using strsplit and emits each
# word with a count of 1
mapper <- function(.,lines) {
  words.list <- strsplit(lines, ' ')
  words <- unlist(words.list)
  return(keyval(words, 1))
}

# The reducer function produces the total sum of
# the counts of all words emitted by the mapper
reducer <- function(word, counts) {
  keyval(word, sum(counts))
}

wordcounter <- function (input, output) {
  mapreduce(input=input,
            output=output,
            input.format="text",
            map=mapper,
            reduce=reducer)
}

# Load input data from HDFS using from.dfs
functionfrom.dfs(wordcounter('/data/my_file.txt','/output')
```

Summary

R is the most popular open-source language for expressing statistical analysis work-flows. Many statisticians and mathematicians spend a great deal of time using R, and it is a commonly taught language in academic environments. Distributed computing makes the collection and processing of data more accessible, and tools like R help make sense of this data. Unfortunately, R was originally designed to run on datasets that are much smaller than the available system memory of a single machine. Despite this limitation, R's flexibility and widespread usage means that it may be advantageous to find ways to deploy it even when datasets become large. It can often be practical to ensure that the R users in your organization are able work just as effectively as data sizes grow.

Even when using a very powerful workstation, it can be difficult or impossible to fit data into the amount of memory that the system has allocated to R. In order to work with datasets that are larger than available system memory, we must either use a different strategy or take advantage of an existing R package to overcome these challenges. R installations on 32-bit machines are often limited to much less memory than the overall system has available. The most important first step to addressing memory limitations is to use R on a 64-bit system, which will help ensure that as much system memory can be used by R as possible.

There are several types of problems that one can encounter when working with large datasets from R. One issue is that the amount of memory available to R may be sufficient to load a dataset, but additional operations can be prohibitively slow or impossible to accomplish. Another type of challenge occurs when the dataset of interest is far larger than the entire amount of memory available to the system.

Before exploring additional workarounds for these challenges, consider using a method that does not require such large amounts of data. It is often not necessary to use an entire dataset to obtain a statistically significant result. Consider random sampling of large datasets to scope down the amount of data necessary for analysis. There are many R modules available that allow reading a subset of data from a database. Consider if it is appropriate to use methods such as sampling and tests of significance to gain statistical insight without having to interact with the entire dataset.

When a dataset is smaller than available system memory, it is possible to use a package such as bigmemory to improve the way R interacts with available RAM. The bigmemory package is an R interface to an underlying set of C++ functions that improve the use of available memory. bigmemory provides a new R data type called "big.matrix," which acts similarly to standard R matrices.

When data sizes are so large that they overwhelm the total amount of system memory, R developers should consider using features from the ff package. ff attempts to provide support for very large datasets by using disk access that looks as much like native, memory-based R as possible. Like bigmemory, ff provides specialized data structures such as the ff data frame. Data objects from the ff package can be stored and even used across different R sessions.

Linear regression is a very common strategy for exploring the potential for numerical variables to be related. For very large datasets, the biglm package allows developers to run regression analysis and create generalized regression models using datasets that are larger than available R system memory.

When building data applications, it's common to require a number of different solutions to work in tandem. Hadoop is a commonly used open-source framework for data processing tasks. RHadoop is a collection of packages that provides the ability to access Apache Hadoop's MapReduce functionality as well as data contained in HDFS and Hbase.

## 12

Building Analytics Workflows Using Python and Pandas

A central theme of this book is that of accessibility. The availability of new, powerful open-source software has been a driving force to help a growing number of developers and analysts gain access to tools they need to solve their data challenges. The open-source movement brings more than just the software alone; another advantage is the momentum of the community of developers who work with those tools. For example, the programming language R, a leading programming environment for statistics and mathematical computing, is not only a language but also offers a huge community of people who contribute code, modules, and other tools.

The R community is large and vibrant, but its focus has always been statistics and scientific computing. In practice, this means that a module for dealing with almost every common type of mathematical computation likely already exists. R is great for interactive and exploratory data needs. However, in order to build fully functional applications, it makes sense to take advantage of software that already has a great deal of built-in functionality. Despite the popularity of specialized languages such as R, more and more scientists, statisticians, and data-application developers are turning to a language that at first glance may not seem like a natural fit for high-performance data processing: Python.

In other chapters, we've already looked at examples of using Python to simplify interacting with data processing tools such as the Hadoop Streaming API. This chapter will cover how to use Python for more applied, CPU-intensive tasks as well as how to work with Python as part of an interactive workflow.

The Snakes Are Loose in the Data Zoo

A lot of attention has been paid to the open-source software commonly associated with large-scale data processing over multiple machines. As discussed in previous chapters, Hadoop is a tool used to distribute processing tasks over a number of machines using a computational strategy called MapReduce. This type of processing works by breaking larger problems into smaller ones and then farming out the small problems to individual machines. In this type of system, the smaller problems are not always particularly challenging and can be tackled by the average server quickly. However, the entire system is limited by how fast the results of these smaller tasks can be passed back to coordinating machines. These systems can be referred to as **IO-bound**: Performance of these types of applications is generally limited more by performance of input and output (IO) of data between nodes than by the CPUs in the machines themselves. The classic MapReduce problem of trying to count all the words in a large set of documents is a great example of this. Counting words is not a particularly CPU-intensive problem; once the processor receives the instruction, it should be able to return the answer faster than new data comes in.

Not all data problems are best solved by attempting to break a problem into smaller pieces and farming the shards out to a cluster of separate machines. Mathematical and statistical problems often require that the CPU handle most of the heavy lifting. **CPU-bound** problems are those in which the speed of the processor is the limiting factor in the system, as other processes must wait while the CPU crunches away on some difficult algorithm. In cases like this, faster, more powerful processors are better. When calculating the answer to complex math problems, a CPU that runs faster will solve the problem faster.

In addition, expressing complex mathematical algorithms is also challenging, so a great deal of specialized software exists to make scientific and statistical computing accessible. There are many commercial tools and languages for numerical computing, including SAS, SPSS, MATLAB, and many more. In the open-source world, R and Julia are popular domain-specific languages for scientific computing, and that old stalwart Fortran is still popular, especially for supercomputing applications.

A language that wasn't originally designed for high-performance numerical computation is Python. Python's core design philosophies include readability, brevity, and efficiency but not raw performance. How can an interpreted scripting language primarily known for text processing be useful for serious scientific and data analytics? To find out, we need to take a look at some practical problems with existing numerical-computation languages.

Choosing a Language for Statistical Computation

Before we discuss using Python for data analysis, let's take a look at R, the de facto exploratory language for statistical computing. R is popular for a variety of reasons. It's open-source and freely available on many platforms. As a language informed and influenced by other functional languages, it's easy to express mathematical concepts naturally in R. Like Python, R is an interpreted language, meaning that you don't have to wait for a compilation step before running commands. In fact, you can run R from the command line, allowing quick iterative exploration of data.

Aside from all these useful features, the biggest benefit of using R might simply be the enormous amount of open, community-based software packages available. **CRAN** (or "Comprehensive R Archive Network") is a worldwide repository containing R code for all kinds of statistics applications. Not only does CRAN contain packages for many common statistical applications such as linear regression, clustering, and hypothesis testing, but there are also plenty of modules available for the long tail of specific scientific-computing needs. Developers can find R code that addresses such domain spaces as baseball, astronomy, and even tools to visualize and statistically analyze animal movement. In short, if there is a statistical need, there is a chance someone has contributed a useful R package that addresses it—and in many cases, there are several packages that address the same problem.

R is popular and useful, and features an enormous collection of open-source code for multiple problem domains. So why try to replace it with something else? The first reason is that the widespread popularity of Python gives it a much larger community of experienced developers. Within the field of statistics applications, R is often cited as the most popular language for asking statistical questions about a dataset. Although it's difficult to track exactly who is using which programming language, it's almost certainly true that the Python community has more developers overall than those using statistical- and scientific-focused languages like R or Julia.[1]

The TIOBE Programming Community index is an attempt to use rankings from popular search engines to rate the popularity of programming languages. Although TIOBE is probably not the most scientific way to measure programming-language popularity, in April 2013 Python ranked eighth in the index, whereas R was ranked twenty-sixth. The RedMonk Programming Language Rankings, which uses data from popular programming-community Web sites such as GitHub and Stack Overflow, ranked Python fourth to R's seventeenth in their February 2013 rankings. RedMonk's Stephen O'Grady went on to say that the "first tier of languages [including Python] does not appear to be relinquishing its hold on developer time and attention" whereas "R has seen steady traction but little growth,"[2] which was ascribed to competition from other platforms.

Extending Existing Code

R is a special-purpose language that puts a large emphasis on the mathematics and statistics domains. Python, on the other hand, is much more of a general-purpose language, meant to handle general programming tasks. To put the scale of Python development into perspective, the Python Package Index, or PyPI, contains nearly 10 times as many libraries as CRAN.

An advantage to using Python for data analysis is that it might be something you are already using. Python is excellent for general text processing. In fact, if you've done any kind of scripting work at all, you have probably already used Python for parsing, extracting, or ordering text. Python's list data type is a core aspect of the language, and the many available list methods make it easy to slice and extract sequential data. Python, of course, has a great deal of other functionality built in as well, including frameworks for networking and writing Web applications. All of this, along with

---

1. http://redmonk.com/sogrady/2012/09/12/language-rankings-9-12/
2. http://redmonk.com/sogrady/2013/02/28/language-rankings-1-13/

bindings for many types of database software, makes it possible to develop your entire data processing and analysis software using Python.

As a programming language, Python has always had a reputation for simplicity and readability. Python's syntactical design results in programming concepts that can often be expressed in very few lines of code. Python also supports a culture of having fun and has a developer community that is active and organized.

Tools and Testing

Popular general-purpose languages such as Python can provide another big advantage over languages with a smaller user base. General-purpose languages often have the best tools for robust application development and testing.

This is the same reason why one might choose to build data workflows using Java and the Cascading framework rather than a special-purpose language such as Apache Pig (see Chapter 9, "Building Data Transformation Workflows with Pig and Cascading"). By using a general-purpose language like Python, you automatically get all the benefits, including debugging, testing, and functionality. of these popular tools. Most importantly, you also gain access to a large number of programmers who are used to working with these languages in the first place.

Python Libraries for Data Processing

Python is often described as a well-designed language, with many core principles that help developers build powerful applications using very little code. Python is easy to learn and read, because it has a very limited core syntax, and statements use common English words instead of symbols when possible. One thing that Python is not optimized for is speed. As an interpreted language, Python's ease of use is emphasized over raw performance. For many scientific applications with lots of data processing needs, speed is essential; how can Python be effective in this domain? One way is to write new Python modules that are optimized for computational speed, and the most popular library for this purpose is NumPy.

NumPy

The fundamental data structure used in Python is the list, or what well-known Python author Mark Pilgrim calls Python's *workhorse data type*.[3] Python lists are objects that provide a large number of operations on sequential data, including index-based retrieval, splicing, and the ability to iterate over elements using loops or list comprehensions. Lists are excellent for a large number of use cases, but for scientific data analysis, it's often more important to run an operation on all fields at once.

NumPy is the fundamental Python module for scientific and statistical computing. NumPy provides two very important extensions to Python's core data types. First of

---

3. www.diveinto.org/python3/native-datatypes.html

all, NumPy provides a new data type: a multidimensional array. The NumPy array data type uses contiguous memory, and operations are implemented in the C language for raw speed. As a result, operations on this data type, even over very large datasets, are very fast.

In order to provide the raw speed necessary to operate on large, multidimensional arrays, NumPy imposes a few restrictions that might be unfamiliar to users of the very flexible core Python data types. First of all, once a NumPy array is defined, it can't be altered directly. (You can, however, create new arrays as a result of slicing and mathematical operations.) Unlike regular Python lists, NumPy arrays are homogeneous, meaning that they can hold only one type of data; in other words, a NumPy array can't represent both integer and floating-point numbers at the same time.

Another useful feature of NumPy arrays is that operations are broadcast to every element in the array at once. It's possible to run calculations across the entire dataset at once, rather than being forced to manually loop through every field separately. Even better, it's possible to broadcast an operation involving multiple arrays. You can multiply all the values in respective cell locations of two arrays together in a single command.

The examples in Listing 12.1 demonstrate the basics of using the NumPy array data type. A simple two-dimensional array can be generated by using two lists containing the same type of data. In the example that follows, we initialize our array with integer values, but we have defined the array as having floating-point numbers.

Listing 12.1   NumPy fundamentals

```
# Conventional method of importing NumPy module
> import numpy as np

# Initialize a NumPy array
sample_array = np.array([[3, 4, 5],
                        [6, 7, 8]], float)

# Returns the value of cell 0,1
> print sample_array[0,1]
4.0

# Generate a 3x3 array of random sample data
> np.random.random_sample((3, 3))

array([[ 0.73292341,  0.22336877,  0.71491504],
       [ 0.54102249,  0.47380184,  0.40844874],
       [ 0.8506573 ,  0.23022121,  0.19739788]])

# Broadcast examples
# Multiply every cell by 3
> print sample_array * 3
[[  9.  12.  15.]
  [ 18.  21.  24.]]
```

```
# Multiplies each cell with the corresponding
# value in another cell
> print sample_array * sample_array
[[  9.  16.  25.]
 [ 36.  49.  64.]]
```

These examples just scratch the surface of what is possible with NumPy arrays, including the ability to concatenate, copy, slice, and reshape data.

SciPy: Scientific Computing for Python

It's easy to see why the multidimensional array data type provided by NumPy can be so useful for scientific analysis. NumPy's use of in-memory arrays makes calculations and data manipulation with Python very fast. Fortunately, many of the most common computational algorithms have been already created and packaged into a related Python module called SciPy. NumPy handles the underlying data structures needed for scientific computing, whereas **SciPy** provides functions for regularly used algorithms, constants, and graphical tools used in mathematics and science applications.

SciPy's huge number of available features are organized into various packages. The statistics package provides dozens of probability distributions and statistical tests. For the visual and audio analysts, there's an entire package devoted to Fast Fourier Transformation algorithms. There's even a package full of constants, featuring the greatest hits of science rocks stars like Avogadro, Planck, Boltzmann, and Faraday.

Listing 12.2 demonstrates a few simple use cases for SciPy. A common use case in the business world is using clustering algorithms to attempt to bucket customers into broad groups. SciPy provides several useful cluster algorithms, including the popular k-means method (also illustrated in Listing 12.2).

Listing 12.2 **Using SciPy**

```
> import scipy.constants

# Value of PI
> print scipy.constants.pi

3.141592653589793

# Run a K-means clustering operation on a NumPy array
import numpy
from scipy.cluster.vq import kmeans2
my_values = numpy.array([[4.0,5.3],
                         [4.1,9.1],
                         [2.4,7.4],
                         [2.1,3.5]])
clusters = 2
centroids, index_of_closest_centroid = kmeans2(my_values,clusters)
```

Using SciPy with Image Data

What is the resolution of your laptop? The ubiquity of laptops, smartphones, and tablets have pushed screen-resolution specs into the public consciousness, and conversations about the width and height in pixels of the latest device are not uncommon.

The images produced on your flat screen monitors are really just collections of pixels arranged in a rectangle. Therefore the properties of these pixels (such as the hue, brightness, etc.) can be naturally expressed in a multidimensional array indexed by the location of the pixel. Because SciPy uses NumPy's underlying multidimensional array data type, it's both fun and easy to convert your image data into a format that can be manipulated using methods in the SciPy ndimage package.

The example in Listing 12.3 illustrates how to use Python's urllib and PIL classes to download an image from the Web, pull the raw representation of the information into a NumPy array, and then apply a Gaussian blur using the SciPy ndimage package.

Listing 12.3   **SciPy for image data**

```
from scipy import ndimage, misc

from urllib import urlopen
from PIL import Image
from StringIO import StringIO

# Retrieve the Python logo from the Web
url = 'http://www.python.org/community/logos/python-powered-w-200x80.png'
python_logo = Image.open(StringIO(urlopen(url).read()))

# Convert image to a NumPy array
image_array = misc.fromimage(python_logo)

# Apply a Gaussian blur to the image
blurred = ndimage.gaussian_filter(image_array, sigma=4)

# Save the image to local disk
misc.imsave('blurred_image.png', blurred)
```

The blurred image result is saved as a new local file. It's also possible to use SciPy's image methods on a succession of video stills. There are a lot of possibilities for digital image processing and analysis, and many transformations can be done in just a few lines of code. Using SciPy to manipulate images programmatically is a great way to learn about how digital effects are implemented.

The Pandas Data Analysis Library

NumPy and SciPy are powerful tools in their own right, and can form the basis of some of the same types of data analysis that one can do with R. However, these tools still leave a gap in the type of applications that can be built, as practical use cases bring additional challenges to address. Common processing tasks usually require an even higher-level approach to data modeling. For example, what if we need to make radical changes to our data's structure? How do we combine datasets of different shapes? What's the best way to work with records with missing data? How do we label data in rows and columns? These real-world data challenges come up time and time again. Fortunately, **Pandas** (short for the Python Data Analysis Library, not named for the adorable animal *Ailuropoda melanoleuca*) augments the utility of NumPy and SciPy by addressing some of these real-world data processing tasks.

Note

The first thing I did after I learned about Pandas was to type "pandas" into a search engine to learn more. It dawned on me at the time that, because Pandas shares a name with a popular animal (among other things), I would always have to add something about data or statistics to find the project homepage. That's no longer the case; judging by recent search-engine ranking, questions on Stack Overflow, and mentions on blog posts, the Pandas library has become quite popular, making information about it pretty easy to find.

Pandas Data Types

Like SciPy, Pandas is based heavily on the data structures provided by the underlying NumPy. Pandas provides a variety of useful data types, including a list-like type called a **Series**. The bread-and-butter Pandas data type is reminiscent of one of the most powerful types in R—the *data frame*. A Pandas **DataFrame** is a two-dimensional data structure in which each column may contain different types of data. An example might be a table featuring three columns in which the first column is a person's name, the second is the person's age, and the third might represent the person's height.

A Pandas DataFrame can be created by passing input from various sources, such as a NumPy array or even a Python dictionary containing lists. One of the differences between a DataFrame and a NumPy array is that a DataFrame can also contain labels for rows and columns.

In my professional data work, I am always amazed how often I worry about the index or schema of the data I am working with. One of the *aha* moments I had with the Pandas library was when I discovered the excellent indexing and alignment methods available for DataFrame objects. It's also great to be able to inspect data quickly. Something I often do when working with data is to take a look at the first few rows of a file or print out the end of a file to sanity check whether my application worked properly. For Pandas DataFrames, use the `head` or `tail` methods to output lines from the top or bottom of your file.

Time Series Data

Pandas was originally developed as a tool for looking at financial data. Wall Street quants and econometricians are heavy users of **time series data**, which is essentially a collection of data indexed over regular time intervals. Time series data is often subjected to regression analysis, which can help explain the connection between different variables over time.

Time series data can be tricky to deal with. Time zones are always a pain, even for automated systems. How do you compare data series from two different time zones? Another issue is the sampling rate of data. If the data you have is the result of a reading taken once an hour, is it possible to fill in or extrapolate values when you compare this data to points taken every minute? Pandas makes a great effort to help abstract all of these problems away.

Let's take a look at some basic time series manipulations using daily historic stock values for a company that has been around for a while: IBM. The Yahoo! Finance[4] Web site provides a useful Web interface for downloading historical stock data in CSV format. The raw data used in this example is a simple CSV file containing the date as a string (in YYYY-MM-DD format) along with a collection of values for various aspects of the stock price. The labels for these columns are contained in the first row of the file. See Listing 12.4 for an example.

The `read_csv` method tells Pandas to take the CSV file and import it as a DataFrame. We also direct Pandas to set the index of the DataFrame to the date and to parse the strings found in the `Date` column into timestamps.

In my experience, dealing with data from multiple time zones is a common challenge, especially with data from computer logs. When faced with the problem of comparing datasets from two different time zones, it's often a good idea to normalize values to Coordinated Universal Time, or **UTC**. Pandas's time series methods make it easy to both set and convert a DataFrame's original data to a particular time zone. Because our data about IBM's valuation comes from a U.S. stock market listing, let's assume that these dates are measured in the U.S. Eastern time zone. We can set this time zone using the `tz_localize` method and if necessary convert the result to UTC using `tz_convert`.

Finally, let's resample the data. Our original data is sampled per day, meaning that we have a single set of data points for each day. We can up- or downsample the granularity of our data using the Pandas `resample` method, effectively changing the number of time stamps we have for our data points. If we resample this data to reflect values taken every five minutes, we won't automatically have the data for that granularity level. Using the raw data we have here, it's impossible to tell what IBM's stock price was in the five-minute period between 10:00 a.m. and 10:05 a.m. However, it is possible to interpolate, or fill, those values based on the data we do have. We could, for example, tell Pandas to fill in all of those missing values with the value we have for the whole day. In the example ahead, we resample our data the other way to be granular to the week. We can tell Pandas to also convert the values using a number of methods; in the example in Listing 12.4, we've asked for the max value of daily values to be used.

---

4. http://finance.yahoo.com/q/hp?s=IBM

Listing 12.4   **Using Pandas for time series data**

```
# Historical IBM stock price, 1962 to 2013
# IBMstock.csv
Date,Open,High,Low,Close,Volume,Adj Close
2013-02-22,199.23,201.09,198.84,201.09,3107900,201.09
2013-02-21,198.63,199.07,198.11,198.33,3922900,198.33
....
1962-01-03,572.00,577.00,572.00,577.00,288000,2.54
1962-01-02,578.50,578.50,572.00,572.00,387200,2.52

# Read CSV file and create a Pandas DataFrame
> import pandas as pd
> stock_data = pd.read_csv('IBMStock.csv',
                        index_col='Date',
                        parse_dates=True)
> print stock_data.head(3)

            Open    High    Low     Close   Volume   Adj Close
Date
2013-02-22  199.23  201.09  198.84  201.09  3107900  201.09
2013-02-21  198.63  199.07  198.11  198.33  3922900  198.33
2013-02-20  200.62  201.72  198.86  199.31  3715400  199.31

# Create an Eastern Time Zone localized DataFrame
> eastern_stock_data = stock_data.tz_localize('US/Eastern')
> print eastern_stock_data.head(3)

                            Open   High    Low    Close  Volume  Adj Close
Date
2013-02-22 00:00:00-05:00  199.23 201.09 198.84 201.09 3107900 201.09
2013-02-21 00:00:00-05:00  198.63 199.07 198.11 198.33 3922900 198.33
2013-02-20 00:00:00-05:00  200.62 201.72 198.86 199.31 3715400 199.31

# Convert this data to a UTC time series
> utc_stock_data = eastern_stock_data.tz_convert('UTC')
> print utc_stock_data.head(3)

                            Open   High    Low    Close  Volume  Adj Close
Date
2013-02-22 05:00:00+00:00  199.23 201.09 198.84 201.09 3107900 201.09
2013-02-21 05:00:00+00:00  198.63 199.07 198.11 198.33 3922900 198.33
2013-02-20 05:00:00+00:00  200.62 201.72 198.86 199.31 3715400 199.31

# A resampled DataFrame with the weekly max of each value
> print utc_stock_data.resample('W',how='max').sort(ascending=False).head(3)
```

```
           Open    High    Low     Close   Volume    Adj Close
Date
2013-02-22 199.23  201.09  198.84  201.09  3107900   201.09
2013-02-21 198.63  199.07  198.11  198.33  3922900   198.33
2013-02-20 200.62  201.72  198.86  199.31  3715400   199.31
```

Building More Complex Workflows

One of the advantages of using Python for data analysis is that we have access to an enormous number of additional general-purpose libraries along with Python's brevity and clean syntax. The ability to build applications entirely in Python, incorporating other popular libraries into your data workflows, makes it great for turning exploratory scripts into full production applications. To demonstrate, let's take a look at an example of something that might be a bit cumbersome to do with R but is very easy to do in Python.

Twitter provides APIs for interacting with public tweets. The Twitter Streaming API can be a lot of fun for people learning how to work with data streams, as it simply unleashes a nonstop barrage of randomly sampled public tweets along with metadata about each tweet, conveniently packaged in a JSON object. In this example, we use the Python Twitter Tools module[5] to read and extract the hashtags found in tweets from the Twitter public sample stream API. Once running, our script will read new tweets from the Twitter sample stream until we hit 1,000 total public tweets. As we collect tweets, the relevant information we want will be stored in a Python dictionary. We then convert the dictionary into a Python DataFrame and gain access to the available Pandas methods for analysis.

In addition to the Twitter API and tweetstream, we will incorporate one of my favorite Python libraries, the Natural Language Toolkit (or NLTK). **NLTK** is a popular and well-supported library for problems in the natural-language processing domain. One of these domains is the study of n-grams, which are phrases of a certain regular term length. For example, a phrase with three separate words is called a 3-gram, and one with five terms would be called a 5-gram. NLTK is great for generating collections of n-grams from otherwise unstructured text blobs (such as tweets). It also provides excellent libraries for parsing text with regular expressions, word stemming, and much more.

Listing 12.5 provides an example of Twitter Streaming API statistics.

Listing 12.5   **Twitter Streaming API statistics example**

```
import json

from pandas import Series
from nltk.tokenize import RegexpTokenizer
from twitter import OAuth, TwitterStream
```

---

5. http://github.com/sixohsix/twitter

```python
# OAuth credentials to access the Twitter Streaming API
# Visit dev.twitter.com/apps to register an app
auth = OAuth(
    consumer_key='[your app consumer key]',
    consumer_secret='[your app consumer secret]',
    token='[your app access token]',
    token_secret='[your app access token secret]'
)

# Create an NLTK Tokenizer
tokenizer = RegexpTokenizer('#[a-zA-Z]\w+')



hashtags = {}
tweet_count = 0

# Connect to the Twitter Streaming API
twitter_stream = TwitterStream(auth=auth)
iterator = twitter_stream.statuses.sample()

for tweet in iterator:
  text = tweet.get('text')
  if text:
    words = tokenizer.tokenize(text)
    if len(words) > 0:
      for word in words:
        hashtags[word] = hashtags.get(word, 0) + 1
    tweet_count += 1
    if tweet_count % 100 == 0:
      print "Looked at %d tweets..." % tweet_count
    if tweet_count > 1000:
      break

# Print out a summary of Tweet statistics using Pandas
s = Series(hashtags)
print 'Top Hashtags in this dataset:'
print s.order(ascending=False)[0:15]

print 'Hashtag dataset statistics'
print s.describe()
```

We've combined a collection of different, powerful Python libraries and have built the beginning of a useful data-analysis application in just a few lines of code.

Working with Bad or Missing Records

Dealing with real data means that you will inevitably come across missing values. Pandas makes it easy to ignore, drop, or even fill in values that are missing. The isnull DataFrame method returns a Boolean when a cell contains no value. The fillna method enables you to replace missing values with some default. There are even interpolation methods that provide the ability to backfill missing data. Listing 12.6 provides examples.

Listing 12.6   **Pandas: Examples of working with broken data**

```
> from pandas import DataFrame, isnull
> from numpy import random

# Generate some random data; in this case, scores
> scores = DataFrame(random.random_integers(1,9,size=(5,2)),
                    columns=['Score 1','Score 2'])

    Score 1  Score 2
0         2        6
1         6        3
2         4        3

# Add a new column, setting all values to None (Null)
> scores['Score 3'] = None
# Change some Null cells to a new value
> scores['Score 3'][2] = 17
> scores['Score 3'][2] = 13

    Score 1  Score 2 Score 3
0         2        6    None
1         6        3    None
2         4        3      17

# Which cells are Null?
> isnull(scores)

   Score 1 Score 2 Score 3
0   False   False    True
1   False   False    True
2   False   False   False

# Find the mean; include or exclude columns
# that contain Null values

> scores.mean(skipna=False)
```

```
Score 1    6.2
Score 2    5.8

> scores.mean(skipna=True)

Score 1     6.2
Score 2     5.8
Score 3    15.0

# Fill in missing data explicitly
> scores['Score 3'].fillna(0)

0     0
1     0
2    17
3     0
4    13
```

Taken together, NumPy, SciPy, and Pandas can accomplish a lot of tasks that would normally be in the realm of what can be done in R. The underlying data structures are very performant, the syntax of these tools is very "Pythonic," and the code produced can be very readable.

For small scripting tasks using common computational algorithms, there's really not much of a difference between using R and Python. In general, R can be very useful for exploratory statistical tasks, and there's no question that there are far more ready-to-use modules already written in R for a large variety of tasks, especially uncommon computational domains.

In terms of scientific computing, Python excels when an application needs to grow into anything more than a simple exploratory or interactive script. As soon as an interactive test starts to become something requiring robust application development, it's hard to argue against using Python. Many statisticians and mathematicians have knowledge of R, but a programmer on your staff might be more familiar with Python than with a more domain-specific language.

iPython: Completing the Scientific Computing Tool Chain

It wouldn't be right to talk about Python's data-centric modules without mentioning **iPython**, a popular interactive Python shell that, over time, has blossomed into a full-fledged scientific-computing environment. After winning the 2012 Free Software Foundation award for his work, iPython's creator Dr. Fernando Perez stated that the project started as "sort of a hybrid of an interactive Python console and a Unix shell, but it has grown into a set of components for scientific computing from interactive exploration to parallel computing, publication, and education."[6] In fact, iPython has seen quite a lot of growth among scientific users, and as a result the project has also been awarded a grant by the Sloan Foundation to help drive development of more collaborative and interactive visualization tools.

iPython adds an important tooling layer to the standard Python shell, including features such as autocomplete and the ability to access interactive help. It's very easy to incorporate existing Python scripts into iPython's interactive workflow. iPython also has an excellent notebook mode that provides iPython's features through an interactive Web application. When starting up iPython with the **notebook** command, a Web server will be launched directly on the workstation, and a browser-based interface becomes available on a local URL. Python commands and output can be run directly in the browser window, and best of all, these notebooks can be saved, exported, and shared with others.

Parallelizing iPython Using a Cluster

As we've mentioned before, one of the advantages of distributed-processing frameworks such as Hadoop is the ability to wrangle multiple machines to help solve large data problems quickly. For many people, Hadoop is the de facto method of running such tasks, but it's not always the best fit for the job. Although Hadoop is becoming more and more automated, there's often quite a lot of administrative overhead when initializing and running a Hadoop cluster, not to mention a great deal of work in writing the workflow code (see Chapter 9, "Building Data Transformation Workflows with Pig and Cascading," for more on Hadoop workflow tools). Often, all we want to do is simply farm a task out to a number of machines or even a set of processors on a multicore machine with as little effort as possible.

iPython makes it easy to run tasks in parallel, by coordinating running Python commands across a distributed network of machines (which iPython calls **engines**). iPython takes advantage of the very fast message-passing library called ØMQ (a.k.a. ZeroMQ) to coordinate messaging between multiple machines. Even if you don't have a cluster of machines available, you can observe some of the advantages of parallel computing on a multicore local machine. As with Hadoop, it's possible to test iPython scripts locally before extending them to run across a cluster of machines. Even better, iPython enables you to run these scripts interactively.

Let's look at a simple example meant to tax the CPU a bit. In Listing 12.7, we use the NumPy random package to generate a list of 1000 integers between 1,000,000 and 20,000,000, and we'll try to identify if they are prime numbers by brute force. Essentially, we will divide (using a modulo operation) each number by every integer from two up to the square root of the number itself. If the resulting remainder is zero, the number will be returned as not prime. This solution basically requires thousands of large division calculations per potential prime. Our first try will be a simple nondistributed solution. Next, we will demonstrate a solution using iPython's parallel library.

---

6. www.fsf.org/news/2012-free-software-award-winners-announced-2

Listing 12.7   **Identifying prime numbers**

```
# prime_finder.py: nonparallel prime-number finder
import numpy as np

# Generate some random large integers
np.random.seed(seed=12345)
possible_primes = np.random.random_integers(1000000, 20000000,
    1000).tolist()

def prime_check(num):
    # Check all integers between 2 and num
    for test in range(2, num):
        # Divisible by test number?
      if  num % test == 0:
            return False
    return True

def find_primes(potential_list):
  for number in potential_list:
    print '%d is prime? %r' % (number, prime_check(number))

find_primes(possible_primes)

time ipython prime_finder.py
17645405 is prime? False
19173348 is prime? False
3993577 is prime? False
7164478 is prime? False
4555874 is prime? False
8708189 is prime? False
14679361 is prime? True
16363190 is prime? False
5246897 is prime? False
9002190 is prime? False
# ... etc ...
1667625154 is prime? False
time output:
real    0m9.249s
```

Even on a fast workstation, running the code in Listing 12.7 will take a few seconds. On a fairly new laptop, the example above took over nine seconds to run over only 1000 large numbers. Although the problem is partially CPU bound, this data challenge is one that can easily be made to run in parallel, so it makes more sense to farm this out to multiple processing cores.

Even if you don't have a cluster of machines available, you can observe some performance gains using a local machine with a multicore processor. In the following example, we take advantage of iPython's *direct interface*, which makes it easy to apply a Python function to a collection of objects in parallel. The DirectView object exposes a map function that works a lot like the standard Python map, applying the same function to each potential prime number. The difference here is that iPython can farm out the prime-number checks to any core available rather than trying to run them in sequence.

To start a new cluster, create an iPython profile to hold the configuration information needed for the local test cluster. Simply run iPython's `profile create` command, and then use the `ipcluster` command to start the cluster engines (see Listing 12.8). It's also very easy to activate local parallel engines using the iPython notebook with controls under the cluster tab.

To augment our original prime-number script, we will start by importing the Client class from the *IPython.parallel* package. This will enable our script to connect to the individual engines in our running cluster. Because our engines do not have access to the prime-number-checking functions that we've defined in their namespace, we use the `dview.push` command to add them to all engines. Now we pass our prime-number-reporting function as a parameter in our client's `dataview.map` method with our list of potential prime numbers as the other input. iPython's cluster-management API will handle the complexities of our parallel computation automatically. See Listing 12.8 for the code.

Listing 12.8 **Parallelizing a computationally intensive task**

```
# Create a new profile to hold parallel configuration
> ipython profile create --parallel -profile=testprofile
# Start a cluster with 4 engines using the testprofile configuration
> ipcluster start --n=4 --profile=testprofile



# parallel_prime_finder.py: iPython parallel prime-number finder
from IPython.parallel import Client

import numpy as np

# Create an iPython parallel client instance and DataView
rc = Client()
dview = rc[:]

# Check if an integer is prime
def prime_check(num):
    # Check all integers between 2 and num
    for test in range(2, int(num**0.5) + 1):
        # Divisible by test number?
        if num % test == 0:
            return False
    return True
```

```
# Returns a message about number being checked as prime or not
def find_primes(number):
  #For each number in potential_list:
  print number
  return '%d is prime? %r' % (number, prime_check(number))


# Add our functions to the namespace of our running engines
dview.push({'find_primes': find_primes})
dview.push({'prime_check': prime_check})


# Generate some random large integers
np.random.seed(seed=12345)
possible_primes = np.random.random_integers(1000000, 20000000, 10).tolist()


# Run the functions on our cluster
results = dview.map(find_primes,possible_primes)


# Print the results to std out
for result in results.get():
  print result


# time ipython prime_finder.py
# Result:
# 17645405 is prime? False
# ...
# 1667625154 is prime? False
# time output:
# real 0m1.711s
```

On my multicore-processor laptop, the parallelized version using six engines took only just over 1.7 seconds, a significant speed improvement. If you have access to a cluster of multicore machines, you could possibly speed this type of brute force application up even more, with some additional configuration work. Remember that at some point the problem becomes IO-bound, and latency in the network may cause some performance issues.

Summary

R's functional programming model and massive collection of libraries has made it the de facto open-source science and statistics language. At the same time, Python has come of age as a productive programming language for memory-intensive data applications. The sheer number of Python developers and the ease of development give Python a unique advantage over other methods of building CPU-bound data applications. Python can often be the easiest way to solve a wide variety of data challenges in the shortest amount of time. Building an application using a more general-purpose programming language provides useful benefits, such as access to a suite of well-supported networking libraries, Web application stacks, testing and development tools, and, most importantly, a large pool of knowledgeable developers.

NumPy provides Python with a fast multidimensional array data type along with broadcasting functions. NumPy also provides a strong foundation for other data-analytics modules such as SciPy. The Pandas library adds an additional layer of tooling for common data-analysis tasks, working with time series data, dealing with missing data, and much more. Pandas's DataFrame, inspired by a similar data type available in R, is very flexible and provides a large number of useful data methods.

Finally, iPython provides a useful interactive and collaborative environment for scientific computing. Taken as a whole, the tools provided by modules such as NumPy, SciPy, Pandas, iPython, and a number of other data libraries bridge the gap between interactive data-analysis workflows and more robust programming models. It's possible to interactively analyze data from the command line and then share and develop this work collaboratively. Although the tools available to the Python community lack some of the features and scientific models available for R or MATLAB, Python's advantages, along with the very active developer community, make it an excellent choice for many data-analytics challenges.

VII

Looking Ahead

## 13

When to Build, When to Buy, When to Outsource

Throughout this book, we've explored the best choices of technologies for a variety of use cases. We've taken a look at systems that collect data at a rapid pace and scale up accordingly. We have covered strategies for collecting large amounts of data in real time and for asking questions about this data quickly. We've even looked at ways to store and share huge amounts of data.

As with any highly innovative and cutting-edge technology, the range of software for dealing with data challenges exists in a variety of states for both development and adoption. This places people who are trying to solve data problems in a bind. Does the solution require investment in hardware administration and software development, or does the answer mean purchasing services from a commercial data-solution vendor?

There is no universally correct answer to this question, but we can look at common patterns to help inform us of the right choices. In this chapter, we will take our earlier principles of choosing just the right data technology—understanding the use case, planning for scale, and avoiding managing infrastructure when possible—to help understand when to buy versus when to build.

Overlapping Solutions

Here we go again! With each new technology revolution, an age-old IT problem rears its head: Should we build our own solution, or should we buy an existing product? The build versus buy conundrum appears so often that a whole range of consultants and methodologies exist to inform decision makers about the best course of action. For those working with new technologies that fall under the Big Data umbrella, this question is coming up more and more often. Although open-source software has often been the driver of new innovations in data technology, more and more commercial products are appearing. Simultaneously, the growth of cloud computing has also provided the ability to use hosted virtual servers instead of traditional server- or appliance-based solutions. Unlike other technology cycles, in the data world there's an added wrinkle that complicates the decision process greatly: the frequent need to deal with hardware.

Data scientists must be proficient with a number of different technologies to gain value from data. We are still in the early days of data-science technology. Open-source software has helped large-scale data technology become more accessible, but as is the nature of this type of software, there are currently many overlapping projects in various states of maturity. In a more mature market, such as the traditional relational database industry, there are a huge number of commercial products available to choose from. However, the world of MapReduce frameworks and nonrelational databases hasn't quite reached the same point yet.

Another characteristic of a more mature technology market is the presence of a pool of customers who feel that there is little risk in choosing various technologies. Currently in the data space, there are many early adopters who will try just about anything and others who are simply trying to make sense of the hype. This leads to some organizations taking the plunge and building solutions using whichever open-source software is available while others wait on the sidelines as spectators.

The current state of data technologies mirrors the multifaceted skill sets that data scientists are required to have. Some technologies require infrastructure skills, including tasks such as hardware monitoring and log management. In other engineering professions, proficiency with a particular type of software is an important skill. Sometimes, a strong theoretical background is the primary skill needed for success. In the world of large-scale data analysis, often all three are expected.

Some of the technologies featured in this book are developer tools; they are designed to be used to build other software. Other technologies we cover are essentially interfaces aimed at data analysts, not developers. And yet others are a combination of the two—requiring analysts to write scripts to define systems that process data.

Data technology is currently in a state of flux, with different aspects of these three pillars maturing at different rates. As a data scientist, it's perfectly reasonable to find yourself in a situation in which there is no obvious solution, whether commercial or not, for solving a data challenge.

Another consequence of the organic growth of data technology is that different software projects can often address very similar use cases. A great example in this space is the choice of R versus Python for scientific computing (technologies that we cover in Chapter 11, "Using R with Large Datasets," and Chapter 12, "Building Analytics Workflows Using Python and Pandas"). R is an extremely popular programming language for statistical and mathematical computing. Python is an extremely popular language for general-purpose programming. Both R and Python can be used for scientific and statistical computing, but currently R is more mature in this space and is more likely to have a greater number of available modules and libraries for specific tasks. Both can be used for general-purpose programming, but it's difficult to argue that R would make a better choice than Python for this purpose. Choosing one over the other depends on a range of factors, including your available personnel. In addition, within the statistical space, there are numerous commercial software packages available, such as SAS or MATLAB, further complicating software decision making.

In Chapter 9, "Building Data Transformation Workflows with Pig and Cascading," we took a look at how to build transformation pipelines with Hadoop. Here is another case of using overlapping technologies: One can choose to build a pipeline solution programmatically using Cascading or stick to a higher-level abstraction by using Apache Pig. Both technologies were developed independently and cover some of the same use cases. A software company building a data processing application on top of Hadoop would obviously use Cascading, whereas a data analyst is more likely to use a tool such as Pig.

In the midst of this flux, developers, analysts, and data scientists all have practical problems to solve and rarely have unlimited time or money to solve them. In some cases, we'll want to pay someone else do the hard work; in others, we will need to dig in and build our own solutions. Let's take a look at some basic guidelines to help us figure out how to navigate the constantly evolving data landscape.

Understanding Your Data Problem

Let's revisit a central theme of this book, which is to understand the data problem before working out a solution. It seems obvious, but when working with difficult data problems many pitfalls can be avoided by flushing out both the end goals and the audience you are trying to serve.

When deciding on what to build in-house and what to outsource, business strategists often talk about understanding your organization's "core competencies." Technology strategist and author Geoffrey Moore, well known for his work on innovation and technology adoption cycles, has written a great deal about this concept. In Moore's view, organizations should concentrate energy on building core technologies—those that help an organization differentiate itself from others.[1] In contrast, other activities are "contextual"; they can help the organization maintain parity with everyone else, but will not help it distinguish itself. The conventional wisdom around this concept is that an organization should devote energy to building unique technology that provides competitive differentiation. While doing this, they should outsource other technology problems to outside vendors. This concept is key for small organizations trying to focus on work that will help them gain a foothold in the market. Why administer a mail server when it's much easier and likely cheaper overall to pay for a Web-based email service?

Although this idea comes from specific, corporate business management cases, the concept is not just for corporations. A small research organization, an academic unit, a game startup, and a data journalist each has a particular core focus. In each of these cases, it's likely that the user would want the technology to get out of the way as much as possible. Even the hackers who love to dabble in the latest and greatest (and believe me, I know how fun it can be) have deadlines to meet and budgets to stay below.

The key lesson here is to understand whether the data challenge you are facing is one that you *must* solve yourself or one that is commonplace enough that someone has

---

1. Moore, Geoffrey A. "Managing Inertia in Your Enterprise." Chap. 11 in *Dealing with Darwin: How Great Companies Innovate at Every Phase of Their Evolution.* New York: Portfolio, 2008.

already built a solution. Because of the rapid innovation and experimentation in the data-technology field, the idea of sticking to core competencies is not always so cut and dry. In the case of Big Data technology, there hasn't been much time for industry best practices to be fully fleshed out, and early adopters are still coming up with success stories. If data technology that you are evaluating is a core aspect of your organization that will help provide differentiation, then building solutions in-house might be the right choice. In contrast, organizations that care more about data technology getting out of the way should start by attempting to purchase a solution rather than devoting time to building one.

Some commercial software vendors provide large, scalable databases with support personnel, hardware, and training for a premium fee. However, if you know that all you need to do is process a large amount of last year's sales data for a year-end report, it might be more reasonable to stay flexible and build a solution using available open-source technologies. If you have determined that you only need to collect some data and query it quickly, then it is probably a sign that you should be looking at a solution built with an open-source technology such as Hadoop and Hive, or Spark and Shark.

In my experience, there are three major considerations when trying to determine whether to build your own solution or buy. The first is the most obvious: What is the cost of solving the problem? This factor is complex; the cost of maintaining software can be hard to predict, and the ability to execute on the solution is highly dependent on organizational personnel. Another factor is how to deal with future scalability. How will the solution you develop change as data volumes grow? Will the system need to be completely rebuilt if either data volume or throughput changes? Finally, there is understanding the audience: For whom is the solution ultimately being developed? Consider an organization trying to analyze a large amount of internal data. Later on, if the same organization needs to provide external access to some of this data for its customers, it may need to deploy a Web-based dashboard or an API. The technologies needed to provide a solution for this new audience may require a completely different set of technologies.

A Playbook for the Build versus Buy Problem

Some of the concepts and technologies of distributed data systems are still in their early stages of adoption. There is not yet a huge amount of literature that describes popularly accepted best practices for making decisions about data technologies. Furthermore, many of the innovative technologies that have been around the longest, such as the Apache Hadoop project, are already starting to see disruptive competition from newer frameworks such as Spark.

There are many ways you can approach the problem of building solutions versus buying. In the currently murky world of large-scale data challenges, there are some patterns that I have observed that work well to help navigate the process of evaluating build versus buy scenarios. First, evaluate your current investments in data technologies and infrastructure with a particular understanding of the personnel and culture of your organization. Next, gain some insight into actual pain points by investing in proof-of-concept projects. Finally, go through the process of understanding potential pitfalls when you need to scale-up data processing tasks.

What Have You Already Invested In?

Before you do anything, understand the technologies in which you've already made investments. Do you already have access to an internal data center? As we've seen, there are many advantages to using clusters of virtualized servers in the cloud over physical hardware in house. This includes flexibility in pricing models and the ability to expand or contract the number of nodes as necessary. These advantages might not be valid if your organization already has made an investment in physical hardware and maintenance.

Your organizational culture will also help dictate which data technologies you ulti-mately use. Is your group already proficient in using a particular database or platform? If so, consider sticking with the technology that your team knows best, even if it is not commonly accepted as the most scalable or cost-effective solution. An example of this approach can be found in the posts of the *ServerFault* blog, home of popular Web site Stack Exchange's engineering team. In one post, entitled "Why Stack Exchange Isn't in the Cloud," Kyle Brandt explains, "We don't just love programming and our Web applications. We get excited learning about computer hardware, operating systems, history, computer games, and new innovations."[2] The post goes on to explain that the entire engineering team has the skills and interest to maintain hardware, and this core competency helps determine what they do. Obviously, the Stack Exchange team has the experience and organizational culture to handle the tasks and optimize the costs of infrastructure management. Other organizations may not have this level of expertise or passion for handling hardware.

Starting Small

You've clearly defined your use case and your audience, and you've scoped out your existing resources. Now it's time to collect and crunch those large, valuable datasets—right?

A common red herring in the world of data science is to immediately start big. It's dangerous to latch on to a trendy Big Data technology to solve a problem that could just as easily have been approached with traditional database tools or desktop software. Organizations are feeling the pressure to derive value from large datasets. The Apache Hadoop project has been hyped to no end by technology media as the be-all and end-all accessible solution to a variety of data use cases. However, the Hadoop framework, which provides an accessible way to distribute MapReduce-based jobs over a cluster of servers, is not always the best solution for the job.

When trying to make a decision about software, one strategy that often pays off is to build proof-of-concept solutions using small samples of data. In doing so, the goal

---

2. http://blog.serverfault.com/2011/11/17/why-stack-exchange-isn%E2%80%99t-in-the-cloud/

is to remove as many variables as possible to try to evaluate the pain points in building a system from scratch. If there are prohibitive factors involved in deploying a solution for a small subset of data, then certainly a larger data challenge should be solved using a commercial solution.

Proof-of-concept projects can even be handled on single workstations. Processing data using scripting tools such as Python, sed, and awk on a local machine can sometimes be all that's needed. Many of the distributed-data tools featured in this book, such as Apache Hadoop, can be run in single-server mode locally on a workstation. Even better, much of the same code used for defining batch processes can be reused on a cluster environment.

Planning for Scale

From your explorations with a proof of concept, you might have gotten some ideas about the types of skills necessary to build your tools with existing open-source technologies. Perhaps, for example, you now have a plan for analyzing the last month's worth of data you have collected. What happens when you want to analyze all the data you've collected for the past five years? Will the technology that you are evaluating be easy to use when data sizes grow? Will you need additional hardware, personnel, or organizational practices in the event of additional data growth?

A common pattern when dealing with ever-growing data sizes is to start with a familiar, mature technology and then face the need to radically change that as data sizes grow. An example is beginning a data collection and processing challenge using a well-known relational database (such as MySQL) on a single server. Then, as the problems of scale begin to appear, the solution must be moved to an entirely different infrastructure, often involving a nonrelational database. Depending on the problem being solved, some commercially available solutions become prohibitively expensive at scale or may not even be performant over certain data sizes.

Some database designs lend themselves well to being distributed across multiple machines (see Chapter 3, "Building a NoSQL-Based Web App to Collect Crowd-Sourced Data"). However, the amount of effort required to actually implement them can be nontrivial. In such cases, it may make sense to purchase the services of a cloud-based nonrelational database solution (such as Amazon's Dynamo DB) rather than invest in the effort to consistently administer an ever-growing cluster of Redis machines. In summary, never invest in a course of action before having a plan for dealing with data as it grows. If working with a commercial solution, determine the vendors' recommended limits, and make sure there is a method for working with additional technologies if there is a possibility for your data challenge to overwhelm these limits.

My Own Private Data Center

The state of the art in large-scale data analysis software is often based on distributed systems of many servers deployed directly on physical hardware or as virtual machines and linked together in a network. As network communication can often be the bottleneck in these systems, latency may be reduced by having the machines in close proximity to one another. This means we need to have direct control of the computer hardware itself to solve our problem. We will also need space, plenty of power, a backup power supply, security, and cooling systems. In other words, we need to build and maintain our own data center.

Or do we? Computing is on its way to becoming a utility, and in the future, a lot of the computing resources we consume will be available in much the same way as water and power: metered service right out of the tap. For many software applications, most of the heavy lifting will take place on platforms or virtual machines with the bulk of processing taking place far away in large data centers. This trend is already very visible on the Web and with mobile applications. From Yelp to Netflix to your favorite social games, how many apps on your smartphone are essentially just interfaces to cloud-based services?

Unfortunately, many hurdles must be overcome before the cloud can become the de facto home of data processing. A common mantra of large data processing is to make sure that processing takes place as close to the data as possible. This concept is what makes the design of Hadoop so attractive; data is generally distributed across server nodes from which processing takes place. In order to use cloud systems for the processing of large amounts of in-house data, data would need to be moved using the relatively small bandwidth of the Internet. Similarly, data generated by an application hosted on one cloud provider might need to be moved to another cloud service for processing. These steps take time and reduce the overall performance of the system in comparison to a solution in which the data is accessible in a single place. Most importantly, there are a range of security, compliance, and regulatory concerns that need to be addressed when moving data from one place to another.

The disadvantages of using a public cloud include an inability to make changes to the infrastructure. Also, the loss of control might even result in greater costs overall. Maintaining hardware can also provide some flexibility in wringing every last bit of performance from the system. For some applications, this might be a major concern.

Currently, it's possible to access cloud computing resources that are maintained in off-site data centers as a service. These are sometimes referred to using the slightly misleading term *private clouds*. It is also possible to lease dedicated servers in data centers that don't share hardware with other customers. These private clouds can often provide more control over the underlying hardware, leading to the potential for higher performance data processing.

A potential advantage of not dealing with physical infrastructure is that more time can be devoted to data analysis. If your company is building a Web application, why divert engineering resources to dealing with all the administrative overhead necessary to administer the security and networking needed to run a cluster of computers? In reality, depending on the type of application being built, managing clusters of virtual server instances in the cloud might be just as time consuming as managing physical hardware. To truly avoid the overhead of managing infrastructure, the best solution is to use *data processing as a service* tools (discussed later in this chapter).

Infrastructure can always be a major investment. Perhaps the most important advantage to using virtualized public-cloud providers for distributed-data applications is the ability to use a bare minimum of processing without investing in fixed hardware costs. Even if the data processing and latency can't be absolutely controlled, it may be more important to keep costs and maintenance time down. Let someone else do this work for you while you concentrate on solving your data challenge.

There are many cases in which building and maintaining your own hardware is advantageous. The time it takes to export a great deal of in-house data into a cloud system (or even from one cloud provider to another) can often be prohibitive. Control over higher-performance applications might be a useful consideration. If the cost of maintaining both hardware and staff are acceptable for your organization, it can also be possible to achieve much better performance-per-price characteristics with in-house hardware. With the right administrative expertise, the total cost of ownership might be lower as well. In most other cases, it makes more sense to do whatever it takes to avoid dealing with the management of hardware.

For many data processing applications, it is advisable to avoid buying or leasing physical infrastructure whenever possible. The fixed costs of investing in physical hardware are so great that this solution should only be used when necessary. For distributed-data applications, always first consider using virtualized systems on a public cloud. Even when starting a large-scale data project, building a proof of concept using cloud infrastructure is a good way to test the application without over-investing in hardware.

Understand the Costs of Open-Source

As is commonly said about the open-source software communities, the English language doesn't have separate words for "free" as in "freedom" and "free" as in "free of charge." Open-source software is always free the way speech is free—but this doesn't mean that it will always cost nothing to implement. Although it can often be free, as in "free beer," there are always costs associated with doing things yourself.

A common criticism (or rather, fear) about open-source software projects focuses on the myth that there are no support options. This is sometimes true, especially around bleeding-edge technologies. However, for more mature projects, the developer and user communities around popular open-source data technologies is vibrant. The *Hadoop* tag on popular tech question-and-answer site StackOverflow has well over 6,000 questions on its own, which doesn't even include the hundreds of tagged posts for related technologies such as "map-reduce," "hive," and "hdfs." Similarly, companies such as Red Hat have shown that it is possible to build viable business models around support and training involving open-source solutions. The popular open-source document database MongoDB is supported by the company 10gen, which provides enterprise support for a fee.

Using open-source software can also be technically rewarding. The experience of working through installation, use, and even modification of open-source code needed to solve data problems can enhance overall engineering skills.

Despite the advantages of using open-source solutions for solving data challenges, many nonobvious costs arise in the course of building-out solutions. One is simply the time necessary for members of your organization to research and deploy a robust solution.

The flexibility and cutting-edge features found in many open-source data-software packages means that your engineering teams can move quickly to solve problems for which commercial product solutions are either nonexistent or prohibitively expensive. The major takeaway is to strive to keep your organization honest about the total costs of developing in-house solutions using open-source technology, including development time, salaries, and the cost of using resources that can better be used somewhere else.

Everything as a Service

Organizations are quickly embracing cloud technologies to solve a wide range of problems. Cloud-based solutions for CRM and accounting software and business productivity programs for tasks such as email and word processing are becoming more commonplace. Many businesses are starting to view cloud-based business productivity tools as a primary platform, falling back to more traditional in-house deployments as a secondary option.

Avoiding physical infrastructure investments is one thing, but having someone manage scalable software services can be even better. As organizations figure out the best ways to solve data challenges, companies are emerging to provide repeatable solutions for new customers. There are already many examples of this phenomenon happening right now. Cloud-based services, such as Amazon's Redshift and Google's BigQuery, provide completely managed services for tasks that until recently were handled by software deployed using expensive in-house appliances. Hosted batch-processing services are also being developed, as companies are exploring how to reduce the administrative barriers to frameworks such as Hadoop.

In the future, Internet speeds will inevitably get faster, commodity hardware will get cheaper, and more organizations will find business opportunities in solving repeatable problems. Where will all this lead? The most likely scenario is that, eventually, a majority of common data-processing tasks will be done using tools that provide various types of data analytics as a service. As the growth of utility computing continues, this trend should make large-scale data collection, processing, and analysis more accessible.

Summary

As organizations find new ways to derive value from their data, the number of commercial and open-source data technologies is rapidly growing to provide solutions. The most accessible innovations in data software have come from the vibrant and flexible open-source community. However, the organic growth of open-source data solutions has resulted in a variety of tools that address overlapping use cases. Some tools are specifically geared toward developers for building new software but are not the right fit for analysts. Other tools require a great deal of hardware-infrastructure management, whether for virtual or physical machines. This makes for an environment that is difficult to navigate. People looking for data solutions must accept the reality that the current state of ambiguity around best practices is normal. Similarly, in the current landscape, it may not be possible to purchase commercial-software solutions to solve every use case. In many cases, there will be a need to build parts of a data pipeline.

Large data challenges are often best solved using distributed software that runs on a cluster of commodity hardware. Examples of this type of technology include the open-source Apache Hadoop framework and many available distributed databases. Building an in-house cluster of physical machines can provide good performance per cost for some applications, but the overall cost may be prohibitive when maintenance and software administration are included.

For many solutions, it makes more sense to use clusters of virtual servers hosted by an off-site data center. This can take the form of either a *private* cloud, featuring dedicated leased hardware, or a *public* cloud, which is typically a collection of virtualized servers running on underlying hardware shared by many customers. Both of these cloud models can be more cost effective than managing physical hardware in house. The public cloud model is especially useful for organizations that are in the process of evaluating new software or scaling up capacity. Distributed computing instances can be grown or shrunk with demand, helping to keep costs manageable. As a rule, avoid dealing with physical hardware investments whenever possible.

In the IT world, there are many guidelines and best practices for determining when to make an investment in an existing product. Often dedicated hardware or software solutions may not even be necessary to solve a particular data problem. In order to determine whether your organization has the skills necessary to build and maintain an in-house data solution, start by implementing a small proof-of-concept project. If the audience for your data solution consists mainly of analysts within your organization, look to buy solutions that focus on ease of use and stability. On the other hand, if solving the data challenge may provide a considerable competitive advantage, consider focusing first on evaluating the potential for building custom solutions.

Reduce the number of variables necessary to understand the requirements for building a solution. If your organization is considering building a solution to cope with a data challenge, it can be effective to scope the evaluation effort using a small subset of data and a single machine proof-of-concept. Next, consider the potential challenges that will come from scale. Some software solutions have the ability to be used at greater and greater scale, but this may take a great deal of engineering effort to implement.

Overall, the software tools available for collecting, processing, and analyzing large datasets are in a state of flux, and best practices and common patterns are still being developed. As the field matures, look for more examples of data solutions being offered as hosted services.

14

The Future: Trends in Data Technology

An exciting and inevitable future is approaching, and it's no exaggeration to say that the future will be fueled by data. Despite political and economic roadblocks, billions of people around the world have gained access to the Internet. As of 2013, the estimated number of Internet-connected mobile devices surpassed that of desktop computers worldwide. Although the growing number of mobile computing devices is by itself significant, consider the fact that we tend to use our smartphones a bit differently than we do a traditional PC. Many keep phones continuously on their person and active at all times (how many of you use your phone as an alarm clock?). Wearable computers, although still in their infancy, are coming soon as well.

Mobile devices are becoming ubiquitous, are often tied to a user's identity, and are always connected to the network. Yet managing and securing personal data on a local device can be difficult; who hasn't lost data due to hardware failure? Constant network connections enable mobile devices to offload processing and storage to cloud services and essentially serve as a user's interface to the network itself. Offloading both data and processing to the network also helps to enable device independence, meaning that any device can be used to access an authenticated user's data. As many technology thinkers have predicted, this pattern is not unlike how we consume electricity from our wall sockets. In other words, computing is quickly becoming a utility.

The growth and adoption of technologies that contribute to this pattern of utility computing is accelerating quickly. Massive social networks such as Facebook, Twitter, Tumblr, and many others have shown that users are willing to spend a great deal of time generating online content to maintain social interactions. New innovations in all-electronic payment systems, self-driving cars, and consumer devices with always-on network connections are also on the horizon. In order to be effective, these devices will need to communicate with users, central servers, and each other. Data that is generated by these devices will be used for aggregation, analysis, and, ultimately, improving applications and decision making.

Whether future inventions will be as groundbreaking as smartphone-based Star Trek universal translators or as questionable as Internet-enabled toasters, the common enabler for this inevitable, ubiquitous computing future is data. More specifically, this vision requires that the huge amounts of data can be collected, stored, processed, and analyzed in a useful way.

As a result, anyone who is involved with any aspect of data-processing technology currently finds themselves in the middle of a very exciting but confusing era. To grok Big Data means to have an awareness of the upcoming potential of the data generated in the era of utility computing. Web-scale technology companies, including Yahoo!, Google, Amazon, Facebook, and many others, have driven early innovations in distributed data processing, such as the MapReduce framework. Web companies were forced to innovate in order to be successful. However, these use cases are just a precursor to the potential data tidal wave that is coming soon.

Future predictions of technology are always doomed to face the judgment of retrospect; there is a disproven urban legend that IBM CEO Thomas J. Watson once said, "I think there is a world market for about five computers." Current trends in data are driven by an inevitable need to provide easy easy-to-use tools to deal with growing amounts of data being generated by both people and machines connected to the ever-growing network.

Hadoop: The Disruptor and the Disrupted

"Big Data is Falling into the Trough of Disillusionment" reads the title of a blog post by Gartner Research Director Svetlana Sicular.[1] In her post, Sicular claims to use a methodology called the "Gartner Hype Cycle curve" to postulate that, as of January 2013, comments from a recent Hadoop conference indicate growing disdain for the promise of Big Data.

Perhaps the most interesting thing about this blog post was neither the sensationalist title nor the amusement that comes from pondering the veracity of the "Gartner Hype Cycle." Sicular brings up examples that solely revolve around Hadoop. The Apache Hadoop project has become synonymous in the media with Big Data and for good reason. The Hadoop ecosystem is huge, and there are many well-funded companies who support its tools, including Cloudera, Hortonworks, MapR, and others. Established database giants such as IBM and Oracle are mentioning Hadoop more and more. Countless companies are working to improve, extend, and profit from Hadoop's reach.

Despite both the hype and success, Hadoop is not the be-all and end-all of large-scale data-processing technologies. The sentiment expressed in Sicular's blog post points toward some of the deficiencies that Apache Hadoop has in covering all aspects of data collection, storage, and processing. Hadoop provides the ability to distribute storage

---

1. http://blogs.gartner.com/svetlana-sicular/big-data-is-falling-into-the-trough-of-disillusionment/

and processing tasks across a scalable number of separate machines or virtual servers. The ecosystem of tools built with Hadoop can provide a very favorable value proposition depending on the use case. For some applications, Hadoop enables great performance per dollar for data-processing tasks. For others, Hadoop can be the only way to accomplish some warehousing and querying tasks economically. Others see Hadoop as a promising technology that lacks the enterprise features necessary to merit investment.

Consider the use of Hadoop with the open-source Hive package as a data-warehousing solution. Hadoop excels at flexibility, but sometimes this comes at the cost of performance for specific applications. Hive enables users to turn SQL-like queries on data stored in a Hadoop cluster into MapReduce jobs that return the query result. Although MapReduce can be flexible for expressing many different kinds of data-transformation and processing tasks, this is not always the most efficient architecture for running aggregate queries. Furthermore, as it stands, the Hadoop ecosystem currently lacks many of the enterprise features found in traditional data warehouse solutions such as reliability and failover, automated backups, and interoperability with existing filesystems.

In other words, Hadoop's MapReduce-based processing model has been overloaded to address data problems that might better be solved in other ways. This does not mean that Hadoop-based data tools are not also benefitting from feature convergence that we will discuss later in this chapter. For example, Facebook, Hortonworks, and other companies are sponsoring projects to help speed up the performance of Hive queries.

However, users are starting to take a look at other data technologies that don't depend specifically on the Hadoop framework. Consider the growth of new **analytical databases**, designed specifically to provide very fast aggregate query results over large databases. Often these analytical tools use columnar-based data structures along with distributed, in-memory processing that completely sidesteps the MapReduce paradigm. These include projects inspired by Google's Dremel, including Cloudera's Impala and MapR's Drill.

Using the ecosystem of tools built on top of Hadoop as solutions to data challenges can be both a great enabler and a potential dead end. In any case, one of the amazing results of the popularity of Hadoop is that it has changed the conversation about the accessibility of large-scale data processing. Businesses no longer have an excuse for not being able to store and process massive amounts of data, and entrenched database vendors are starting to pay attention to the groundswell. In terms of technology culture, Hadoop has empowered users to gain access to some of the technology previously available only to large Internet companies or huge organizations with a great deal of resources.

Everything in the Cloud

I've often met people who consider Internet applications, such as Web-based email, as just another reincarnation of the days when it was commonplace for users to share time on a central, powerful mainframe. This sentiment is accurate in superficial ways. Certainly the concept of using the network to access data and then processing it somewhere else is the same, but dig a bit deeper and you'll notice that there is something much more profound happening.

Like Big Data, the term *cloud computing* is a buzzword that is often used to refer to any number of concepts, from Web applications to Internet services to virtualized servers. The real difference between what is known in the mainframe world as time-sharing and cloud computing is that, rather than being tied to a single computer across a network, users are increasingly served by a dynamic computing fabric. No longer is user data tied to a single, powerful machine; data is sharded, replicated across many data centers, and made redundant to protect against catastrophic failure.

Security maven Bruce Schneier once wrote, "The old time-sharing model arose because computers were expensive and hard to maintain. Modern computers and networks are drastically cheaper, but they're still hard to maintain."[2] Indeed, managing machines can be challenging. Individual machines break, and maintaining hardware can be expensive and time consuming. Network access to an account on a single mainframe was once the only way to achieve powerful computing resources because the mainframe itself was very expensive. Now the common administrative challenges are being abstracted, and specialists in massive data centers focus on security, connectivity, and data integrity. Computing as a utility is possible because economies of scale and access to the network have made compute cycles very cheap.

A decade into the 21st century has brought out claims by tech punditry that the PC is dead. The reality is a bit more complicated. In an era of device independence, a user, whether on a laptop, on a phone, in the car, or at check-in at an airport kiosk can access the same data connected to their identity. An average consumer can find a great number of conveniences from utility computing, such as not having to worry about the integrity of data on their local hardware and easy sharing of documents.

User data is already moving off of local machines and into utility computing environments. As this goes, so does the need to process data locally. Until networking speeds become faster (and they may never be fast enough), it's most efficient to process data where it lives. In many cases, data is already living in the data center thanks to the growth of Web and mobile applications.

Moreover, many Web applications require huge compute clouds to function at all. Search engines like Google use massive data-processing algorithms to rank every public page on the Internet. The social graphs that power LinkedIn and Facebook could not be built without the huge amounts of user data being generated everyday. The cloud is hungry, and it eats data. As a result of all of this, there is a great deal of interest in Web services that live completely in the cloud. Data processing as a service is a trend we will see more and more of as the field matures.

---

2. www.schneier.com/blog/archives/2009/06/cloud_computing.html

The Rise and Fall of the Data Scientist

When a reputable business magazine proclaims the "Sexiest Job of the 21st Century," it is certain to attract attention. So it happened in 2012, in a *Harvard Business Review* article written by Thomas H. Davenport and Greylock Partners' data scientist in residence, D.J. Patil.[3] According to the authors, this sexy job is—surprise!—the data scientist. Despite the assumed sex appeal, some analysts predict that demand for this role will outpace supply. A McKinsney report claims that by 2018, the United States will be short by at least 140,000 of these sexy data scientists. Who are these important, fetching people, and why do we need so many?

Like many technological buzzwords, **data scientist** can mean different things to different people. Because of the current state of data technology, people who are successful in this field often have to wear many hats. They must possess an understanding of systems and software necessary to collect and extract the data they need. They will often have at least enough statistical and measurement knowledge to understand whether they are asking the right questions.

So what exactly are these people? Are they developers? Are they statisticians? Davenport and Patil assert that a data scientist is a person who possesses a combination of intellectual curiosity, domain knowledge, and the technical chops to solve data challenges. The Davenport and Patil article makes a good point that many organizations already have people like this, perhaps even stretching out of their current positions as developers or statisticians to solve problems. By formalizing and evangelizing the data-scientist role, people like Patil hope to call attention to the success that these contributors have in organizations.

Sean Taylor, at the time a Ph.D. student at NYU, posted an interesting article on his blog called "Real Scientists Make their Own Data." One of Taylor's assertions is that a problem with the term data scientist is that it can be applied to people who are not, in fact, scientists. In Taylor's view, true scientists are people who take the time to build their own datasets. There is something very human about the role of a traditional scientist. Scientists tell stories and then use experimental data to provide convincing evidence for their view. Do data scientists do this as well? Science is often concerned with establishing basic principles through observation and experimentation. Data scientists aren't researching the basic principles of data. Data scientists tend to do the kind of applied, practical work that we normally think of as engineering.

It may come to pass that the term data scientist turns out to be a poor one. A more useful question might be, "What are the skills that make people in this role successful?" Proponents of data analysis technology often debate whether or not the components of the skill set necessary to collect, analyze, and manage massive datasets is something that can be automated. Some claim that the skill sets necessary to deal with current data challenges comprise a new type of job category, one that will be around

---

3. http://hbr.org/2012/10/data-scientist-the-sexiest-job-of-the-21st-century/

for many years. Others claim that software tools will mature to the point of making many of the most technical tasks of this work completely automated.

Some make the analogy that the role of the data scientist of today is a bit like that of the "Webmaster" role of the late 1990s[4]: a person who had an adequate understanding of the collection of technologies necessary to create and maintain a Web site. These skills included a bit of server administration, a smattering of design, some knowledge of JavaScript and Perl, and enough familiarity with HTML to know that the `<blink>` and `<marquee>` tags should only be used ironically. Decades later, it's clear that for many professional Web development jobs, specialized knowledge is required. An established Web startup may employ a graphic designer, a frontend developer, a systems developer, and even a user-experience researcher. Developers who work on frontend and mobile versions of an application require different skills and knowledge of different toolsets than those who are tasked with maintaining the health of the application's backend systems. Many applications are now built on fully managed systems such as Amazon Web Services, Rackspace, or platforms such as Heroku. The tasks given to the Webmaster were improved by adding specialists, whereas others became automated thanks to utility computing.

I am skeptical of the longevity of a do-it-all data-scientist role. Certainly many professional statisticians are great programmers—and vice versa—but I have a hard time believing that the ideal state is somewhere in between. Developers want to write code, and statisticians are passionate about statistics. Many of the pain points around large-scale data projects happen because the software for different parts of a data pipeline is simply not well connected, or the data itself is not normalized. People interested in asking questions about data may be programmers, or statisticians may learn some development skills to get their work done. Sometimes the most accessible solution to a data problem requires mangling … I mean, *managing* a collection of different technologies, but I see all of these as temporary edge cases.

I think the reality is that roles in which we were specialized before the era of MapReduce will continue to be very similar. In many ways, administrating clusters of nodes and writing glue software to connect big data pipes can be fun, but ultimately these tasks will fall into the realm of automation brought on by economies of scale. Innovations will trend toward interoperability, and some of the tricky transformation and collection tasks undertaken by present day data scientists will become more and more invisible.

A better way to look at the highly innovative space of data technologies is to think about which skill sets in the field are the most susceptible to disruption. Disruptive technologies often find footholds in industries in which one aspect is "good enough" to be useful and provides a collection of enormous benefits that incumbents cannot provide. The same might be said of professional roles. A statistician or math specialist may be able to provide just enough programming know-how to get a task done.

---

4. http://blogs.msdn.com/b/microsoftenterpriseinsight/archive/2013/01/31/what-is-a-data-scientist.aspx

Another example from the realm of statistics involves the role of large datasets and model building. When dealing with census or population data, is the ability to collect and process all of the data the end of statistical sampling? In some limited cases, having access to an entire, massive dataset is useful when doing something like looking for anomalies in data for fraud detection. However, when attempting to gain insight from a dataset for statistical analysis or to produce correlation or clustering data, it's not necessary to use every single record in the dataset. What is more important is that the statistician knows exactly what types of questions to ask and how to tell a compelling story using the data. In other words, the types of issues that were important before the era of collecting and processing hundreds of gigabytes of data in seconds are the same types of issues that are important now.

Convergence: The Ultimate Database

In the early 1970s, the lifeblood of what we now know as the Internet was a collection of incompatible networking protocols.[5] Early Internet pioneers knew that each of the various protocols had unique technological advantages, but as they were designed separately, they were rarely inoperable. A pattern for a better set of protocols was developed, borne from the lessons learned on other projects. Eventually the now familiar TCP/IP protocol was created, and we still use this protocol extensively today.

A similar pattern is currently taking place in the world of data technology. Nonrelational databases, such as document and object stores (often lumped together as "NoSQL" databases), evolved because the pressure to deal with the avalanche of Webscale data collection trumped the requirements of the relational database's consistency model. Even the idea of using SQL has been called into question; asking questions about the data contained in some nonrelational data stores might be better suited to writing custom functions using a programming language or a nonstandard query language. However, this doesn't mean that users revolted against the concepts of strong consistency. It just means that, for a specific use case, relational features didn't always score as the highest priority.

If I could snap my fingers and create an ideal database without technological limitations, it would be an always-available, infinitely scalable relational database in the cloud. This database would support standard SQL so that I wouldn't have to retrain my new analytics employees to use a different system. The database could scale horizontally so that no matter how much data I added queries would run very quickly, and the database would be accessible via a Web service. Most importantly, this magic, ideal database would be completely invisible and forgotten by the majority of my developers. It would be stable and reliable. It would just work, much as we expect our other business tools to work.

The always-available, infinitely scalable relational database in the cloud doesn't exist—at least, not yet. But a real trend is happening in which the best features of

---

5. www.garykessler.net/library/tcpip.html#evol

different database models are being swapped and shared. The proliferation of nonrelational database technology was a reaction to the limitations of the relational model for dealing with Web-scale data. Over time, key design concepts from nonrelational databases have started to appear in traditional relational databases and vice versa. Some relational databases are becoming easier to run in a distributed setting. Scalable databases are starting to recognize the benefits of providing an SQL interface. An example is the open-source database RethinkDB. RethinkDB advertises itself as a having "an intuitive query language, automatically parallelized queries, and simple administration." Firebase, a commercial database product optimized for application backends, claims that it is a "cloud database designed to power real-time, collaborative applications." Another example of a product born from the concept of feature mashup is CitusDB's *SQL on Hadoop* product. CitusDB runs PostgreSQL instances on individual Hadoop data nodes to enable users to run queries without kicking off costly MapReduce jobs.

Finally, another example comes from the company that published the first paper about the MapReduce paradigm as well as many early ideas about nonrelational database models. Google's new F1 database, built on top of Spanner and described in a publicly available paper,[6] is another example of a trend to combine the best of many worlds. Simply put, F1 is a mostly relational database that attempts to achieve a strong consistency model using the Spanner storage layer that is distributed geographically across multiple data centers. This planetary-scale consistency comes at the expense of the speed that it takes to fully commit data, but techniques in the application layer of programs that use Spanner help to minimize delays. The query language used in Spanner is a variant of SQL, which the research paper claims was due to strong user demand.

The future will result in popular database-technology tools converging toward a bare minimum of features for continued utility and growth. The end result of this evolutionary period will hopefully be an era in which the most "good enough" data solutions become commonplace, reliable, and invisible.

Convergence of Cultures

Although data technologies are in the midst of a Cambrian-like period of evolutionary feature swap, an interesting corollary is also happening on the human front. In this book, a common theme is the tension between the traditional enterprise worlds of the data warehouse and business analyst versus the world of developer-driven, MapReduce-based tools such as Hadoop. This clash is often played out between open-source and proprietary database products. These cultural silos mirror the physical data silos that thwart gaining the maximum value from organizational data.

---

6. http://static.googleusercontent.com/external_content/untrusted_dlcp/research.google.com/en/us/archive/spanner-osdi2012.pdf

As examples, I've observed experts in the world of star schemas baffled by a lack of SQL-92 compliance in a cutting-edge analytical database, even while the system was tearing through terabytes of data. I've also observed Web developers using a sharded and schemaless MongoDB document store wondering why their analyst wants them to provide a specific schema that can describe any object in the database. In these debates over utility, the reality is that everybody is sort of right. The greatest value comes from systems that are interoperable. The major trend we are seeing is that the different camps of entrenched users are peeking over the wall, checking each other out, and asking questions about how the other systems work.

Summary

Although the state of data-analysis technology is innovation and rapid change, there are patterns emerging that help elucidate future trends. Clearly the growth of utility computing as a solution to power Web and mobile applications is driving both user data and applications that process this data into the cloud. The result is the growth of new applications that live completely in the cloud. Not only are these types of applications generating a great deal of data, but the tools that can process this data are being built with utility-computing resources as well.

The Apache Hadoop project has become synonymous with tech hype around Big Data solutions. With a huge user base and a growing collection of corporate shepherds, the Hadoop ecosystem will obviously grow and evolve to become more enterprise friendly and interoperable with existing business-analytics tools. However, tools built on top of the Hadoop ecosystem are not always the best solution to data challenges. The appearance of gaps exposed when trying to use a MapReduce framework for some use cases has meant that the spotlight is beginning to be directed to other types of data tools. The growth of new distributed analytical databases is a good example of the type of non-MapReduce technology that is being added to the mainstream data landscape. These insights are also helping people understand best practices around when to use MapReduce and when to stick with traditional tools such as relational databases and spreadsheets.

The role of developers, analysts, and systems administrators who work in this space will certainly change as well. For a short time, it appears that there will be demand for growth in the profession of the do-it-all data scientist—a role that includes being able to both ask the right questions and have the technical skills to navigate the sometimes disparate collection of tools necessary to find the answer. Generally, the roles that require building narratives and telling stories with data will likely remain much as they were before tools like Hadoop were available. The need for statisticians, applied mathematicians, model builders, and researchers seems poised not only to grow but perhaps to become greater than ever. Administrative work involving more technical aspects of what is currently considered "data science," such as being able to administer clusters of virtual servers, is likely moving toward software automation.

Another exciting trend in data technology is the convergence between various data technologies that have developed in isolation. There's a growing pool of users who have enough experience with MapReduce, nonrelational databases, and cloud technologies to begin to demand tools that combine the best of all worlds. The best features of various classes of technologies are gradually crossing over to appear in others. New nonrelational databases are taking on aspects of relational databases. Business-oriented ETL tools are integrating with MapReduce frameworks. Eventually, we can look forward to a time in which major data software incorporates the best features of many models of data technologies. What is innovative now will eventually become more commonplace and even invisible to many users.

Finally, it's interesting to witness the culture clash between traditional business analysts, statisticians, data-application developers, and others start to become more of a melting pot. Statisticians are debating the pros and cons of working with massive datasets. Researchers are able to use tools previously available only to huge Web companies. Business analysts are considering how best to work with the hackers of Hadoop. And a number of projects and startups are vying to try to fill the gaps between these spaces. Hopefully the cross-pollination will result in people learning how to ask the right questions about their data and use the best technologies available to help find the best answers.

Index

Video Training for Professionals Working with Data

informit.com/awdataseries

ISBN: 978-0-13-335895-7

Working with Big Data: Infrastructure, Algorithms, and Visualizations LiveLessons presents a high-level overview of big data and demonstrates how to use key tools to solve your data challenges.

Paul Dix is the author of *Service Oriented Design with Ruby and Rails* (Addison-Wesley, 2011) and a frequent speaker at conferences and user groups, including Web 2.0, RubyConf, RailsConf, The Gotham Ruby Conference, and Scotland on Rails. Paul is a cofounder at Errplane, a cloud-based service for monitoring application performance and metrics.

ISBN: 978-0-13-339282-1

This ***Hadoop Fundamentals LiveLessons*** tutorial demonstrates the core components of Hadoop, including Hadoop Distributed File Systems and MapReduce and explores how to use Hadoop at several levels, including the native Java interface, C++ pipes, and the universal streaming program interface.

Douglas Eadline, Ph.D., is a consultant to the HPC industry and writes a monthly column in *HPC Admin Magazine*. Both clients and readers have recognized Dr. Eadline's ability to present a "technological value proposition" in a clear and accurate style.

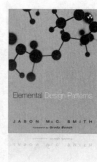

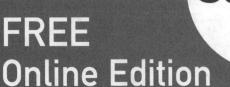

FREE
Online Edition

Your purchase of *Data Just Right* includes access to a free online edition for 45 days through the **Safari Books Online** subscription service. Nearly every Addison-Wesley Professional book is available online through **Safari Books Online**, along with thousands of books and videos from publishers such as Cisco Press, Exam Cram, IBM Press, O'Reilly Media, Prentice Hall, Que, Sams, and VMware Press.

Safari Books Online is a digital library providing searchable, on-demand access to thousands of technology, digital media, and professional development books and videos from leading publishers. With one monthly or yearly subscription price, you get unlimited access to learning tools and information on topics including mobile app and software development, tips and tricks on using your favorite gadgets, networking, project management, graphic design, and much more.

Activate your FREE Online Edition at
informit.com/safarifree

STEP 1: Enter the coupon code: EBINOGA.

STEP 2: New Safari users, complete the brief registration form.
Safari subscribers, just log in.

If you have difficulty registering on Safari or accessing the online edition,
please e-mail customer-service@safaribooksonline.com